A COMMEN

ON THE

New Testament Epistles

BY

DAVID LIPSCOMB

EDITED, WITH ADDITIONAL NOTES,

BY

J. W. SHEPHERD

I, II Thessalonians,
I, II Timothy,
Titus, and Philemon

GOSPEL ADVOCATE CO.

Nashville, Tenn. 37202

1989

Complete Set ISBN 0-89225-000-3
This Volume ISBN 0-89225-010-0
Paperback   ISBN 0-89225-442-4

COMMENTARY ON
THE FIRST EPISTLE TO THE
THESSALONIANS

INTRODUCTION

In presenting this commentary to the public, the editor does so fully conscious of the great weight of responsibility that rests upon him. As an author and editor it is not a new venture. He is the author of several books, all of which are meritorious and exceedingly helpful to the studious and ambitious servant of the Lord, and especially so to those who teach and preach the gospel of Christ.

His educational advantages and scholarly attainments make him well fitted to command the attenton of the intellectual reader. His deeply spiritual nature, coupled with a high sense of honesty and unquestioned integrity, will commend him to the honest searcher after truth. He has given his life to the study of the Bible, and his careful, painstaking methods of study have left nothing to speculation or guesswork. In his efforts to arrive at the truth he has studied carefully the setting, the circumstances, the people, their manners and customs, and the language of the text. He has compared translations, encyclopedic references, and commentaries. He has not done his work to establish or to support any theory of religious thought nor to propagate any personal or private opinion, but solely to find the truth: What does God say?

The basis of this commentary, of course, is the notes and observations of the venerable and lamented David Lipscomb accumulated through the years while he was editing the *Gospel Advocate*. These writings were placed in the hands of J. W. Shepherd to be edited and published by him. To those who knew David Lipscomb, these writings breathe the atmosphere of honesty and truth as he saw it. His rugged honesty and sincerity, coupled with loyalty and devotion to truth, as also his firmness and humility, and his deep and profound reverence for the word of God, made him a safe and trustworthy exponent of the Bible. He was big enough and humble enough to say, "I don't know," and would not venture to speculate on untaught things in the Book of God. In the early days of the Nashville Bible School, now David Lipscomb College, have I heard him say in answer to some question referring to an obscure passage of Scripture: "Well, I don't know." He did not presume to speak where God had not clearly revealed his will.

In this work the editor has interposed notes and comments of his own in addition to those of D. Lipscomb, but has been careful to keep them separate, setting his notes, etc., off in brackets [like this], and thus there is no danger of confusion or commingling of ideas. He has faithfully kept a distinction between Shepherd and Lipscomb.

In giving this series of commentaries on the Epistles of the apostle Paul, the editor has made a very valuable contribution to religious instruction; for, to my mind, there has been no safer teacher of the Bible than David Lipscomb. I believe he had a deeper insight to the meaning and sense of the Scriptures than any other man since the days of Alexander Campbell, if not from the days of the apostle Paul. In many ways I consider him greater than Campbell.

I commend this volume to those who look for truth and want to know and do God's will, and hope for it a place in the home of every lover of God and truth.

I. B. BRADLEY

Dickson, Tennessee, January 20, 1942.

CONTENTS

INTRODUCTION TO THE FIRST THESSA-LONIAN EPISTLE

I. THESSALONICA

Thessalonica is now known as Salonika, and is situated at the head of the Thermiac Gulf, which deeply indents the Macedonian shore, and it covers the irregular slope which runs, not very steeply, from the water's edge to the crest of the hill, which forms a semicircular barrier round the upper extremity of the gulf. With a rich district in the rear and the open sea in the front, the city rapidly became one of the most important Mediterranean ports, its position being at once suitable for commerce and capable of defense. The prosperity of the city justifies the wisdom of its founders. When the Romans divided Macedonia into four governments, Thessalonica was made the chief city of the second province, and ultimately became the metropolis of the whole. At the time of Paul's visit it enjoyed the rights of a free city, being governed by seven polytarchs, who, though responsible to the Roman proconsul, were elected by the citizens themselves.

Into this important city Paul came over the great Roman road, which connected the region north of the Ægean Sea with Rome. The First Epistle gives evidence (2: 9) that he readily found employment, and felt himself at home among the workingmen and tradespeople of the city. This coincides with the fact that one of the staple manufactures of the city was goat's-hair cloth. The sound that follows the ear as one walks through Salonika today is the straining vibration of the loom and pendulumlike click of the regular and ceaseless shuttle.

Another allusion (1: 8) reminds us that not only must such a city have had special attraction for Paul as likely to give a favorable hearing to the gospel message, but that its commercial and seafaring population would rapidly spread what they themselves might receive. Every ship that left the harbor, and every wagon that turned inland, carried some account of the riot at Thessalonica and the extraordinary man who had been the occasion of it. But though in such a short time Paul planted here the second church that rose on the European continent, those on whose aid he might naturally have counted, his own countrymen, made it so dangerous for him and Silas to remain that the brethren sent them by night to Berea. (Acts 17: 10.)

Although, therefore, the population was largely Jewish, the Epistle bears evidence of being written to a church composed almost entirely of Gentile Christians. (2: 14.) There are no allusions to the tenets of Judaism or to the facts of Jewish history, nor are there any references to the Old Testament either in the way of illustration or of proof. The account Paul gives of preaching among them (1: 9, 10) precisely tallies with the report of his address given to the Athenians (Acts 17: 22, 23), and shows that in introducing the gospel to the Gentiles, he was at that time accustomed to announce the coming of the judgment, to proclaim Jesus as raised from the dead, to judge the world, and the Saviour of all who believed him.

II. THE OCCASION AND OBJECT OF THE EPISTLE

We are now prepared to consider the circumstances of the church at Thessalonica which drew forth this letter. Paul had twice attempted to revisit Thessalonica and had both times been disappointed. Thus prevented from seeing them in person, he had sent Timothy to inquire and report to him as to their condition. (3: 1-5.) Timothy had returned with most favorable tidings, reporting not only their progress in the faith and practice, but also their strong attachment to Paul. (3: 6-12.) And this Epistle is the outpouring of his gratitude on receiving this gratifying news.

At the same time, Timothy's report was not unmixed with sorrow. There were certain features in their condition which called for Paul's interference: (1) The very intensity of their faith in Christ, dwelling too exclusively on the day of the Lord's coming, had been attended with evil consequences. On the one hand, a practical inconvenience had arisen. In their feverish expectation of his coming, some had been led to neglect their ordinary responsibilities as if the daily duties of life were of no account in the immediate presence of so vast a change. (4: 11; 2 Thess. 2: 1, 3, 6, 11, 12.) On the other hand, a theoretical difficulty had arisen. Certain members of the church had died, and there was great anxiety lest they should be excluded from any share in the glories of the Lord's coming. (4: 13-18.) Paul rebukes the irregularity of the former and drives away fears of the latter. (2) Persecution had broken out, and the Thessalonians needed consolation and encouragement under their sore trial. (2: 14; 3: 2-4.) (3) An unhealthy feeling with regard to spiritual gifts was manifesting itself. They needed to be reminded of the superior value of prophesying —teaching—compared with other gifts of the Spirit which they exalted at its expense. (5: 19, 20.) (4) There was danger of relapsing into their old heathen habits of profligacy. Against this Paul offers words in season. (4: 4-8.)

Notwithstanding all these drawbacks, the condition of the Thessalonian church was satisfactory, and most cordial relations existed between Paul and his converts. This honorable distinction it shares with the Philippian church. At all times, and amid every change of circumstance, it is to the Macedonian churches that Paul turns for sympathy and support.

III. TIME AND PLACE OF WRITING

Paul, accompanied by Silvanus, came to Berea, and soon thereafter was joined by Timothy. Thence, Paul and Timothy proceeded to Athens, leaving Silvanus at Berea. Timothy was most likely sent back from Athens to Thessalonica to strengthen and encourage the church there. At Athens Paul intended to remain until the arrival of his fellow helpers, for he had sent "a commandment unto Silas and Timothy that they should come to him with all speed." (Acts 17: 15.) It seems, however, that he left Athens without them, for unforeseen circumstances had prevented them from complying with his request, and they did not join him until after his arrival in Corinth. Inasmuch as Paul joins the names of Silvanus and Timothy in the address of the Epistle, it is evident that it was not written until after their arrival. Some time also must have elapsed between the establishment of the church in Thessalonica and the writing of the Epistle. Paul had twice attempted to visit them and failed (2: 7, 8), Timothy had been sent by Paul to Thessalonica and had returned from his mission and reported that the faith of the Thessalonians had been spread abroad throughout Macedonia and Achaia (1: 7, 8). The interval, however, could not have been long. Timothy returned at the beginning of Paul's residence at Corinth, and Paul's anxiety for the Thessalonians induced him to write the Epistle immediately on receiving the information given by Timothy. He speaks of his absence from them as lasting only a short time. (2: 17.) We may,

therefore, fix the time of writing the Epistle toward the close of
A.D. 52 or the beginning of 53 and during the early part of Paul's
residence at Corinth, possibly six months after planting the church
at Thessalonica.

COMMENTARY ON THE FIRST EPISTLE TO THE THESSALONIANS

SECTION ONE

PAUL'S PAST AND PRESENT RELATIONS WITH THE THESSALONIANS AND HIS LOVE FOR THEM
1: 1 to 3: 13

1. THE SALUTATION AND GREETING
1: 1

1 Paul, and Silvanus, and Timothy, unto the church of the Thessalonians in God the Father and the Lord Jesus Christ: Grace to you and peace.

---

1 **Paul,**—There was no need to add "apostle" to the name of Paul in writing to a church with which his relations were so familiar and cordial.

and Silvanus,—Silvanus is the Silas of Acts of Apostles. Paul first met him when he went to Jerusalem from Antioch to seek a settlement of the question of circumcising the Gentile Christians. He was sent with Paul to communicate the decision of the apostles and elders. (Acts 15: 19, 25, 29.) When Paul declined to take John Mark with him on his second missionary journey, and parted with Barnabas, he chose Silas as his companion, and the two were beaten and imprisoned together at Philippi. (Acts 16: 19-29.) He was with Paul during the riot at Thessalonica (17: 4), and was sent away with him to Berea, remaining there after Paul had been obliged to depart, and joined him again in Corinth (18: 5). In that city he was an esteemed coworker with Paul. (2 Cor. 1: 19.)

and Timothy,—Timothy was the well-known companion and assistant of Paul. The terms which he applies to him— "my beloved and faithful child in the Lord" (1 Cor. 4: 17), "my true child in faith" (1 Tim. 1: 2)—indicate not only Paul's love for him, but also that he had been the means of his conversion. At any rate, it is clear that, when on his first missionary journey, Paul visited Lystra, and Timothy's mother and grandmother were led to Christ, and that Timothy was then old enough to be instructed in the way of the Lord. He became a disciple of Christ and a companion of Paul. He was gifted of the Spirit. (1 Tim. 4: 14; 2 Tim. 1: 6.) When these and other teachers were with Paul, he usually associated them with himself in writing to the churches. They were both with him when the work of the Lord was begun in Thessalonica.

unto the church of the Thessalonians—This is the local description. The only New Testament parallel is "the church of the Laodiceans." (Col. 4: 16.)

in—[This word is frequently used by Paul to express intimacy of union, and is not readily explained by any simpler term. Here it introduces the spiritual relation and may be paraphrased thus: in relationship with God as Father and with Jesus Christ as Lord.] They were baptized "into the name of the Father and of the Son and of the Holy Spirit." Hence, were in these divine persons.

God the Father—[God's everlasting power and divinity is manifest in creation (Rom. 1: 20); his Fatherhood is subject of revelation (Matt. 11: 27; John 17: 25); it is not universal (Matt. 13: 38; John 8: 23-44); but is asserted only in relation to those who have been born anew (John 1: 12, 13; Gal. 3: 26; 1 John 3: 1; 5: 1). Being our Father God looks to his children for honor (Mal. 1: 6) and confidence (Matt. 6: 25, 34), while he deals with them in pity (Psalm 103: 13, 14) and in love (John 16: 27).]

and the Lord—[Christ himself assumed this title. (Matt. 7: 21, 22; 9: 38.) His purpose did not become clear to the disciples until after his resurrection from the dead, and the revelation of his deity consequent therein. Thomas, when he realized the significance of the presence of a mortal wound in the body of a living man, immediately joined with it the absolute title of Deity, saying: "My Lord and my God." (John 20: 28.) In Peter's sermon on the day of Pentecost he said, "Let all the house of Israel therefore know assuredly, that God hath made him both Lord and Christ, this Jesus whom ye crucified" (Acts 2: 36); and in the house of Cornelius he said, "He is Lord of all" (10: 36). And Jude speaks of some "denying our only Master and Lord, Jesus Christ," and in the next verse applies the term Lord to God. (Jude 4, 5.) The title *Lord* as given to the Savior in its full significance rests upon the resurrection (Acts 2: 36; Rom. 10: 9; 14: 9), and is realized only "in the Holy Spirit" (1 Cor. 12: 3). While he is still rejected alike by Jew and Gentile, angels (Matt. 28: 6) and saints (Rom. 10: 9) acknowledge him in it, but in the day of his manifested glory every tongue in the universe shall "confess that Jesus Christ is Lord, to the glory of God the Father" (Phil. 2: 11). Those who acknowledge him as Lord now are his servants. (Eph. 6: 6, 7), and to them he looks for obedience (Luke 6: 46; Rom. 6: 16), and on that condition graciously admits them to his friendship (John 15: 14, 15).]

Jesus—[This name was given to the Son of God while he dwelt on earth in the flesh as his personal name in obedience to the command of the angel to Joseph, the husband of his mother, Mary, shortly before he was born. (Matt. 1: 21.) By this name he was generally known throughout the gospel narrative. While he was on earth in the flesh, no one of his disciples is recorded as having addressed him by his personal name; but it is plain that the custom was common among believers in the apostolic age that they confessed with the "mouth Jesus as Lord" (Rom. 10: 9), and it is, therefore, the pattern for Christians till time shall cease.]

Christ:—[In the Epistles of James, Peter, John, and Jude, men who had companied with the Lord in the days of his flesh, *Jesus Christ* is the invariable form of the name and title, for this was the order of their experience; as *Jesus* they knew him first, that he was the *Messiah* they learned finally in his resurrection. But Paul came to know him first in the glory of heaven (Acts 9: 1-6), and his experience being thus the reverse of theirs, the reverse order, *Christ Jesus*. In Paul's Epistles the order is in harmony with the context. Thus Christ Jesus describes the exalted one who emptied himself (Phil. 2: 5-7) and testifies of his pre-existence; Jesus Christ describes the *despised* and *rejected* one who was afterwards glorified (Phil. 2: 11) and testifies to his resurrection. Christ Jesus suggests his *grace;* Jesus Christ his *glory.*]

Grace to you and peace.—Paul's usual salutation is extended to them. Grace properly means favor and includes those blessings that are applicable to Christians in common, denoting an ardent prayer that all the mercies and favors of God for time and eternity might be conferred upon them.

2. THANKSGIVING FOR THEIR RECEPTION OF THE GOSPEL AND HIS LOVE FOR THEM
1: 2-10.

2 We give thanks to God always for you all, making mention *of you* in our prayers; 3 remembering without ceasing your work of faith and labor of

---

2 We give thanks to God always—Paul knew the facts concerning their conversion and the trials which they endured under the fierce persecutions through which they passed.

for you all,—There was not one of them that he knew for whom he did not give thanks. The whole church was what it should be.

making mention of you in our prayers;—He made special mention of them in asking God's help and blessing to rest upon them. The number of persons and churches Paul mentions in his prayers is remarkable. It shows how much Paul regarded special and direct prayers for persons.

3 remembering without ceasing your work of faith—He had seen its manifestation when among them and remembered it. The work of faith was the work and consecration to which faith led them in their work of service to the Lord under the fierce persecutions to which they had been subjected. [Faith is the response of the soul to the life-giving word of God (Rom. 10: 8-17), producing a change of life and a cheerful courage under trial.]

and labor of love—The labor and fatiguing toil to which they were led by their love to God and to their brethren. This love had been manifested by the untiring and devoted toils which they had undergone to help their brethren in distress. Love makes us willing to labor and suffer for those we love. [Love to God is expressed in obedience (John 14: 15, 21, 23); to man in considering the interest of others rather than our own (Phil. 2: 4).]

lŏve and ¹patience of hope in our Lord Jesus Christ, before ²our God and Father; 4 knowing, brethren beloved of God, your election, 5 ³how that our ⁴gospel came not unto you in word only, but also in power, and in the Holy

¹Or, *stedfastness*
²Or, *God and our Father*
³Or, *because our gospel &c.*
⁴Gr. *good tidings;* and so elsewhere; see marginal note on Mt. 4. 23

and patience of hope in our Lord Jesus Christ,—Hope of future blessings and joy led them to bear with patience the ills brought upon them. [The word patience is frequently used by Paul. It is fortitude in suffering, endurance in toil or trial. Rightly to suffer is harder than rightly to work. The persecutions to which the Thessalonian Christians had been and were still exposed gave large room for the exercise of steadfastness.]

before our God and Father;—God looks upon us and will reward and bless us for our endurance for his sake. [It was a hope which they had through the merits of the Redeemer and which they were permitted to cherish before God; that is, as in his very presence. When they thought of God, when they remembered that they were soon to stand before him, they were permitted to cherish this hope. It was a hope which would be found to be genuine even in the presence of a holy and heart-searching God.]

4 **knowing, brethren beloved of God,**—They knew that God had accepted them—the Gentiles—in Christ so could fully realize that they were under his care and supervision.

your election,—All who believe and obey the gospel of Jesus Christ are the elected of God. This applies especially to the Gentiles who believed in him. The Jews had been the elect or chosen of God. Now the Gentiles who believed in Christ were elect. They knew that God had accepted them in Christ so could fully realize that they were under his care and supervision. Their election was their acceptance in Jesus when they believed and obeyed him.

5 **how that our gospel came not unto you in word only, but also in power,**—Paul calls it "our gospel" because it was the gospel which they preached. He did not mean that the gospel had been originated by them, but only that they delivered the good news of salvation unto them. [It did not come to them

Spirit, and *in* much *assurance; even ye know what manner of men we
showed ourselves toward you for your sake. 6 And ye became imitators of
us, and of the Lord, having received the word in much affliction, with joy of

*Or, *fulness*

in word only, for it was conveyed in human speech, even
though not in enticing words of man's wisdom, but it passed
beyond the word. It did not merely sound in the ear or touch
the understanding, but it came in power on the part of the
preachers with an overwhelming force and persuasiveness so
that their "faith should not stand in the wisdom of men, but in
the power of God." (1 Cor. 2: 5.)]

and in the Holy Spirit, and in much assurance;—The presence of the Holy Spirit gave them much assurance, and they
preached with a conscious conviction of the truth of their
message. This conviction of its truth on their part added to
the momentum with which it penetrated the hearts of their
hearers and wrought in them a full assurance of its truth.

**even as ye know what manner of men we showed ourselves
toward you for your sake.**—Neither Paul nor his associates
sought any selfish end or purpose, but conducted themselves
in the most unselfish manner, following in the footsteps of the
Lord Jesus, so far as practical, that they might set before
them the true example to be followed.

6 And ye became imitators of us, and of the Lord,—By becoming imitators of Paul and of his fellow laborers, they became imitators of the Lord. Paul said: "Be ye imitators of
me, even as I also am of Christ." (1 Cor. 11: 1.) The point of
imitation did not consist in their cordial reception of the gospel, for that could not apply to Christ; but in their joyful endurance of suffering. The force of the word is that what they
became at conversion must be diligently continued thereafter.

having received the word in much affliction,—Luke tells us
that when they first heard the gospel Paul and his fellow
workers went into the synagogue, "and for three sabbath days
reasoned with them from the scriptures, opening and alleging
that it behooved the Christ to suffer, and to rise again from
the dead; and that this Jesus, whom, said he, I proclaim unto
you, is the Christ. And some of them were persuaded, and
consorted with Paul and Silas; and of the devout Greeks a

great multitude, and of the chief women not a few. But the Jews, being moved with jealousy, took unto them certain vile fellows of the rabble, and gathering a crowd, set the city on an uproar; and assaulting the house of Jason, they sought to bring them forth to the people. And when they found them not, they dragged Jason and certain brethren before the rulers of the city, crying, These that have turned the world upside down are come hither also. . . . And they troubled the multitude and the rulers of the city, when they heard these things." (Acts 17: 2-8.) It was under affliction like this that the Thessalonians received the gospel.

with joy of the Holy Spirit;—The preaching was the result of the Holy Spirit directing and guiding in the work. The Spirit dwells in the word of God as the principle of life dwells in the seed. Jesus said: "It is the spirit that giveth life; the flesh profiteth nothing: the words that I have spoken unto you are spirit, and are life." (John 6: 63.) "The seed is the word of God." (Luke 8: 11.) Paul says: "The Spirit giveth life." (2 Cor. 3: 6.) The Spirit gives life through the word. On the day of Pentecost the Spirit in the apostles spoke to the people and gave them life. The Spirit is the representative of the Godhead who imparts life. The Spirit appeared miraculously in the beginning of the human race and imparted life to the body of Adam; he then gave laws to perpetuate this life to Adam's descendants as much as he gave life to Adam in the beginning. Just so the Holy Spirit gave life miraculousy on the day of Pentecost, and since has imparted life through the word of God which is the seed of the kingdom. This is the very point of likeness between the natural and spiritual laws according to Jesus and the Holy Spirit. Peter said: "Repent ye, and be baptized every one of you in the name of Jesus Christ unto the remission of your sins; and ye shall receive the gift of the Holy Spirit." (Acts 2: 38.) The Spirit is in the seed, the word. He goes with the word into the heart, but develops into the distinct and active life only at birth. The same process that brings a Man into Christ fits him to enjoy the blessings that dwell in Christ. [So the consolations which they received, in consequence of hearing and obeying the word of God, delivered unto them through Paul, more than

the Holy Spirit; 7 so that ye became an ensample to all that believe in Macedonia and in Achaia. 8 For from you hath sounded forth the word of the Lord, not only in Macedonia and Achaia, but in every place your faith to God-ward is gone forth; so that we need not to speak anything. 9 For they

counterbalanced all the afflictions which they suffered from their persecutors.]

7 so that ye became an ensample to all that believe in Macedonia and in Achaia.—The Thessalonians followed these teachings with such faithfulness that they became an ensample to others. At the time this Epistle was written Greece was divided into the provinces of Macedonia and Achaia. Thessalonica was the capital of Macedonia and Corinth of Achaia.

8 For from you hath sounded forth the word of the Lord, not only in Macedonia and Achaia,—It was sounded by living men and women in their daily conduct. It seems that Paul had in mind the influence of their heroic endurance of the persecutions and spiritual prosperity, and of the missionary labors of evangelists sent out by them.

but in every place your faith to God-ward is gone forth;—This strikingly describes the report that spread far and wide from Thessalonica, and the story of what had taken place among them prepared the way for the reception of the gospel in other places. The loudest, clearest, most eloquent, and most unanswerable proclamation of the gospel is the unconscious testimony of Christian living. It may be sounded forth in great power in the midst of the severest afflictions—and often is. The troubles they endured for the name of Christ tested and revealed their faith, and so led to the fuller proclamation of the gospel.

[The lesson that we should learn from the zeal of the early Christians is that success in the service of the Lord is to be accomplished only through the spirit of self-denying labor and devotion. At the present time the great need is men of zeal —self-denying zeal and earnestness—who are willing to surrender all worldly honor, wealth, and fame to work for God and the salvation of lost and ruined men; not simply to revive religion, but to restore in its divine simplicity and power the true faith and works of the church of God as he himself or-

themselves report concerning us what manner of entering in we had unto you; and how ye turned unto God from idols, to serve a living and true God,

---

dained them. God intends his message to be conveyed to men only through those Christlike enough to deny self to carry it to their dying fellow men. God demands these sacrifices, not of the preacher alone, but of everyone who would serve him.]

so that we need not to speak anything.—Their faith certainly had the solid stamp of reality, for otherwise it would never have produced such a widespread notoriety. [By the going of the report of their faith great service was done. In preaching the gospel in new places it was Paul's custom to hold up what it had done for other places. With regard to Thessalonica, he was placed in an exceptional position. In Berea, in Athens, in Corinth, or wherever he went, he needed not to labor to create an impression of what the gospel had done for Thessalonica. He needed not to say anything for the work was already done for him.]

9 **For they themselves report concerning us what manner of entering in we had unto you; and how ye turned unto God from idols,**—The facts concerning the conversion of the Thessalonians were well known throughout the regions in which he traveled. They were acquainted not only with the fact that Paul had preached in Thessalonica, but also with the results of his preaching. The results had been greater among the Gentiles than among the Jewish population. Luke says: "Some of them were persuaded, and consorted with Paul and Silas; and of the devout Greeks a great multitude, and of the chief women not a few." (Acts 17: 4.) They were to turn to God from whatever kept them from him, to turn because they believed in him and loved him, and meant to listen, study, and obey him in conversion. Conversion implies faith in God through Christ, and repentance is turning away from sin. The intention with which they turned to God is described, in which the two grand features of the Christian life are signalized.

to serve—To serve God is a comprehensive expression including the various thoughts, feelings, and acts whereby a godly person seeks to please God.

10 and to wait for his Son from heaven, whom he raised from the dead, *even* Jesus, who delivereth us from the wrath to come.

---

a living and true God,—The God to whom they had now turned is living and real. Jesus said: "And this is life eternal, that they should know thee the only true God, and him whom thou didst send, even Jesus Christ." (John 17: 3.) *True* means real, genuine, as opposed to that which is pretended, which has no real existence.

10 **and to wait for his Son from heaven,**—The second coming of the Lord Jesus Christ was an element in Paul's teaching which made a very deep impression on the Thessalonian believers; it was to them a great object of Christian hope. They not only believed he would come again; they were eager for his coming. They, in their suffering and distress, like the apostle John, were ever ready to say: "Amen: come, Lord Jesus." (Rev. 22: 20.) It is a matter of fact that hope in this sense does not hold its ancient place in the hearts of many professed Christians of today. So far from being a power of God in the soul, a victorious grace, it is a sure token that God is absent. Instead of inspiring, it discourages; it leads to numberless self-deceptions; men *hope* their lives are right with God when they ought to search them and see. This, when our relations to God are concerned, is a degradation of the very word. The Christian hope is laid up in heaven. The object is the Lord Jesus. (1 Tim. 1: 1.) It is not precarious, but certain; it is not ineffective, but a great and energetic power. Anything else is not hope at all. The operation of true hope is manifold. It is a sanctifying grace, for "every one that hath this hope set on him purifieth himself, even as he is pure." (1 John 3: 3.)

whom he raised from the dead, even Jesus,—The apostle connects the raising of Jesus from the dead with the deliverance of the Christian from the wrath to come. A destruction awaits all sinners before God. [This is the fact, which, when they came to understand it, brought Peter and the other disciples into a new life of hope, for he says: "Blessed be the God and Father of our Lord Jesus Christ, who according to his great mercy begat us again unto a living hope by the resurrection of Jesus Christ from the dead." (1 Pet. 1: 3.) This fact,

when he came to know it, changed the life of Saul the persecutor into the bond servant of Jesus Christ. (Acts 9: 1-9; 1
Cor. 9: 1; Gal. 1: 16.) That the historic fact—"Jesus Christ
risen from the dead" (2 Tim. 2: 8)—is the complete vindication of the truth of the gospel is declared by the Lord himself:
"Thus it is written, that the Christ should suffer, and rise
again from the dead the third day; and that repentance and
remission of sins should be preached in his name unto all the
nations, beginning from Jerusalem." (Luke 24: 46, 47.)]

who delivereth us from the wrath to come.—Jesus came to
save his people from their sins, that they might be delivered
from the wrath of God against all sin and ungodliness. This
freeing from sins and the consequent deliverance from the
wrath by Jesus Christ is the good news that was sounded out
from Thessalonica to all places around.

3. HE REMINDS THEM OF THE CHARACTER OF HIS LIFE AND MINISTRY AMONG THEM
2: 1-12.

1 For yourselves, brethren, know our entering in unto you, that it hath not
been found vain: 2 but having suffered before and been shamefully treated,
as ye know, at Philippi, we waxed bold in our God to speak unto you the
¹gospel of God in much conflict. 3 For our exhortation *is* not of error, nor

¹Gr. *good tidings:* and so elsewhere; see marginal note on Mt. 4. 23

---

1 For yourselves, brethren, know our entering in unto you,
—Paul's purpose in these words was to stir up their minds
with stirring memories of their conversion. Not only did
strangers report the power and efficacy of their preaching
among them, but they themselves were experimentally acquainted with its effects on their own hearts and lives.

that it hath not been found vain:—It was not fruitless or
without permanent results. [On the contrary, it was mighty,
energetic, and powerful.]

**2 but having suffered before and been shamefully treated, as
ye know, at Philippi,**—They came to Thessalonica from Philippi, where Paul and Silas had been publicly scourged with
rods and cast into prison and their feet made fast in stocks.
(Acts 16: 22-24.) Their treatment had been unlawful and
brutal.

of uncleanness, nor in guile: 4 but even as we have been approved of God to

we waxed bold in our God to speak unto you the gospel of God in much conflict.—But notwithstanding the injury and violence they had suffered, they were bold in the strength and power to preach unto them. [Disregarding the sufferings they had had to endure after preaching at Philippi, God had given them courage to resume his work at Thessalonica.]

3 **For our exhortation**—His exhortation to turn to God was not a desire to lead them into error for selfish purposes. [The word *exhortation* has a twofold signification, denoting both exhortation and consolation; when it refers to moral conduct, it denotes exhortation; but when it is an address to a sufferer, it denotes consolation. In the gospel these two meanings are blended together.]

is not of error,—Without any direct evil intent to lead them into error for selfish ends.

nor of uncleanness,—Not from a desire to gratify lusts, as was so often the case with idol worshippers. [This also refers to false teachers, which are described thus: "For, uttering great swelling words of vanity, they entice in the lusts of the flesh, by lasciviousness, those who are just escaping from them that live in error; promising them liberty, while they themselves are bondservants of corruption; for of whom a man is overcome, of the same is he also brought into bondage." (2 Pet. 2: 18, 19.) Both in Corinth and in Thessalonica gross vice was consecrated to religion.]

nor in guile:—[The preceding words deny a wrong motive; this denies a wrong method. Not only were their motives sincere and pure, but their manner of dealing was straightforward, with no ends to serve for the attainment of which they needed to use deceit, for as Paul says: "For we are not as the many, corrupting the word of God: but as of sincerity, but as of God, in the sight of God, speak we in Christ" (2 Cor. 2: 17), and "but we have renounced the hidden things of shame, not walking in craftiness, nor handling the word of God deceitfully" (2 Cor. 4: 2). This verse treats Paul's ministry negatively as to its truthfulness, its motives, and its methods.]

4 **but even as we have been approved of God to be intrusted with the gospel, so we speak;**—Of his preparation for this mo-

be intrusted with the ¹gospel, so we speak; not as pleasing men, but God

mentous work it is said that after his baptism "he was certain
days with the disciples that were at Damascus. And straight-
way in the synagogues he proclaimed Jesus, that he is the Son
of God." (Acts 9: 19-20.) After this it was ten years before
Barnabas came to him in Tarsus to find a fellow worker and
to introduce him into a wider sphere of service. (Acts 11: 25,
26.) [Up to this time he had visited Arabia, returned to Damascus, and thence after three years went to Jerusalem,
where he was with the disciples "going in and going out . . .
preaching boldly in the name of the Lord: and he spake and
disputed against the Grecian Jews; but they were seeking to
kill him. And when the brethren knew it, they brought him
down to Cæsarea, and sent him forth to Tarsus." (Acts 9:
28-30.) Of his residence in Tarsus nothing is revealed, but he
had commended himself and had become so widely known
that Barnabas sought his assistance at a critical stage of the
important work at Antioch. (Acts 11: 25.) This was a period of testing, but his days of probation were not yet fulfilled.
Three years more of new and varied experiences had to pass
before he was definitely called by the Holy Spirit and separated by his brethren to the work among the Gentiles, for
which God had set him apart, and concerning which the Lord
Jesus had spoken to him on the Damascus road some fourteen
years before, saying: "I am Jesus whom thou persecutest.
But arise, and stand upon thy feet: for to this end have I appeared unto thee, to appoint thee a minister and a witness
both of the things where in thou hast seen me, and of the
things wherein I will appear unto thee; delivering thee from
the people, and from the Gentiles, unto whom I send thee, to
open their eyes, that they may turn from darkness to light and
from the power of Satan unto God, that they may receive remission of sins and an inheritance among them that are sanctified by faith in me." (Acts 26: 15-18.)]

not as pleasing men,—He had been faithful to preach the
gospel, but not to please and make himself popular with men.
[The desire to be pleasing to men is to use them for one's own
exaltation, to make them the steppingstones on which he
seeks to rise to eminence. To put oneself in that relation to

others is an ungodly thing. Such men give ground to slander, and bring reproach on the cause of Christ. True devotion to God is love, the nature of which is not to take, but to give.]

but God—His purpose was to please God who had entrusted him with the gospel of his Son, which is to save all men from sin and suffering.

who proveth our hearts.—God proves and test the heart. He accepts no service save as it comes from the heart. He contrasts the service which comes from the heart with that which is to gratify the flesh. The fleshly heart is the center and active force in stirring and using all the faculties of the fleshly body. Without the activity of the heart, the eyes could not see, nor the ears hear, nor the brain think. The eye is not the body or the fleshly heart, yet it is a faculty of both, so are all the senses and organs of the body. Within the fleshly body dwells the spiritual body. That body has faculties, members, and organs; only they are spiritual faculties and organs. The mind, the emotions, the volitions are all members or organs of the spiritual body, but no one of them is the body. The spiritual heart is the center and the life of this spiritual body and directs and uses these faculties. The *heart* is frequently used to represent the whole inner or spiritual man. It thinks through the mind; loves or hates through its emotions; sees, wills, and purposes through the volition; and believes and trusts, decides and acts, through the harmonious action of all its faculties. Common experience ought to show that the mind alone is not the heart. Many things are memorized and retained in the mind, of which the heart does not take hold at all; they do not arouse the emotions or volitions, consequently do not affect the heart. The mind perceives, discriminates, and decides what is true or false; carries this decision to the heart; and the heart believes or disbelieves. The Bible nowhere says the mind believes; the heart believes; and the scriptures require that the gospel shall be believed with the whole heart. The intellect approves, the emotions lay hold of the truth, and the volition, or the will, acts on it. [God, who at first approved of Paul as fit for the

words of flattery, as ye know, nor a cloak of covetousness, God is witness;
6 nor seeking glory of men, neither from you nor from others, when we
might have ²claimed authority as apostles of Christ. 7 But we were ³gentle
in the midst of you, as when a nurse cherisheth her own children: 8 even
so, being affectionately desirous of you, we were well pleased to impart unto

²Or, *been burdensome* ver. 9; comp. 1 Cor. 9: 4 ff.
³Most of the ancient authorities read *babes.* Comp. 1 Cor. 14. 20

work among the Gentiles, continued to approve him throughout the whole of his discharge of its functions.]

5 **For neither at any time were we found using words of
flattery, as ye know,**—He did not flatter his hearers and did
not seek popularity of them. Jesus said: "How can ye believe, who receive glory one of another, and the glory that
cometh from the only God ye seek not?" (John 5: 44.) Paul
was always true to that truth, and never sought honor of men.

nor a cloak of covetousness, God is witness;—Neither did
he make his preaching a cloak to make gain. He appealed to
them because his course had been so decided in that respect
that they could not mistake it. [This passage exhibits to us,
in the charges brought against Paul, those vices which even
bad men can see to be wholly inconsistent with the Christian
character. No matter how we cloak it—and we always cloak
it in one way or another—it is incurably unchristian.]

6 **nor seeking glory of men.**—He did not seek a high and
honorable position in the midst of these nor yet of others. So
guarded was he in this matter that he did not even use the
power he might have to be supported as an apostle of Jesus
Christ. Jesus, in sending out his apostles, told them to carry
nothing with them, that "the laborer is worthy of his hire."
(Luke 10: 7.)

**neither from you nor from others, when we might have
claimed authority as apostles of Christ.**—He did not use this
right to live of the gospel lest he should be burdensome to
them as an apostle of Christ.

7 **But we were gentle in the midst of you, as when a nurse
cherisheth her own children:**—He nourished and cared for
them instead of allowing them to support him. [Paul felt for
them the affectionate solicitude which a mother does for a
child at her breast.]

8 **even so, being affectionately desirous of you, we were well
pleased to impart unto you, not the gospel of God only, but**

you, not the ¹gospel of God only, but also our own souls, because ye were become very dear to us. 9 For ye remember, brethren, our labor and travail: working night and day, that we might not burden any of you, we preached unto you the ¹gospel of God. 10 Ye are witnesses, and God *also*, how holily and righteously and unblamably we behaved ourselves toward you

also our own souls, because ye were become very dear to us. —He was moved by a sincere love for them instead of making gain of them; he was willing not only to impart unto them the gospel of Christ, but his own soul. This is a similar expression to what he said of his own Jewish people: "I could wish that I myself were anathema from Christ for my brethren's sake, my kinsmen according to the flesh." (Rom. 9: 3.) These are strong expressions, showing the intense desire he had for their salvation. [Such labor as Paul's in and for the church was really an impartation of his life. Health and energy and life were given out constantly in his preaching and sufferings from persecution, along with exhausting manual labor night and day.]

9 **For ye remember, brethren, our labor and travail: working night and day, that we might not burden any of you,—** These words are intended to bring out strongly the very hard and exhausting labor in which Paul was involved by his desire to support himself while ministering the gospel to them. This he did lest they should suspect him of selfish motive so that the gospel would be hindered. He would not have refused to receive their help after their conversion to help him preach the gospel to others.

we preached unto you the gospel of God.—It was the gospel of God inasmuch as it came as a glad message from God. They looked to God as their God, who had commissioned them to deliver his message.

10 **Ye are witnesses, and God also,**—They were the witnesses of his outward conduct, and God of the motives which actuated him in the service he rendered.

how holily—This denotes his pious disposition and conduct toward God.

and righteously—This denotes his conduct toward his fellow men. How just and fair in all his dealings with them.

and unblamably—This expresses the negative side of both particulars. He was cautious and extremely careful to give

that believe: 11 as ye know how we *dealt with* each one of you, as a father with his own children, exhorting you, and encouraging *you,* and testifying, 12 to the end that ye should walk worthily of God, who ⁴calleth you into his own kingdom and glory.

⁴Some ancient authorities read *called*

---

no cause or ground of blame to anyone. [That no charge could be maintained, whatever charges might be made.]

we behaved ourselves toward you that believe:—His life was holy, consecrated to God, just and fair to all men. [We should ever remember that utmost fidelity in word and deed is due to believers, as well as to unbelievers. Our example is potent for good or evil in the church as well as out of it.]

11 as ye know how we dealt with each one of you,—He particularizes the carefulness he had shown for individuals. He dealt with each one, exhorting them to follow the better way, comforting them in their trials and troubles. [This shows that the success of the apostles was not easily won, that converts were not made in masses, but by the slow, toilsome affectionate application of the gospel to individuals, one by one. Without this personal and individual dealing, the public preaching is not so effective.]

as a father with his own children,—When they failed he encouraged them to try again, and warned them of the danger of turning aside as a father does his own children.

exhorting you,—[The father should not merely tell his children their duty but also to exhort them warmly to duty, especially from his own experiences in life. So it is the part of the minister of the word of truth not only to hold up scripture teaching, but also, fatherly, warmly to urge its observance.]

and encouraging you,—It is also the part of a father to hold out encouragement to the performance of duty. Nothing can be more fatal to the young than a discouraging tone. [It is the part of a worker in the Lord's vineyard not to be harsh, censorious, despondent, but fatherlike to catch a geniality and hopefulness from his message, and may be said to have come from the Fatherhood of God.]

and testifying,—[There are times when a father addresses his children as with a dying breath, conjures them by all that he holds dear and sacred by a consideration of their best interests, not to give way to temptation, but to follow in the path of duty. There are times when it becomes necessary for the Lord's servant to concentrate his earnestness, and to address his brethren as with a dying breath, conjuring them by the authority of God, by the blood of Christ, by the dreadful issues at stake, by the solemnity of the judgment not to allow themselves to be cheated out of eternal life in the presence of God and the redeemed.]

12 to the end that ye should walk worthily of God,—[This was the object of the exhortations. Men can profess to accept God's calling and yet live very much as they had done before; hence, they needed to be told to walk worthily of God. And it is a consideration which helps those who are seeking godliness that God has associated them with himself. As men are helped by their position to live up to it, and as children naturally strive to be worthy of their parents; so those who know God and are connected with him are stimulated to higher efforts.]

who calleth you into his own kingdom and glory.—God had called them out of the world, freed them from sin, and translated them into his own kingdom that through fidelity to him in that kingdom they should come to partake of his glory.

4. THE SUFFERINGS OF THE THESSALONIANS THE SAME AS THOSE ENDURED BY THEIR JEWISH BRETHREN
2: 13-16

13 And for this cause we also thank God without ceasing, that, when ye received from us ⁵the word of the message, *even the word* of God, ye accepted *it* not *as* the word of men, but, as it is in truth, the word of God,

⁵Gr. *the word of hearing.* Gal. 3. 2, 5

---

13 And for this cause we also thank God without ceasing, —Here Paul falls back into the thankful strain with which he began the Epistle. The very words, "we give thanks to God always for you all" (1:2), is caught up. Having given out his strength in preaching them, he had unceasing cause of thanksgiving to God in the result.

that, when ye received from us the word of the message,— In setting forth the result, the word is described from the point of view of the Thessalonians in relation to the message which he delivered to them.

which also worketh in you that believe. 14 For ye, brethren, became imitators of the churches of God which are in Judæa in Christ Jesus: for ye also

---

even the word of God,—They did not receive his teaching
as that of a man without authority, but they received it, as it
was in truth, the word of the living God.

**ye accepted it not as the word of men, but, as it is in truth,
the word of God,**—A truth accepted as the word of God has
much more power than the same thing would have if believed
to be only as the word of men; but they had accepted it, ap-
propriating it to the life, not as originating with man, but
with God. The word of God works effectually in all that believe; that is, it brings those who believe it truly into obedience
to the word of God. It is an evil heart of unbelief that causes
men to turn from God's law and to substitute the ways of men
for the appointments of God. Keeping the appointments of
God and obeying his law is the test of faith in God. Only
faith that works benefits. "For in Christ Jesus neither circumcision availeth anything; nor uncircumcision; but faith
working through love." (Gal. 5:6.) "Even so faith, if it have
not works, is dead in itself." "Was not Abraham our father
justified by works, in that he offered up Isaac his son upon
the altar? Thou seest that faith wrought with his works, and
by works was faith made perfect." (James 2: 17, 21, 22.)
Faith working in the heart produces love. "If ye love me, ye
will keep my commandments. And I will pray the Father,
and he shall give you another Comforter, that he may be with
you for ever." (John 14: 15, 16.)

which also—This marks the contrast between those who
merely heard the gospel and those who hearing believed.
Many had received the gospel with the ear, some had accepted
it in the heart; in these its claim to be from God was vindi-
cated by its active power in their lives. (Heb. 4: 12.)

worketh in you that believe.—The word of God is described
as "living and active"; by it the new birth is effected (1 Pet.
1: 23); the soul saved (James 1: 21), sanctified (John 17: 17;
1 Tim. 4: 5), and edified (Acts 20: 32). It bears fruit and in-
creases throughout the world and grows and prevails might-
ily. (Acts 19: 20.) Like the seed (Mark 4: 26, 27), the word
of God bears its life power within itself, hence its manifold ac-

suffered the same things of your own countrymen, even as they did of the
Jews; 15 who both killed the Lord Jesus and the prophets, and drove out us,

---

tivities and its boundless increase. It is compared with fire
against that which is false and with a hammer against that
which is strong (Jer. 23: 29); it is light in the midst of darkness (Psalm 119: 105); and it is the sole weapon in the Christian's warfare (Eph. 6: 17).

14 **For ye, brethren, became imitators of the churches of
God which are in Judaea in Christ Jesus:**—I do not understand that they tried to fashion after the example of the Jewish churches; but following the same law, meeting the same
difficulties, they had developed into the same likeness; became
imitators of them by following the same laws. This was said
for the encouragement and strengthening of the Thessalonians, for as unbelieving Jews persecuted the Christians in
Judea so they had done here to them. The unbelieving Jews
stirred up the persecution at Thessalonica, but it was prose-
cuted by unbelieving Gentiles.

**for ye also suffered the same things of your own country-
men,**—It was always the Jewish policy to persecute by means
of others. By making a wily appeal to political passion the
Jews had aroused the Gentiles to attack Paul; thence followed
the persecution of the church at Thessalonica, which had not
at the time of writing subsided. [We do not know to what
extremity the enemies of the gospel had gone in Thessalonica;
but the distress of the Christians must have been great when
Paul could make this comparison. He had already told them
(1: 6) that much affliction, with joy of the Holy Spirit, is the
badge of God's children; and here he combines the same stern
necessity with the operation of the word of truth in their
hearts. The effect of receiving the gospel is in the first instance a new character, a character not only distinct from that
of the unconverted, but antagonistic to it, and more directly
and inevitably antagonistic, the more thoroughly it is wrought
out, so that in proportion as God's word is operative in us, we
come in collision with the world which rejects it. To suffer,
therefore, is to Paul the seal of faith. It is not a sign that
God has forgotten his people, but a sign that he is with them;
and that they are being brought by him into fellowship with

and please not God, and are contrary to all men; 16 forbidding us to speak
to the Gentiles that they may be saved; to fill up their sins always: but the
wrath is come upon them to the uttermost.

---

the apostles and prophets, and with the Son of God himself.
It is a subject for gratitude that they have been counted worthy to suffer for his name.]

even as they did of the Jews;—In Palestine there were no
others but Jews who could be excited against Christians, and
they were obliged to appear as the persecutors themselves.

15 who both killed the Lord Jesus and the prophets,—Here
is a fearful picture of the results of the wicked course of the
Jews. They instigated and led to the death of Jesus. Christ
told how they had killed the prophets. (Matt. 23: 31-37.)
[This was a terrible indictment against the Jews, the purpose
of which was to show the deep sympathy of Paul with the
persecuted Thessalonians, and his indignation against the persecutors, and to make them see more deeply the value of their
faith by the effort to keep it from them.]

and drove out us,—This refers to Paul and his companions,
the record of which was given by Luke. (Acts 17: 5-9.)

and please not God,—They had shown by their history that
they could not meet with the divine approval. They made
great pretensions of being the peculiar people of God, and it
was important to show that their conduct demonstrated that
they had so such claims. Their opposition to the Thessalonians, therefore, was no proof that God was opposed to them,
and they should not allow themselves to be troubled about
such opposition.

and are contrary to all men;—They worked evil to all men,
both Jews and Gentiles. Their spirit and policy may be seen
from our Lord's great denunciatory discourse against the
scribes and Pharisees, and his arraignment of their leaders for
their impiety and inhumanity when he said: "Woe unto you,
scribes and Pharisees, hypocrites! because ye shut the kingdom of heaven against men: for ye enter not in yourselves,
neither suffer ye them that are entering in to enter." (Matt.
23: 13.)

**16 forbidding us to speak to the Gentiles that they may be
saved;**—They did not object to the Gentiles becoming Jews

by circumcision and adoption into the Jewish commonwealth; but their chief persecution of Paul arose on account of his preaching to the Gentiles and teaching both Jews and Gentiles that the Gentiles were equal with the Jews in the grace of God while uncircumcised. [When the Jewish nation set itself relentlessly to prohibit the extension of the gospel to the Gentiles—when the word passed round to the synagogues from headquarters that this renegade Paul, who was summoning the pagans to become the people of God, was to be thwarted by fraud or violence—God's patience was exhausted.]

to fill up their sins always:—In thus rejecting God, and fighting against man, they heaped up the measure of their iniquity. God permits men to go far in wickedness because he is long-suffering and gives time for repentance as in the days of Noah. (1 Pet. 3: 20; 2 Pet. 3: 9; Rom. 2: 4.) On the other hand, God permits the evil things he sees in man to grow and develop until they become manifest to eyes other than his own that his righteous judgment may be put beyond dispute. (Psalm 89: 2, 14.) So he dealt with the Amorites. (Gen. 15: 16.) So with the Jews. (Matt. 23: 32.)

but the wrath is come upon them to the uttermost.—Their sins are full, their iniquities are complete in the rejection of Christ and the persecution of his servants. So the final ruin and dispersion of the nation was at hand. [The wrath which had been often previously manifested in preemptory calamities was not to exhaust its whole force upon them.]

5. PAUL'S EFFORT TO SEE THEM
2: 17-20

17 But we, brethren, being bereaved of you for ⁶a short season, in presence not in heart, endeavored the more exceedingly to see your face with

⁶Gr. *a season of an hour*

17 **But we, brethren, being bereaved of you for a short season,**—This he says lest they should think he had deserted them while so great an emergency demanded his presence. If he could not give them the comfort of his presence, he gave them the comfort of knowing that he would have been with them had it been possible.

in presence not in heart,—His heart was still with them.

great desire: 18 because we would fain have come unto you, I Paul once and
again; and Satan hindered us. 19 For what is our hope, or joy, or crown of
glorying? Are not even ye, before our Lord Jesus at his ⁷coming? 20 For
ye are our glory and our joy.

⁷Gr. *presence.* Comp. 2 Cor. 10. 10

This is an elegant and touching expression used to denote
affection for absent friends. Paul's absence from them gave
him a greater yearning for their presence.

**endeavored the more exceedingly to see your face with
great desire:**—[His affection for them was so far from being
diminished by his leaving them that it had been the more in-
flamed.]

**18 because we would fain have come unto you, I Paul once
and again;**—[This was not a sudden impulse that quickly subsided by his leaving them, as we see sometimes happen, but
that he had been steadfast in this purpose, inasmuch as he
sought various opportunities to visit them.]

and Satan hindered us.—How and when Satan hindered his
visiting them is not revealed, though some adversity, some
imprisonment, or hindrance was thrown in his way. [When-
ever the wicked molest us, they fight under Satan's ban-
ner, and are his agents for harassing us. When our endeavors
are directed to the work of the Lord, it is certain that everything that hinders proceeds from Satan.]

19 For—[This word introduces his reason for so ardently
desiring to be with them again; this is conveyed in the form
of a question to express his deep feeling more effectively than
a mere statement would have done. This accounts for his earnest desire to visit them. He thus longed to see them for
there was nothing that afforded him its same immediate enjoyment, or the same substantial satisfaction as his spiritual
children in Thessalonica.]

what is our hope, or joy, or crown of glorying?—The highest point in his future was their acceptance as true and faithful Christians by the Lord Jesus at his coming.

Are not even ye, before our Lord Jesus at his coming?—
They would be at the day of Jesus Christ as the fruits of his
labors, the hope of his glorying in that day. Paul frequently
calls his converts his *crown* of glory. "We are your glorying,

even as ye also are ours, in the day of our Lord Jesus." (2 Cor. 1: 14.) "Holding forth the word of life; that I may have whereof to glory in the day of Christ, that I did not run in vain neither labor in vain." (Phil. 2: 16.)

20 For ye are our glory and our joy.—They were the fruit of his life and labors. As an apostle of Jesus Christ, and as such he gloried and rejoiced in them. In his mind he saw them grow daily out of the taint of heathenism into the purity and love of Christ. He saw them, as the discipline of God's instruction had its perfect work in them grow from babes in Christ, and grow in the grace and in the knowledge of the Lord, to the measure of the stature of perfect men. He saw them presented faultless in the presence of the Lord in the great day. To witness that spiritual transformation which he had inaugurated carried on to completion gave the future a greatness and a worth which made Paul's heart leap for joy.

6. HE SENDS TIMOTHY TO LEARN THE STATE OF THE THESSALONIAN CHURCH
3: 1-10

1 Wherefore when we could no longer forbear, we thought it good to be left behind at Athens alone; 2 and sent Timothy, our brother and ⁸God's

⁸Some ancient authorities read *fellow-worker with God*

---

1 Wherefore when we could no longer forbear, we thought it good to be left behind at Athens alone;—Paul's anxiety for the Thessalonian Christians was so great that he could endure the strain no longer while he was at Athens and preferred to be left alone.

2 and sent Timothy,—[Immediately upon reaching Athens, Paul sent word back to Macedonia by the brethren who had escorted him "that they should come to him with all speed." (Acts 17: 15.) It is, therefore, most reasonable to suppose that Silas and Timothy joined Paul forthwith at Athens, and were almost as soon sent back into Macedonia—Silas to Berea or Philippi, and Timothy to Thessalonica. This explains Paul's being left *alone*. This also explains how both Timothy and Silas came from Macedonia to Corinth. (Acts 18: 5.) "To be left behind" was a great trial to Paul's affectionate nature. Such a sacrifice may well impress the Thessalonians

minister in the °gospel of Christ, to establish you, and to comfort *you* concerning your faith; 3 that no man be moved by these afflictions; for your-

°Gr. *good tidings;* see ch. 1. 5

with the strength of his love for them. He mentions this as if it had been a great sacrifice, and it certainly was so for him. He seems to have been in many ways dependent on the sympathy and assistance of others and of all places he ever visited Athens was the most trying to his ardent temperament. It was filled with idols and exceedingly religious; yet it seemed to him more hopelessly away from God than any city he had ever visited. Never had he been left alone in a place so completely unsympathetic; never had he felt so great a gulf between the minds of others and his own; and Timothy had no sooner gone than he made his way to Corinth.]

our brother and God's minister in the gospel of Christ,— [Paul bestows these commendatory titles on Timothy partly from his affection for his young fellow worker and partly to show still further his love for the Thessalonians which enabled him to part with so dear and valuable a companion.]

to establish you, and to comfort you concerning your faith; —The Thessalonian Christians were, at the time this Epistle was written, with only partial gifts of the Spirit and the remembrance of what Paul had taught them when he was with them. Paul knew they needed a fuller instruction in the completed will of God that they might be established more strongly in the faith. The more complete their knowledge of God's will, the better they knew how to walk in God's ways; and the stronger and the more fixed their faith in him, the greater joy and comfort they had in doing his will. One's enjoyment of the assurance which faith gives depends on the strength of that faith enlightened and directed by the will of God. [Paul feared that their faith might fail under the persecution to which they were exposed. Timothy's mission was in the interest of their faith to impress upon them that the troubles in which they were involved were no proof that their faith was vain and to encourage them to continue steadfast in it.]

3 that no man be moved by these afflictions;—Their love for Paul was so great that his afflictions unduly moved and

selves know that hereunto we are appointed. 4 For verily, when we were
with you, we told you ¹beforehand that we are to suffer affliction; even as it
came to pass, and ye know. 5 For this cause I also, when I could no longer
forbear, sent that I might know your faith, lest by any means the tempter

¹Or, *plainly*

excited them and they felt discouraged and disheartened that
Paul, the leader of the Christians, an inspired man of God,
should so suffer. [But the afflictions to which he especially
refers are most likely the persecutions which began with the
establishment of the church and still continued.]

for yourselves know that hereunto we are appointed.—
[From the very beginning God declares to his people that they
may expect to be tried and therefore when trial comes they
cannot be inclined to suppose that God is forgetful of them.]
The afflictions of God's children do not result from chance,
but are the necessary consequence of being his children; they
arise from the appointment and ordinance of God. We must
be conformed to Christ in his sufferings. To his disciples
Jesus said: "In the world ye have tribulation: but be of good
cheer; I have overcome the world." (John 16: 33.) When the
Lord called Paul to the apostleship, he showed him how many
things he must suffer for his name's sake. (Acts 9: 16.) All
the apostles suffered persecution, and, concerning Christians
in general, Paul asserts that "through many tribulations we
must enter into the kingdom of God." (Acts 14: 22.)

**4 For verily, when we were with you, we told you before-
hand that we are to suffer affliction;**—They should not have
been surprised at the consequences of their acceptance of the
gospel, for he did not withhold from them the inevitable consequences of their accepting the gospel. [There was every reason to apprehend that they would meet with opposition on account of their becoming Christians, and it was natural that
Paul should prepare their minds for it beforehand.]

even as it came to pass, and ye know.—[This refers to the
time when Paul, Silas, and Timothy were driven away from
Thessalonica, and when the church was so much agitated by
the violent opposition of the Jews. (Acts 17: 5-8.)]

**5 For this cause I also, when I could no longer forbear, sent
that I might know your faith,**—Because of their knowing of
his sufferings and the discouragement, when he could no

had tempted you, and our labor should be in vain. 6 But when Timothy came even now unto us from you, and brought us glad tidings of your faith

---

longer restrain his anxiety about the effect of his sufferings on them, he sent Timothy that he might know their fidelity, or steadfastness in the gospel. [The word *know,* as it occurs here, suggests fullness of knowledge rather than progress in knowledge.]

lest by any means the tempter had tempted you,—[Paul had just referred to the hindrances to his own movements that Satan had been able to throw across his path. (2: 18.) He now writes of a more serious Satanic opposition in the temptation of the young Thessalonian church to unfaithfulness. He is anxious lest during his absence the fierce enmity of the Jews, either by some more violent attack on the church or by the harassing of incessant persecution, may at length have broken down their fidelity and faithfulness. The dangers in which these lay besets Christians in all ages, though the form in which it presents itself varies much.]

and our labor should be in vain.—[Paul feared that Satan might have succeeded in weakening their faith, and that his labors in their behalf might therefore finally come to naught. This recognition of the dependence of his final success upon the steadfastness of those who became obedient to the faith under his labors appears particularly in the following exhortation: "So then, my beloved, even as ye have always obeyed, not as in my presence, only, but now much more in my absence, work out your own salvation with fear and trembling; for it is God who worketh in you both to will and to work, for his good pleasure. Do all things without murmurings and questionings; that ye may become blameless and harmless, children of God without blemish in the midst of a crooked and perverse generation, among whom ye are seen as lights in the world, holding forth the word of life; that I may have whereof to glory in the day of Christ, that I did not run in vain neither labor in vain." (Phil. 2: 12-16.)]

6 But when Timothy came even now unto us from you,—Timothy in company with Silas joined Paul at Corinth (Acts 18: 5), and gave him information concerning the condition of the Thessalonian Church. The word *now* qualifies *came,* and

and love, and that ye have good remembrance of us always, longing to see us, even as we also *to see* you; 7 for this cause, brethren, we were comforted over you in all our distress and affliction through your faith: 8 for now we

denotes *just now*. Timothy's return had been anxiously awaited, and no sooner had he arrived and given his report than Paul writes this affectionate and grateful Epistle.

and brought us glad tidings of your faith and love,—[The report that Timothy brought from Thessalonica comforted Paul in all his distress and affliction, and brought him new life and indescribable joy. Timothy was a coworker with Paul from the beginning of the Thessalonian Church; he was greatly devoted to it and came at once into close contact with its real condition and found it full of faith and love. They were standing fast in the Lord. Their common faith had its most signal manifestation in love; it separated them from the world, and bound them close to each other. Faith in God and love to him and to man are the very life of the Christian. It is good news to faithful Christians to hear they exist in a congregation].

and that ye have good remembrance of us always,—They remembered Paul and his teaching in love, and cherished an affectionate regard for him, notwithstanding the efforts which had been made to alienate their affections from him.

longing to see us, even as we also to see you;—There was no disposition to blame him for having left them or because he did not return to them. They were as anxious to see him as he was to see them. [Titus brought a similar message from Corinth to Paul while he was in Macedonia, and that after he had written his severe first Epistle to them. (2 Cor. 7:7.) Writing from Rome, Paul expressed his longing to see again the beloved saints at Philippi (Phil. 1:8), a longing in which Epaphroditus, his fellow worker, shared (2:25). "For in faith ye stand." (2 Cor. 1:24.)]

7 for this cause, brethren, we were comforted over you in all our distress and affliction through your faith:—Paul was much comforted in his affliction with the assurance of their strong and active faith. [Their faith was the essential point concerning which Timothy was sent to inquire (verse 5); if this was steadfast, all would be well. So the Lord Jesus

live, if ye stand fast in the Lord. 9 For what thanksgiving can we render
again unto God for you, for all the joy wherewith we joy for your sakes
before our God; 10 night and day praying exceedingly that we may see your
face, and may perfect that which is lacking in your faith?

prayed for Peter: "But I made supplication for thee, that thy
faith fail not." (Luke 22: 32.)]

8 **for now we live, if ye stand fast in the Lord.**—[When
Timothy came from Thessalonica he found Paul in great need
of comforting words. So extreme was his distress that he
spoke of it by implication as death. But the good report of
the faith and love of the Thessalonians and their joy and glad-
ness brought life to him. This passage shows that Paul was a
man of a high and ardent nature, sensitive in his affections to
a high degree. His whole soul was bound up with the
churches he had founded. (2: 8.) They were his spiritual
"children" (1 Cor. 4: 14, 15), his "beloved and longed for," his
"joy and crown" (Phil. 4: 1). He lived for nothing else.]

9 **For what thanksgiving can we render again unto God for
you,**—Paul puts this question in proof of the strong declaration he had just made; the news that Timothy brought from
them was new life to him, so much so that he could find no
words sufficient to express his gratitude to God for the
abounding joy which filled his heart in thinking of them.

**for all the joy wherewith we joy for your sakes before our
God;**—It was a pure, holy joy which was not hindered, but
heightened, because it was in God's presence; standing in full
view of God, his exultation only swelled to a higher, stronger
degree of thanksgiving for all the joy he had received from
their steadfastness. [The condition of alarm and depression
which Paul had previously experienced made the rebound of
joy the more vivid. Only those who have suffered much
know joy in its full capacity, "as chastened, and not killed; as
sorrowful, yet always rejoicing." (2 Cor. 6: 9, 10.)]

10 **night and day praying exceedingly that we may see your
face,**—His rejoicing issued in prayer all the more constant and
earnest that he might again be with them, not in heart only,
but in person.

and may perfect—[Since perfect means the attainment of its
ends and entire completeness in all its parts, the suffering believer should seek to be perfect in the development of charac-

ter, and entire in the discharge of the duties allotted to his several spheres of life. When this end should be attained, he would be lacking in nothing in Christian conduct.]

that which is lacking in your faith?—[The things that were lacking to attain this end were not so much what was lacking *in* their faith, but that which was lacking to *perfect* their faith. Their faith in itself was steadfast and vigorous. Of their faith Paul says: "Remembering without ceasing your work of faith and labor of love and patience of hope in our Lord Jesus Christ. . . . . For from you hath sounded forth the word of the Lord, not only in Macedonia and Achaia, but in every place your faith to God-ward is gone forth; so that we need not to speak anything." (1: 3, 8; see also 2: 13, 2 Thess. 1: 3.)] The things that were lacking were the things unrevealed. Paul had not, at the time he preached at Thessalonica, received the fullness of the will of God, or they were not capable of understanding it when he was with them. So their faith was deficient on account of the lack of knowledge. Paul was anxious to supply the lack lest they fall from their steadfastness. [The principal things lacking apparently concerned their conduct, their hope, and their mutual relationship in the church, for instruction on these points occupies the remainder of the Epistle.]

7. PRAYER FOR THE THESSALONIANS
3: 11-13

11 Now may [2]our God and Father himself, and our Lord Jesus, direct our way unto you: 12 and the Lord make you to increase and abound in love one

[2]Or, *God himself and our Father*

---

11 Now may our God and Father himself, and our Lord Jesus,—Paul had earnestly endeavored to visit them, but in vain. Satan had successfully opposed him. But Paul made his appeal to God who is overall, and to the Lord Jesus, their Lord and his. God is mightier and wiser than Satan and his servants, so all is well.

direct our way unto you:—[The petition is that God would remove all obstacles so that he could come direct to them. This prayer, though deferred, in about five years afterwards was fulfilled in his return to Macedonia. (Acts 20: 1, 3.)]

toward another, and toward all men, even as we also *do* toward you; 13 to
the end he may establish your hearts unblamable in holiness before [3]our God
and Father, at the [4]coming of our Lord Jesus with all his saints.[5]

[3]Or, *God and our Father*
[4]Gr. *presence.* Comp. 2 Cor. 10. 10
[5]Many ancient authorities add *Amen*

**12 and the Lord make you to increase and abound in love
one toward another,**—Paul so loved them that he could not
rest until he had made known the full will of God to them.
[Taken together the words may be understood as *increase in
love so as to abound.*]

and toward all men, even as we also do toward you;—If
such earnest love that others should know the truth and be
saved was proper for the Thessalonian Christians, it is right
for Christians now.   Christians then inspired with the true
spirit cannot rest without making an earnest effort to make
known the will of God to all men.   [The Christian obligation
to love and to serve is not to be limited in its objects to other
Christians, nor does it in any way depend on the love or hate
that others may show. (Matt. 5 : 44-48.)   There is no limit to
the heart's capacity for love nor to the opportunities afforded
for its exercise in daily life; hence, these repeated exhortations. (4 : 1, 10; 2 Thess. 3 : 5.)]

**13 to the end he may establish your hearts unblamable in
holiness before our God and Father,**—The prayer that God
would make them to increase in love toward one another and
toward all men was to the end that he might thereby establish
their hearts unblamable in holiness before God.

at the coming of our Lord Jesus with all his saints.—This
carries the thought that the heart cannot be established unblamable in holiness before God—cannot be prepared to meet
the Lord at his coming—without a heart abounding in love toward both God and man. "Love worketh no ill to his
neighbor; love therefore is the fulfilment of the law." (Rom.
13 : 10.) He who abounds in love must do what the law requires him to do, both toward God and man.

SECTION TWO

EXHORTATIONS AGAINST VICE, AND COMFORT AND WARNINGS IN VIEW OF THE COMING OF CHRIST
4: 1 to 5: 28

1. WARNINGS AGAINST IMPURITY
4: 1-8

1 Finally then, brethren, we beseech and exhort you in the Lord Jesus, that, as ye received of us how ye ought to walk and to please God, even as ye do walk,—that ye abound more and more. 2 For ye know what ⁰charge

⁰Gr. *charges*

---

1 Finally—[This does not imply that the letter was drawing to a close, but it marks a transition in the subject matter. Hindered from speaking to them by word of mouth, he writes this Epistle to supply that which was lacking.]

then, brethren,—[As he had prayed for their growth in holiness, now he exhorts them to the same end; for the only way to reach that condition is through obedience to the revealed will of God.]

we beseech and exhort you in the Lord Jesus,—Paul *beseeches* them as a matter concerning himself and his interest in them; he *exhorts,* as it concerns them and their own duty and relation to Christ because they are Christians, that such an appeal is addressed to them.

that, as ye received of us how ye ought to walk—*Received* signifies the reception as a matter of instruction. But beside teaching the facts of the gospel they taught its practice—what men should do and what should be the work and effect of their faith (1:3)—as well as what they should believe.

and to please God,—The duty of pleasing God had been emphasized in Paul's instructions, and he had set all other duties in this light. He spoke of himself "not as pleasing men, but God who proveth our hearts." (2:4.) Similarly of the Jews, he says, they "please not God, and are contrary to all men." (2:15.) [Our conduct is always in everything pleasing or displeasing to him, and the earnest Christian finds in this the highest delight in the service of God.]

we gave you through the Lord Jesus. 3 For this is the will of God, *even*
your sanctification, that ye abstain from fornication; 4 that each one of you

---

even as ye do walk,—This he adds lest they should be
grieved by an apparent assumption on his part that they had
failed to heed his former instructions.

that ye abound more and more.—The close relations of the
believer to Christ is the grand motive for striving after true
progress. The grace of God supplies the power; the love of
Christ brings the obligation. By all that he is to us we are
urged to be worthy of him by an even richer and fuller Christian life. [There is no finality to progressive holiness while
the believer remains on earth. Life is marked either by
growth or decay. Hence, Christians are to be "rooted and
grounded in love" (Eph. 3: 17), to be "sound in faith, in love,
in patience" (Tit. 2: 2); for as they "walk in love" toward one
another and toward all men, they walk so as to please God
(Eph. 5: 2). To please God is the highest ambition of the true
Christian; the consciousness of pleasing him is the highest
Christian joy. But walking implies progress. Standing still
is dangerous. They must go on from strength to strength,
forgetting the things that are behind and pressing on to those
that are before.]

**2 For ye know what charge we gave you through the Lord
Jesus.**—He impresses upon them that the commandments he
had given were from the Lord Jesus. Although Paul was inspired, he would not take such responsibilities on his shoul-
ders as many uninspired men do every day. Paul would give
no direction save what Jesus gave him.

3 For this is the will of God, even your sanctification,—All
who have entered into Christ, and have thus obligated themselves to serve him are sanctified in him.

that ye abstain from fornication;—No man can be sanctified
or consecrated to God who does not restrain all lusts, and direct them in a lawful channel. [The foul and heathenish vice
of fornication was prevalent among the heathen and little condemned by public opinion. It was especially the great sin of
Corinth, from which Paul wrote, the patron goddess of which
city was Venus. The purity of the Thessalonian Christians
was imperiled from the condition of society around them, and

know how to possess himself of his own vessel in sanctification and honor, 5
not in the passion of lust, even as the Gentiles who know not God; 6 that no

in many cases from former unchaste habits. The temptations
to licentiousness assailing the first generation of Christians
were fearfully strong, and Paul in all his Epistles gives urgent
warnings upon this subject. The sense of purity had to be
created in men gathered out of the midst of heathen corruption.]

4 **that each one of you know how to possess himself**—
Everyone should know how to govern his lusts within the limits of sanctification and honor and maintain purity and self-
restraint.

of his own vessel—There can be no doubt that he employs
the term to mean body. For everyone has his own body as
his house in which he dwells. He would, therefore, have us
keep our body pure from all uncleanness. The victim of sensual passion ceases to be master of his own person—he is possessed; and those who formerly lived in heathen uncleanness
had now as Christians to possess themselves of their bodies to
win the vessel of their spiritual life and make it truly their
own, and a fit receptacle, for the redeemed and sanctified self.
(Luke 21 : 19.)

in sanctification and honor,—Honorably, for the one who
prostitutes his body to uncleanness covers it with infamy and
disgrace. [In marriage people are to so live that they may be
mutually conscious that with them marriage is an honorable
estate, with nothing in it that makes them ashamed, and that
it promotes their sanctification.]

5 **not in the passion of lust,**—Not giving way to the lusts or
to the will or tendency of unrestrained licentiousness. [Pas-
sion signifies an overpowering feeling, one to which one so
yields himself that he is borne along by evil as if he were its
passive instrument; he has lost the dignity of self-control and
is the slave of his own appetites.]

even as the Gentiles who know not God;—The Gentiles
gave way to the gratification of every lust and evil desire.
[For impurity, often in the most abandoned and revolting
forms, was a prevailing feature of pagan life at the time Paul
wrote. Of their condition, Paul says: "Wherefore God gave

man [7]transgress, and wrong his brother in the matter : because the Lord is an avenger in all these things, as also we [8]forewarned you and testified. 7 For

[7]Or, *overreach*
[8]Or, *told you plainly*

them up in the lusts of their hearts unto uncleanness, that their bodies should be dishonored among themselves : for that they exchanged the truth of God for a lie, and worshipped and served the creature rather than the Creator, who is blessed for ever. Amen. For this cause God gave them up unto vile passions : for their women changed the natural use into that which is against nature : and likewise also the men, leaving the natural use of the woman, burned in their lust one toward another, men with men working unseemliness, and receiving in themselves that recompense of their error which was due." (Rom. 1 : 24-27.) Man first denies his Creator, then, degrades himself.]

6 that no man transgress, and wrong his brother in the matter :—This has reference to the sin of adultery. Each one should restrain his lust within the bounds sanctified and made honorable by God. None should go beyond what is right and violate the marital rights of his brethren.

because the Lord is an avenger in all these things,—Paul says: "Be not deceived; God is not mocked; for whatsoever a man soweth, that shall he also reap. For he that soweth unto his own flesh shall of the flesh reap corruption." (Gal. 6: 7, 8.) "For which things' sake cometh the wrath of God upon the sons of disobedience." (Col. 3: 6.) The law of God, wrought into the constitution of the human body, takes care that we do not escape without paying the penalty. If not at the moment, it is in the future, and with interest in premature old age; in the torpor which succeeds the excesses of man's prime; in the sudden breakdown under any strain put on either physical or moral courage. They are avenged in the soul. Sensual indulgence extinguishes the capacity for feeling; the profligate would love but cannot; all that is inspiring, elevating, redeeming in the passions is lost to him; all that remains is the dull sense of that incalculable loss. This deadening is one of the most terrible consequences of immorality. They who do such things do not escape the avenging holiness of God. Even death, the refuge to which despair so often drives,

God called us not for uncleanness, but in sanctification. 8 Therefore he that rejecteth, rejecteth not man, but God, who giveth his Holy Spirit unto you.

holds out no hope to them. Men and women of the present age need to have impressed on them that God is an avenger of sexual wrongs both in this world and the next.

as also we forewarned you and testified.—[On this subject it appears that Paul at Thessalonica had spoken very plainly and solemnly from the first.]

7 **For God called us not for uncleanness,**—God has not called to practice any lewd and lascivious habits which the Gentiles who know not God practice. The law of God alone can hold back from degrading sins.

but in sanctification.—God constituted marriage: "Let marriage be had in honor among all, and let the bed be undefiled." (Heb. 13: 4.) He ordained that every man should have his wife and cleave unto her alone. [The call of God was from the first a sanctifying call for the Thessalonians, and was attended with holy influences and forbade all uncleanness. Certainly he never intended them to live impure lives when he called them into his own kingdom and glory. (2: 12.)]

8 **Therefore he that rejecteth, rejecteth not man, but God,**— God's test of love is willingness to obey him out of respect and reverence for his will. "This is the love of God, that we keep his commandments." (1 John 5: 3.) It matters not what a man's emotions, sympathies, and attractions may be, if he is not willing to deny himself and reject his own wisdom and obey the will of God, he rejects God. According to this rule, so strongly emphasized by God, if a man do the things commanded by God as the dictate of his own wisdom and not as obedience to the will of God, that doing is not accepted as service to God. The principle and test of love becomes simple under the law of God. Whenever one will forego earthly ends to obey, he loves God better than he loves these ends.

who giveth his Holy Spirit unto you.—God had given to his chosen apostles his Holy Spirit that they might know the mind of God. They delivered this mind or will of God to men; and when they reject or set aside the teaching of the apostles for the wisdom of man they do not reject man, but God. All the efforts to exalt human wisdom and experience to a rule of action for man is to reject the wisdom of God; and those who reject God, God will reject and condemn them with an everlasting destruction.

2. EXHORTATION TO BROTHERLY LOVE AND SOBRIETY OF CONDUCT
4: 9-12

9 But concerning love of the brethren ye have no need that one write unto you: for ye yourselves are taught of God to love one another; 10 for

9 **But concerning love of the brethren ye have no need that one write unto you:**—They already practiced brotherly love. (3: 6.) These words distinguished a remarkable characteristic of the early church. They describe how the first Christians regarded themselves as the members of one family. They felt like the members of one household, like the nearest kindred in one home, and in the spirit of home life they shared their possessions. This was only possible so long as the family spirit pervaded the church. Circumstances altered the habits of the church as it grew in numbers and spread over a wide area. But all through Paul's Epistles the same family affection of Christians is apparent. Love of the brethren one for the other is a leading feature of Christianity.

for ye yourselves are taught of God to love one another;— They showed their love by deeds of kindness and helpfulness to each other. The whole gospel taught them to love one another. As Christ loved the brethren, so in following him they did the same. [When the gospel went abroad in the world, two characteristics of its adherents—their personal purity and love for each other—attracted general attention. Amidst the gross sensuality of heathenism, the Christian stood untainted by indulgence of the flesh, and the utter heartlessness of heathen society, which made no provision for the poor, sick, or the infirm and the aged. The Christians were conspicuous for their brotherly kindness to each other. Personal purity and brotherly love were the new and regenerating virtues which Christ had called into existence in the midst of a dying world.

indeed ye do it toward all the brethren that are in all Macedonia. But we exhort you, brethren, that ye abound more and more; 11 and that ye ⁹study

⁹Gr. *be ambitious.* See Rom. 15. 20 marg.

The principle of brotherly love is the very essence of Christianity. Every believer is taught of God to love the brother who shares his faith; such is the guarantee of our own salvation. Hence, it is said: "We know that we have passed out of death into life, because we love the brethren. He that loveth not abideth in death." (1 John 3: 14.) The brotherly love of the apostolic church was not only visible to the world, it commended it to the world; it brought a new thing into being, a new thing for which the world was pining. The poor in the cities of Asia and Europe saw with wonder and joy and hope men and women united to one another in a spiritual union which gave scope to all their gifts for society and satisfied all their desires for it. The churches were companies of people where love to God and man was the prevailing sentiment, where outward pressure often increased the inward bonds, and where mutual confidence diffused inward joy. Men were drawn to them by the desire to share the life of love.]

10 for indeed ye do it toward all the brethren that are in all Macedonia.—Thessalonica was the natural center of the Macedonian churches, including Philippi and Berea, with other congregations which had sprung up around these principal cities. The Thessalonian Christians were using their position and influence for the good of their brethren around them, and thus giving the proof that they were deeply interested in the Lord's work. Silas and Timothy had recently returned from Macedonia (3: 6; Acts 18: 5), and had doubtless informed Paul of their zeal in behalf of the brethren around them.

But we exhort you, brethren, that ye abound more and more;—[That for which Paul had prayed (3: 12) is now the subject of an earnest exhortation. What had formerly applied to the whole of a God-pleasing course is now applied to brotherly love. He exhorts them to seek opportunities to express their love in brethren beyond Macedonia. Embrace in intellectual and practical interest a wider extent of the brotherhood

to be quiet, and to do your own business, and to work with your hands, even

in Christ. The present obstacle to love is selfishness or exorbitant fondness for one's own interests, for which we have all reason to humble ourselves before God, and give love the unlimited sway of our being, so that we shall ungrudgingly delight in our brethren in Christ, seek their advancement in Christian excellence, and help them in all ways we can.]

11 and that ye study to be quiet,—Not meddlesome, or busybodies in other people's matters. [For the word "study" the margin has "be ambitious to be quiet." Paul here combines words of contradictory meaning in order to give point and force to the exhortation. The love of personal distinction was an active influence and potent for mischief in Greek city life; possibly the Thessalonians were touched with it, and betrayed symptoms of the restless and emulous spirit that afterwards gave Paul so much trouble in Corinth. He makes it an object in prayer: "I exhort therefore, first of all, that supplications, prayers, intercessions, thanksgivings, be made for all men; . . . that we may lead a tranquil and quiet life in all godliness and gravity." (1 Tim. 2: 1, 2.) Eager and active as his own nature was, Paul much admired this kind of a life and deemed it ordinarily the course filled for the cultivation and development of Christian character. Though he may escape the excitements of social and political life, the Christian is exposed to the more subtle dangers of religious excitement, always a chief hindrance to love of the brethren; for as fever prevents the due discharge of the functions of the body, so does excitement the healthy activities of the spirit.]

and to do your own business,—He instructs them to attend to their own affairs, and not to interfere with the affairs of others. This would prevent the impertinent prying into the affairs of others, to which many are prone, and produce that careful attention to their calling in life, which produces thrift, order, and competence. The Lord requires no one to give up an honorable calling, and countenances idleness in no one. [The Christian should be punctual, prompt, and energetic. "It is as when a man, sojourning in another country, having left

as we charged you; 12 that ye may walk becomingly toward them that are
without, and may have need of nothing.

---

his house, and given authority to his servants, to each one his
work, commanded also the porter to watch." (Mark 13: 34.)]

and to work with your hands,—"Jehovah God took the man,
and put him into the garden of Eden to dress it and to keep
it." (Gen. 2: 15.) "And unto Adam he said, Because thou
hast harkened unto the voice of thy wife, and hast eaten of the
tree, of which I commanded thee, saying, Thou shalt not eat
of it: cursed is the ground for thy sake; in toil shalt thou eat
of it all the days of thy life; thorns also and thistles shall it
bring forth to thee; and thou shalt eat the herb of the field; in
the sweat of thy face shalt thou eat bread, till thou return
unto the ground; for out of it wast thou taken: for dust thou
art, and unto dust shalt thou return." (Gen. 3: 17-19.)
Labor was not the curse, mortality or death was the curse.
Labor was the antidote to the curse, as it would employ him
in the ways not hurtful.

even as we charged you;—While he was with them he commanded them to labor with their hands, and this command
had often been given to them. It is a duty that should be
taught to all Christians.

12 **that ye may walk becomingly**—Christians should so
excel in the common decencies and duties of life as to afford
the unbeliever no occasion to upbraid or suspect them. Paul
was ever solicitous about such matters. He says: "Walk in
wisdom toward them that are without, redeeming the time."
(Col. 4: 5.) "Look therefore carefully how ye walk, not as
unwise, but as wise; redeeming the time, because the days are
evil." (Eph. 5: 15, 16.) And of the domestic virtues it is said:
"In like manner, ye wives, be in subjection to your own husbands; that, even if any obey not the word, they may without
the word be gained by the behavior of their wives; beholding
your chaste behavior coupled with fear." (1 Pet. 3: 1, 2.)
And to the husbands he says: "Ye husbands, in like manner,
dwell with your wives according to knowledge, giving honor
unto the women, as unto the weaker vessel, as being also

joint-heirs of the grace of life; to the end that your prayers be not hindered." (3 : 7.)

toward them that are without,—Those who are not Christians, whether Jews or Gentiles, are without. [While they know nothing of the spiritual blessings of the gospel (1 Cor. 2: 14), they do appreciate the difference, order, and confusion between idleness and diligence, between begging and independence. The good effects of the gospel were to be shown in every relation with all men in daily life, lest the way of truth should be spoken against. "And many shall follow their lascivious doings; by reason of whom the way of the truth shall be evil spoken of." (2 Pet. 2: 2.)]

and may have need of nothing.—Two purposes would be filled by their industry: (1) allay the suspicions of those without; and (2) to be well supplied themselves. Paul limits the labor to that which is good: "Let him that stole steal no more: but rather let him labor, working with his hands the thing that is good, that he may have whereof to give to him that hath need." (Eph. 4: 28.) Diligent labor in that which is good that one may supply his own needs and those of his family, be able to pay his debts, act honestly toward others, and have to give to those who need is the law of God. To work the things that are good is to work at those callings which bring good to the world. Christians are forbidden to work at callings that bring evil.

3. CONCERNING THOSE WHO HAVE FALLEN ASLEEP
4: 13-18

13 But we would not have you ignorant, brethren, concerning them that fall asleep; that ye sorrow not, even as the rest, who have no hope. 14 For

---

13 But we would not have you ignorant, brethren,—[This impressive phrase Paul employs as in Rom. 11: 25 and elsewhere to call attention to a new topic concerning which he was especially anxious for his readers to have a clear understanding.]

concerning them that fall asleep;—Some of the members had died, and this aroused a painful fear lest such had lost their share in the Lord's approaching advent. So vivid was the expectation of the Lord's return that it seemed to those newborn children of God that those dying would miss the great hope that had been so precious to them of seeing Christ return to raise the dead. But the glorious revelation here as to the triumphant future of both the dead and living saints dispelled their gloom and comforted their hearts as it has the faithful Christians since. *Death* is sleep to Christians. The Lord Jesus Christ made it the standing name for death among believers. (Luke 8: 52; John 11: 11; Acts 8: 1.) The expression indicates the restful effect on the child of God and also its temporary nature. We sleep but a brief period and then rise to renewed activity. The expression indicates the restful effects of death to the child of God and its temporary nature. It will last no longer than Christ delays his coming. How the word *sleep* must have consoled the Thessalonian mourners!

that ye sorrow not,—[Not the natural sorrow over the departure of loved ones, but the sorrow of distress about their future. They who look for no resurrection sorrow for the dead, but Christians are not to do so. To bewail the condition of the faithful Christian is wholly out of place, though to utter our own grief and bewail our own loss is natural and fitting. Grief for the loss of friends is common to all, and is not inconsistent with acceptance of the will of God, neither does it deny the hope of the Christian. Jesus himself wept in sympathy at the grave of Lazarus. (John 11: 33-35.) Paul was apprehensive of the sorrow into which he would have been plunged had the sickness of Epaphroditus resulted in death. (Phil. 2: 27.) The brethren at Thessalonica grieved not merely for their loss, but they grieved also for the loss sustained, as the survivors supposed, by those of their number who had died. It was to save them from grief on this account that the apostle wrote, showing them that their fears were groundless.]

even as the rest,—The heathens, on the death of their relatives and friends, made a great how of excessive grief by cutting their flesh and by loud crying and lamentations.

who have no hope.—A broad characteristic of all who are not in Christ; they have no hope concerning the future life. Of the unbelieving Gentiles, Paul said they are: "Strangers

if we believe that Jesus died and rosé again, even so them also that are fallen

from the covenants of the promise, having no hope and without God in the world." (Eph. 2: 12.)

14 **For if we believe**—The foundation truth of the gospel was, and is, that all Christians believe that Jesus died and rose again.

that Jesus—[The personal name is appropriate here, as it reminded them that the Deliverer for whom they looked, and who had himself undergone death, which they dreaded, was himself a man, and that his manhood was unimpaired by his death. It was Jesus who died and the same Jesus who rose again. (Acts 1: 11; 2: 32, 36; 9: 5; 1 Tim. 2: 5; 2 Tim. 2: 8.) Death had not been final in his case, neither would it be in theirs.]

died—The first cardinal point of the gospel of God concerning his Son is that he died—"who was delivered up for our trespasses" (Rom. 4: 25) ; "and gave himself up" (Eph. 5: 25) ; "suffered" (1 Pet. 3: 18). This fact is always stated in direct terms. The term as used in the Scriptures refers to two things : (1) The separation of the soul from the body and the cessation of the functions of the body and its return to "dust." (Gen. 3: 19.) In this sense Adam's body at the age of nine hundred thirty years died. (Gen. 5: 5.) In this sense death awaits every human being. (Heb. 9: 27.) (2) The separation of man from God. "For the mind of the flesh is death." (Rom. 8: 6.) Adam died in this sense the day he disobeyed God. (Gen. 2: 17.) The descendants of Adam are born in the same state of separation from God. In this sense death describes the condition of all unregenerated men. (John 5: 24, 25; Rom. 5: 12-21; Eph. 2: 15; 4: 18; 1 John 3: 14.) Death is the opposite of life. It is definitely stated that God created man, called him into existence (Gen. 1: 27) ; but the Scriptures nowhere state that he will ever cease to exist. The term "life" when used of man, as distinguished from the body— "the earthly house of our tabernacle" (2 Cor. 5: 1)—may be defined as conscious existence in communion with God. But when death is used of man, and not merely of the body, it is properly defined as conscious existence in separation from God. All out of Christ are dead, all in Christ have life. But

asleep [10]in Jesus will God bring with him. 15 For this we say unto you by

[10]Gr. *through.* Or, *will God through Jesus*

all, whether living or dead, equally exist and are equally conscious of existence. (Luke 16: 19-31.) If death were no existence, the declaration that Jesus died would convey a thought contradictory to the plain teaching of the Scriptures and would obviously be untrue. Therefore, in whichever sense it is used, it is in the Scripture viewed as the penal consequence of sin, and sinners alone are subject to death; it was as the *bearer* of sin that the Lord Jesus submitted to death on the cross. (Rom. 5: 12; 1 Pet. 2: 24.) And while the physical death of the Lord Jesus was of the essence of his sacrifice, it was not the whole. It is said: "Now from the sixth hour there was darkness over all the land until the ninth hour. And about the ninth hour Jesus cried with a loud voice, saying, . . . My God, my God, why hast thou forsaken me?" (Matt. 27: 45, 46.) The darkness symbolized and his cry expressed the fact that he was left alone in the universe; he was forsaken. Hence, it is that the word of consolation, *"sleep,"* was not used of him in his death. Here, however, since not expiation of sin, but the resurrection of the saints is in view, attention is concentrated on the simple historical fact of the physical death of the Lord Jesus. (John 19: 30.)

and rose again,—That it was not possible that his Son should be held by death is the second cardinal point in the gospel of God concerning his Son. (Acts 2: 24; Rom. 1: 4; 1 Cor. 15: 4.) "When he had made purification of sins, sat down on the right hand of the Majesty on high." (Heb. 1: 3.) [This is the only place in which Paul speaks of the resurrection of the Lord Jesus as his own act. Ordinarily, he speaks of it as the act of God. (1: 10.)]

even so them also that are fallen asleep in Jesus will God bring with him.—Jesus was the first fruits from the dead, and the first fruits were the promise of the coming harvest when all in Christ should come forth from the grave. [The same gospel that carried the assurance of the death and resurrection of the Lord carried also the assurance of the resurrection of all who believe on him.]

the word of the Lord, that we that are alive, that are left unto the [11]coming

―――――――――
[11]Gr. *presence*

15 **For this we say unto you by the word of the Lord,**—Paul now gives the authority for this statement and shows how the dead in Christ shall share in the glorious coming of the Lord. By "the word of the Lord," he evidently means a revelation from the Lord direct to him. In what way prophets and apostles became conscious of supernatural inspiration is not revealed; but elsewhere also Paul speaks of the consciousness of thus being moved. (Acts 18:9; 1 Cor. 7:10; Gal. 1:12; Eph. 3:3-12.) [The things to which reference is made are such as the eye has not seen, or the ear heard, or had entered into the heart of man; they are out of range of the natural man. The words of Paul assert that "we say unto you by the word of the Lord," and thus revealed them to him who spoke them, and certainly in the same words the Lord taught him to use. Evidently the Lord guided him to use these words, not because they were unfamiliar, but perhaps for the very purpose of preventing him from using words that were not familiar.]

that we that are alive,—At the coming of the Lord Jesus, believers will be divided into two classes, even as they were then at Thessalonica, the living and the dead. But the time of that coming has not been revealed; it is among the secret things concerning which Jehovah has kept his own counsel. (Deut. 29:29.) As a consequence in speaking of the coming of the Lord, Paul sometimes associates himself with those looking forward to resurrection (2 Cor. 4:14); sometimes to those looking forward to change (1 Cor. 15:51, 52). It is clear, therefore, that no conclusion can be drawn from Paul's language as to his personal expectations. He certainly shared in what should be the attitude of every generation of Christians—the desire for, and the expectation of, the coming of the Lord Jesus. Throughout his life, as his Epistles clearly show, he maintained the same attitude toward the great alternatives. His example and his words alike teach us to be prepared to meet death with unflinching courage, but, above all things to look for the coming of the Lord.

of the Lord, shall in no wise precede them that are fallen asleep. 16 For the
Lord himself shall descend from heaven, with a shout, with the voice of the

---

that are left unto the coming of the Lord,—These words are
intended to show what is meant by the living. They were not
necessarily the then living, though there was a reasonable
hope that the Lord might come again during the lifetime of
those who would read this Epistle, but those who will be upon
the earth when the Lord comes.

shall in no wise precede them that are fallen asleep.—This
discloses that believers at the time of the Lord's second coming shall have no precedence of those that sleep. The dead in
Christ shall rise before any change of the living saints shall
take place. If there is to be any priority at all, it will be in
favor of the sleeping saints; these will be raised before anything is done for the living; they are to have the foremost
place in the glorious events of the Lord's coming. Though
dead, they are "dead in Christ"—departed "to be at home with
the Lord." (2 Cor. 5: 8; Phil. 1: 23.)

16 **For the Lord himself shall descend from heaven,**—The
Lord is now in heaven at God's right hand. (Acts 7: 55; Heb.
1: 3.) Thence he shall come forth. No apparition will it be,
but an actual and visible descent. The same person who ascended is he who will descend. Angels will accompany the
Lord's coming. (2 Thess. 1: 7; Matt. 25: 30, 31.) They will
have their part to perform in the tremendous events of the
day.

with a shout,—[This word is peculiar and distinctive. It
occurs nowhere else in the New Testament. It is used of an
officer to his troops, or by a sea captain to his crew. It con-
fines itself to a particular class; it is addressed to a distinct
company; hence, is neither universal nor indiscriminate. It is
a signal shout to Christ's own people and to no others. It will
single out those who are asleep in Jesus Christ and pass all
others by; it will be heard and understood and obeyed by the
saints and by no others. For Paul is there dealing with Christians alone; the wicked do not enter the circle the apostle addresses. The like significant fact appears in 1 Cor. 15: 35-58.
Christians only are subjects of that great call. The wicked
dead will certainly be raised and the living nations be judged.

archangel, and with the trump of God: and the dead in Christ shall rise

(John 5: 28, 29; Matt. 25: 31-46.) But here God's people alone are in view. The shout singles out Christ's own dead and quickens them into life. It is an articulate sound, for it is the utterance of the Lord's own voice. (Matt. 24: 31; John 5: 25-29.) But in the passage before us God's people alone are in view. The almighty shout singles out Christ's own from among the dead and quickens them into life. It is not an inarticulate sound that is meant, as a peal of thunder or the loud report of some powerful explosive, as is by some imagined; it is an articulate sound, for it is the utterance of the Lord's own voice. Jesus said: "Marvel not at this: for the hour cometh, in which all that are in the tombs shall hear his voice, and shall come forth; they that have done good, unto the resurrection of life; and they that have done evil, unto the resurrection of judgment." (John 5: 28, 29.) At the tomb of Lazarus "he cried with a loud voice, Lazarus, come forth." (John 11: 43.) The Lord Jesus Christ will utter his voice, will call from above to his sleeping people, and they shall hear and obey the call and come forth in incorruptible and glorious bodies. At his command they shall rise. Round this planet shall that mighty shout ring, penetrating every grave, piercing even the ocean's depth, and it will stir into life and call out into the eternal fellowship of the Lord the whole vast host of the righteous dead.]

with the voice of the archangel,—[The word seems to denote, not chief angel, but chief or ruler of the angels. They will have their part to perform in the tremendous events of that day. The voice of the archangel may be employed to summon the heavenly hosts and marshal the innumerable company of the redeemed, for "they shall gather together his elect from the four winds, from one end of heaven to the other." (Matt. 24: 31.) An army associated with royalty gives an impression of power and grandeur. How exalted is this divine personage whose coming is attended by such a retinue—the marshaled legions of the skies!]

and with the trump of God:—It is God's trumpet because employed in his heavenly service. Paul calls it "the last

first; 17 then we that are alive, that left, shall together with them be caught

---

trump," and adds, "For the trumpet shall sound, and the dead shall be raised incorruptible, and we shall be changed." (1 Cor. 15: 52.) [It is "the last" because it sounds its awful peal in connection with the end. The trumpet, like the voice of the archangel, is but the instrument of God to accomplish his glorious purposes. Through both these the descending Lord accomplishes his sovereign will in the resurrection of his sleeping dead and the change of the living saints.]

and the dead in Christ shall rise first;—Those in Christ who are dead shall rise and ascend before those who are alive at his coming. [So little danger is there that those who die before the Lord comes will suffer loss; they will be the first to share in the glad triumph of their Redeemer. Immediately thereafter living believers will be fashioned anew in their bodies, and so made fit to dwell in Christ in glory. "Behold, I tell you a mystery: We all shall not sleep, but we shall all be changed, in a moment, in the twinkling of an eye, at the last trump; for the trumpet shall sound, and the dead shall be raised incorruptible, and we shall be changed." (1 Cor. 15: 51, 52.) "For our citizenship is in heaven; whence also we wait for a Saviour, the Lord Jesus Christ: who shall fashion anew the body of our humiliation, that it may be conformed to the body of his glory, according to the working whereby he is able even to subject all things unto himself." (Phil. 3: 20, 21.) Just what is in this physical transformation is not revealed; but of some things touching it we may be sure. It will be the identical body and spirit of those then living that will be changed. It will be so complete and perfect that while the identity will be preserved it will be forever freed from all that is earthly, mortal; it will be a "body of glory," like the glorious body of the Son of God. Incorruption and immortality will be the vesture of the saved and glorified.]

17 then we that are alive, that are left,—[The phrase of verse 15 is here repeated, thus distinguishing as in 1 Cor. 15: 51, 52 between those living and those dead in Christ at the time of his advent, marking the different positions in which these two divisions of the saints will be found. Just what is

up in the clouds, to meet the Lord in the air: and so shall we ever be with the Lord. 18 Wherefore ¹comfort one another with these words.

¹Or, *exhort* ch. 5. 11

involved in the physical transformation is not disclosed and speculation is worse than useless.]

shall together with them be caught up in the clouds,—"Together with" implies full association. Sundered as the saints will be the Lord's return, some in their graves, other alive, and all scattered over the whole earth, they then shall be reunited nevermore to part.

to meet the Lord in the air:—Not heaven, not in some sphere infinitely remote from this world, but in the upper regions of the lower atmosphere. As they ascend to meet him their bodies "shall all be changed, in a moment, in the twinkling of an eye" (1 Cor. 15: 51, 52), thus their bodies shall be changed from natural into spiritual bodies, which, being fashioned after the likeness of his glorious body, shall be able to endure the brightness of his presence, which those in the flesh could not (Rev. 1: 17).

and so shall we ever be with the Lord.—On the night before his crucifixion, Jesus said to his disciples: "I go to prepare a place for you. And if I go and prepare a place for you, I come again, and will receive you unto myself; that where I am, there ye may be also. (John 14: 2, 3.) And he prayed on the night of his betrayal: "Father, I desire that they also whom thou hast given me be with me where I am, that they may behold my glory, which thou hast given me: for thou lovedst me before the foundation of the world." (John 17: 24.)

18 **Wherefore comfort one another with these words.**—Because the dead shall be raised, and those who remain alive shall be caught up in the twinkling of an eye, and because this corruptible must put on incorruption, and this mortal must put on immortality. When our brethren in Christ sleep, we must "comfort one another with these words." These promises of the future resurrection to those in Christ should be grounds of comfort to Christians when their brethren in Christ die. It is a sleep, a rest in Christ Jesus, whence they will come forth with new life and vigor and increasing joys.

[What congregation is there in which there is not need of this consolation? One needs the comfort today and another tomorrow; in proportion as we bear each other's burdens, we all need it continually. The unseen world is perpetually opening to receive those whom we love; but though they pass out of sight and out of reach, it is not forever. They are still united to Christ; and when he comes in his glory he will bring them with him. Is it not strange to balance the greatest sorrow of life against words? Words, we often feel, are vain and worthless; they make no difference in the pressure of grief. Of our own words that is true; but those we have been considering are not our own words, but the words of the Lord. His words are living and powerful. Heaven and earth may pass away, but they cannot pass. Let us comfort one another with these precious words.]

4. CONCERNING THE TRUE WAY TO WATCH FOR THE COMING OF THE LORD
5: 1-11

1 But concerning the times and the seasons, brethren, ye have no need that aught be written unto you. 2 For yourselves know perfectly that the

1 **But concerning the times and the seasons, brethren, ye have no need that aught be written unto you.**—The Greek word for *times* denotes space of time, that for *seasons* particular times. The question as to *times* was how long before the Lord comes. What periods will elapse before the Lord comes? As to *seasons,* what events will transpire meanwhile? How will the course of history shape itself? These questions naturally excited their curiosity. But they had been plainly told that they could not know.

2 **For yourselves know perfectly that the day of the Lord so cometh as a thief in the night.**—They had been taught by the apostle that the coming of the Lord would be as a thief in the night. This Jesus taught: "But of the day and hour knoweth no one, not even the angels of heaven, neither the Son, but the Father only. And as were the days of Noah, so shall be the coming of the Son of man. For as in those days which were before the flood they were eating and drinking, marrying and giving in marriage, until the day that Noah entered into the

day of the Lord so cometh as a thief in the night. 3 When they are saying,
Peace and safety, then sudden destruction cometh upon them, as travail upon
a woman with child; and they shall in no wise escape. 4 But ye, brethren,

---

ark, and they knew not until the flood came, and took them all
away; so shall be the coming of the Son of man. . . . Watch
therefore: for ye know not on what day your Lord cometh.
But know this, that if the master of the house had known in
what watch the thief was coming, he would have watched,
and would not have suffered his house to be broken through.
Therefore be ye also ready; for in an hour that ye think not
the Son of man cometh." (Matt. 24: 36-44. See also 25: 13;
Luke 12: 39, 40; 2 Pet. 3: 10.)   No truth seems to have been
more clearly and fully taught than that the Son of man would
come when not looked for by the world.   Yet there is no question connected with the Scripture on which man bestows
more attention, and no question that they seek more earnestly
to determine.   The time has been often set, and as often
proved a mistake.   One, by a righteous and pure life, can be
ready for his coming.   We should not only be ready for him,
but should also love his appearing and desire earnestly the
day of his coming.

3 **When they are saying, Peace and safety,**—In the very act
of their saying, "Peace and safety"—just when men of the
world pronounce everything secure and quiet—then the thief
comes, who steals from them the possessions they imagined
safe from all attack. Such times of security are pregnant with
judgment to the wicked.

then sudden destruction cometh upon them.—[Then suddenly over them stands destruction.   Without a moment's
warning ruin comes—not seen approaching, but first visible
hanging over the doomed sinner.]

as travail upon a woman with child;—This image signifies,
besides the suddenness of the disaster, its intense pain, and its
inevitableness.   The point of comparison is the suddenness of
the birth pang and that of the Lord's coming.

and they shall in no wise escape.—[Instead of peace and
safety destruction surprises them; all for which they have
lived passes away; they awake, as from a deep sleep, to dis-

are not in darkness, that that day should overtake you ²as a thief: 5 for ye are all sons of light, and sons of the day: we are not of the night, nor of darkness; 6 so then let us not sleep, as do the rest, but let us watch and be sober. 7 For they that sleep sleep in the night; and they that are drunken

²Some ancient authorities read *as thieves*

cover that their soul has no part with God. It is too late then to think of preparing for the end; the end has come; and it is with solemn emphasis that the apostle adds, "They shall in no wise escape."]

4 **But ye, brethren, are not in darkness, that that day should overtake you as a thief:**—This does not mean that they will know when the Lord will come, but is an exhortation to be always prepared, always looking, always ready that they may not be taken by surprise, no matter when he comes.

5 **for ye are all sons of light, and sons of the day:**—The light which blesses men is all concentrated in Jesus Christ. As the light imparts new possibilities of life to those who otherwise are hopelessly in trespasses and sins, so the light of Christ enters into the heart through faith and produces a high spiritual order in the life that is thus begotten and sustained, as the apostle says, by "the light of the gospel of the glory of Christ. . . . Seeing it is God, that said, Light shall shine out of darkness, who shined in our hearts, to give the light of the knowledge of the glory of God in the face of Jesus Christ." (2 Cor. 4: 4-6.)

we are not of the night, nor of darkness;—To the sons of the day, who knowing and practicing the truth as it is in Christ, there is no night of darkness. They are always in the light. [Paul recognizes no exceptions, no inner distinctions, among the members of the church; all stand alike so far as grace, privileges, and duties are concerned. The following exhortation shows that it was a matter of each man's free will whether he would sustain his character as a "child of light" or not.]

6 **so then let us not sleep, as do the rest,**—Since we are of the day, let us not be careless, indifferent, or engaging in the works of darkness. [There is a conduct appropriate to every position. Our position as sons of light implies a certain corresponding wakefulness. We are sons of light because we live in Christ; it follows that we look for his appearing, and do not

are drunken in the night. 8 But let us, since we are of the day, be sober,

---

sleep as others may do who do not desire or expect his coming.]

but let us watch and be sober.—[Evidently the term *sober* in
this connection means sober as opposed to being drunk.
Everyone would shrink from being drunk on the great occasion of the Lord's coming; yet the great day of his coming is
associated with a warning against this awful sin. The Lord
warned: "Take heed to yourselves, lest haply your hearts be
overcharged with surfeiting, and drunkenness, and cares of
this life, and that day comes on you suddenly as a snare."
(Luke 21: 34.) Paul warns: "The night is far spent, and the
day is at hand: let us therefore cast off the works of darkness,
and let us put on the armor of light. Let us walk becomingly
as in the day; not in revelling and drunkenness, not in cham-
bering and wantonness, not in strife and jealousy." (Rom. 13:
12, 13.) What horror could be more awful than to be over-
taken in this state?]

7 For they that sleep sleep in the night;—The wicked, the
careless, the licentious are children of the night, and engage in
their sins in the night, when the thief will come unawares
upon them. The children of the day are those who live faithfully, always watching for the Lord's coming. He will come
to the children of the night with sudden destruction and ruin;
but to the children of the day, he will bring deliverance and
eternal salvation. Hence, the exhortation to be faithful children of the light.

and they that are drunken are drunken in the night.—
[These words are to be taken as a simple statement of fact—
what occurs in the ordinary experiences of life. The night is
the season in which sleep and drunkenness occur; whereas the
day is the time for watchfulness and work. The Jews and
heathen considered it disgraceful for a man to be drunk in the
daytime. For this reason the Jews on the day of the Pentecost said of the apostles: "They are filled with new wine. But
Peter, standing up with the eleven, lifted up his voice, and
spake forth unto them, . . . these are not drunken, as ye suppose; seeing it is but the third hour of the day." (Acts 2: 13-
15.)]

putting on the breastplate of faith and love; and for a helmet, the hope of salvation. 9 For God appointed us not unto wrath, but unto the obtaining of salvation through our Lord Jesus Christ, 10 who died for us, that, whether

8 **But let us, since we are of the day, be sober,**—He exhorts those who are of the day to restrain the appetites and passions to proper limits. [While the word sober means freedom from the influence of intoxicants, it also means freedom from credulity and from excitability. As *watch* denotes alertness, so *sober* is in contrast to the lethargy of sleep, so the latter is in contrast to the excitement of drunkenness. (Eph. 5: 18.) Christian sobriety of maturer years is the result of self-control and the study of the Scriptures.]

putting on the breastplate of faith and love;—[Of believers in Christ the apostle says: "For ye are all sons of God, through faith, in Christ Jesus. For as many of you as were baptized into Christ did put on Christ" (Gal. 3: 26, 27), and he is to "put on therefore, as God's elect, . . . a heart of compassion, kindness, lowliness, meekness, longsuffering" (Col. 3: 12), and such is to be the ordinary apparel of the Christian. In this character he is to appear daily in the world. He, however, is enrolled as a soldier (2 Tim. 2: 4), and as such has suitable armor provided for him, and with this he is exhorted to clothe himself (Eph. 6: 11). The whole is summed up in these words: "But put ye on the Lord Jesus Christ, and make not provision for the flesh, to fulfil the lusts thereof" (Rom. 13: 14), for the man who puts on the Lord Jesus Christ stands both in the Christian's dress and in the Christian's panoply.]

and for a helmet, the hope of salvation.—The hope of salvation is the helmet to protect the head—a salvation, the hope of which is to cover the heads in the day of battle.

9 **For God appointed us not unto wrath,**—The design of God in sending his Son into the world was not to condemn it.

but unto the obtaining of salvation through our Lord Jesus Christ,—Those who obtain this salvation and glory do so according to the appointment and calling of God on condition of a willing response to that calling through Jesus Christ.

10 **who died for us,**—No language expresses the office of the death of Jesus Christ so well as that used by the Holy Spirit: "All have sinned, and fall short of the glory of God; being jus-

we ³wake or sleep, we should live together with him. 11 Wherefore ⁴exhort

³Or, *watch*
⁴Or, *comfort* ch. 4. 18

tified freely by his grace through the redemption that is in Christ Jesus; whom God sent forth to be a propritiation, through faith, in his blood, to show his righteousness because of the passing over of the sins done aforetime, in the forbearance of God; for the showing, I say, of his righteousness at this present season: that he might himself be just, and the justifier of him that hath faith in Jesus." (Rom. 3: 23-26.) That is, the blood of Christ was provided for the salvation of all; but only those who, led by faith in God, accept the salvation provided can appropriate that salvation, or God is, by the shedding of that blood, enabled to be just while justifying him who believes in Jesus. This justification and the benefits through it are conveyed to the sinner through the exercise of faith in Christ Jesus, or through walking in the exercise of complying with the conditions sealed by the blood of Jesus Christ, into which he is led by faith in him. It follows then if one's life is saved through the blood of Christ, then Christ is entitled to that life, and man can approach God only through and by virtue of the blood with which he was purchased. He must come to God as the servant of Christ who has redeemed him.

that, whether we wake or sleep, we should live together with him.—[This refers to the anxieties of the Thessalonian Christians regarding their deceased brethren. He assures them that the very object of Christ in dying was to secure to his people a life which no death could interrupt or destroy. Those who have died before his second coming suffer no disadvantage, for he has secured that whether we wake or sleep —live or die—we should live with him. If we live in the flesh, we are to live by faith in the Son of God; we are to live by his grace, under his protection, in his body—the church. If we die, we die unto him, and in some way he reveals himself as nearer to us than when we live here on earth. Thus Paul says: "But I am in a strait betwixt the two, having the desire to depart and be with Christ; for it is very far better." (Phil. 1 : 23.)]

one another, and build each other up, even as alsó ye do.

---

11 **Wherefore exhort one another, and build each other up,** —Because Jesus died that all might live with him, we should encourage, edify, and strengthen one another to continue in the way of life and peace. [It remains with us to watch and be sober; to arm ourselves with faith, love, and hope. Paul says: "Set your mind on the things that are above, not on the things that are upon the earth." (Col. 3:2.) It is left to us as Christians to assist each other in the appropriation and application of these great truths.]

even as also ye do.—[In this new spirit each member sought the welfare of his fellow Christian, not on stated occasions, but as opportunity afforded; and not in any formal way, but as from the heart, thus realizing the intimate relations that exist between those who are members of the one body (Rom. 12:5), and thus giving effectual expression to the unity of all in Christ.]

5. EXHORTATION TO ORDERLY LIVING AND DUE PERFORMANCE OF SOCIAL AND SPIRITUAL DUTIES
5: 12-22

12 But we beseech you, brethren, to know them that labor among you, and are over you in the Lord, and admonish you; 13 and to esteem them

---

12 **But we beseech you, brethren, to know them that labor among you,**—To *labor* is the ordinary expression of Paul for such work as he himself did. Perhaps it refers to the giving of that regular and connected instruction in the truth which followed faith and baptism. It covers everything that could be of service to the church or any of its members. Paul says: "Now I beseech you, brethren (ye know the house of Stephanas, that it is the firstfruits of Achaia, and that they have set themselves to minister unto the saints), that ye also be in subjection unto such, and to every one that helpeth in the work and laboreth." (1 Cor. 16:15, 16.) Those who labor are not necessarily elders or deacons; for some of the best workers in the church are not elders or deacons.

and are over you in the Lord,—They were not over them in worldly affairs, but in things pertaining to the Lord.

exceeding highly in love for their work's sake. Be at peace among yourselves. 14 And we exhort you, brethren, admonish the disorderly, encourage

---

and admonish you;—[Admonition is a somewhat severe
word; it means to speak to one about his conduct, reminding
him of what he seems to have forgotten, and of what is
rightly expected of him. Admonition differs from remon-
strance in that the former is warning based on instruction; the
latter may be little more than expostulation. Eli remonstrated
with his sons (1 Sam. 2: 24), but failed to admonish them.
We are admonished (1 Cor. 10: 11) so to minister the word of
God that they shall depart from unrighteousness (2 Tim. 2:
19).]

13 **and to esteem them exceeding highly in love for their
work's sake.**—The Bible deals but little in mere sentiment of
feeling. It demands action and deeds that flow from kindly
feelings and loving hearts, faith made perfect by works. So
the esteem must show itself in deeds of kindness and helpfulness in whatsoever they need or will aid them in their work.
It involves both moral and material support. [Thus not personal affinity, but actual service rendered to the Lord in labors among his people is the ground on which believers are to
hold their brethren in loving regard.]

Be at peace among yourselves.—Christians must cultivate a
spirit of peace and harmony among themselves. [This instruction suitably follows the foregoing admonitions. They
were not to quarrel with those over them nor let their actions
produce a factious spirit. The church was new among them
and brought them into new and delicate relations with persons of various educational advantages and habits; there were
difficulties and great need of patience and forbearance; but the
order that they live in peace was somewhat modified by these
additional words: "If it be possible, *as much as in you lieth,*
be at peace with all men" (Rom. 12: 18), but not intended to
excuse any evasion of the plain obligation imposed by the
command, but throws the responsibility on every believer who
does not hold himself in obedience to the command.]

14 **And we exhort you, brethren, admonish the disorderly,**
—It is the duty of Christians, as members of the church, to
help one another to a better and more faithful and holy life.

the fainthearted, support the weak, be longsuffering toward all. 15 See that

---

[The disorderly are those who fall short of the Christian standard or who violate the laws of the Lord by irregularities of any kind. Any Christian who sees any walking disorderly has a right to admonish them; it is laid upon him as a sacred duty tenderly and earnestly to do so. We are too much afraid of giving offense and too little afraid of allowing sin to run its course. Which is more godlike: to speak to the one who has been disorderly or say nothing at all to him, but talk about what we find to censure in him to everyone who will listen to us, dealing freely behind his back with things we dare not speak to his face? Surely admonition is better than gossip; even if it is more difficult, it is more Christlike. It may be that our own conduct shuts our mouths or at least exposes us to a rude retort; but unaffected humility and devotion to God can overcome that.]

encourage the fainthearted,—This refers to those who are easily disheartened and discouraged. They lack the energy and boldness in which the disorderly abound. They require constraint as the others require restraint. Sensitiveness to criticism, dread of persecution, a sense of failure to follow the will of the Lord, apprehensiveness concerning the future are among the causes that produce faintness of heart.

support the weak,—Those without spiritual strength, the weak in faith and conscience who do not go forward. It is very conceivable that in so young a church there were yet people, who, like children, easily stumbled. We must hold on to them, not expect or leave them to stand alone. "Now we that are strong ought to bear the infirmities of the weak, and not to please ourselves. Let each one of us please his neighbor for that which is good, unto edifying." (Rom. 15:1.)

be longsuffering toward all.—[Long-suffering is the quality of self-restraint in the face of provocation which does not hastily retaliate nor promptly punish; it is the opposite of anger and is associated with mercy and used of God. (Ex. 34:6; 1 Pet. 3:20.) Christians must learn to be patient, forbearing, persevering, not easily discouraged in helping all men in their weakness and trials.]

none render unto any one evil for evil; but always follow after that which is good, one toward another, and towards all. 16 Rejoice always; 17 pray without ceasing; 18 in everything give thanks: for this is the will of God in

15 See that none render unto any one evil for evil;—The essential temper of Christ is not to render evil for evil; he did not take vengeance. "For hereunto were ye called: because Christ also suffered for you, leaving you an example, that ye should follow his steps; . . . who, when he was reviled, reviled not again; when he suffered, threatened not; but committed himself to him that judgeth righteously." (1 Pet. 2: 21-23.)

but always follow after that which is good, one toward another,—The same spirit of love, forbearance, kindness, returning good for evil, that shone so brightly in the Son of God, must exist in the life and bearing of Christians toward one another.

and toward all.—God requires Christians to maintain and manifest this spirit for their own good, and as Christ's disciples may show his spirit and commend his religion to the world.

16 Rejoice always;—Christians with the blessings and protection of God here on earth, with his everlasting arms underneath them, and with the glories of the eternal world opened to them, should rejoice always. [Paul had learned, and taught the secret, that in sorrow and suffering endured for Christ's sake there is hidden a new spring of joy.]

17 pray without ceasing;—Feeling his own weakness, his shortcomings, and his dependence upon God, the child of God cannot otherwise than pray earnestly and fervently for the help of God in all the difficulties, temptations, and trials of life. He realizes his own weakness and infirmities, and God's power and goodness, and he cannot do otherwise than pray. A spirit of prayer and devotion should be so cultivated and maintained in the Christian's heart that will make every breath he draws fragrant with the odor of prayer. [If prayer is thus combined with all our works, we shall find that it wastes no time, though it fills all. Certainly it is not an easy practice to begin, that of praying without ceasing. It is so natural for us not to pray that we perpetually forget and undertake this or

Christ Jesus to you-ward. 19 Quench not the Spirit; 20 despise not proph-

that without God. But surely we get reminders enough that this omission of prayer is a mistake. Failure, loss temper, absence of joy, weariness, and discouragement are its fruits, while prayer brings us without fail the joy and strength of God. The apostle himself knew that to pray without ceasing requires an extraordinary effort; and in the only passages in which he urges it, he combines it with the duties of watchfulness and persistence. (Eph. 6: 15; Col. 4: 2; Rom. 12: 12.) We must be on our guard that the occasion for prayer does not escape us, and we must take care not to be wearied with this incessant reference of everything to God.]

18 **in everything give thanks:**—The Christian, realizing what God in Christ has done for him and the world, and how transcendently greater are the glories of the eternal world than all the sorrows and misfortunes of this evil world, that amid the deepest misfortunes of earth, lifts his heart in praise and thanksgiving to God. [Failure in thanksgiving for blessings enjoyed is evidence of the alienation of man from God (Rom. 1: 21); thanksgiving under circumstances of adversity and sorrow was characteristic of the Lord Jesus. When the people of certain cities rejected him, he answered and said: "I thank thee, O Father, Lord of heaven and earth, that thou didst hide these things from the wise and understanding, and didst reveal them unto babes: yea, Father, for so it was well-pleasing in thy sight." (Matt. 11: 25, 26.) And when he gave thanks for the bread, the symbol of his death, he knew that in his adversities the will of the Father was being accomplished.]

for this is the will of God—To do the will of God is to yield ourselves to the accomplishment of his design for us.

in Christ Jesus—The servants of God are to do the will of God as expressed in the life of Christ Jesus in his submission to God, which made his heart glad even in the face of death. (Psalm 16: 7-11.) [He not only taught his disciples to rejoice (Matt. 5: 12), pray (Luke 11: 1-13), and to give thanks (John 6: 11-23); but he was the perfect example of all these things (Acts 1: 1). His conduct (John 6: 38; Heb. 10: 7, 9) and his message (John 17: 8, 14) together were the revelation of the

esyings; 21 ⁵prove all things; hold fast that which is good; 22 abstain
from every form of evil.

⁵Many ancient authorities insert *but*

will of God to the world, and in these things Paul could say:
"Be ye imitators of me, even as I also am of Christ" (1 Cor.
11: 1). For as to rejoicing (2 Cor. 6: 10; 7: 4), prayer (Phil.
1: 9), and thanksgiving (2 Cor. 2: 14) they were all expressed
in his daily life.]

to you-ward.—[God not only desires that these things shall
be in his children, but what is taught them may be made effectual in their daily conduct. To this end the apostle says:
"So then, my beloved, even as ye have always obeyed, not as
in my presence only, but now much more in my absence, work
out your own salvation with fear and trembling; for it is God
who worketh in you both to will and to work, for his good
pleasure." (Phil. 2: 12, 13.)]

19 **Quench not the Spirit;**—The spirit dwells within the
Christian and rises within him. It is likened to a fire burning
within him, and is not to be quenched. Not to be restrained,
but its promptings are to be followed. We quench what
dwells within and rises up within us. We resist what ap-
proaches us from without. The Christian is warned not to
quench the spirit that dwells within. The sinner is warned
not to resist the Spirit which appeals to him from without.

20 **despise not prophesyings;**—Prophesying originally
meant foretelling future events. It came to mean, in process
of time, any kind of teaching by supernatural gifts. These
teachers could often teach by the spirit, but were not able to
work miracles to prove it. Under cloak of spiritual gifts false
teachers came in and the disciples were in danger of rejecting
and despising all claims to spiritual gifts of the lower order.
Paul tells them here not to despise these teachers or their
teaching.

21 **prove all things;**—Instead of rejecting these teachings
claiming to be spiritual, they were to prove or test all. The
test was: "If any man thinketh himself to be a prophet, or
spiritual, let him take knowledge of the things which I write
unto you, that they are the commandment of the Lord." (1
Cor. 14: 37.) Conformity in his teachings and prophesyings

to the teachings and writings of the apostles was the test by which all claims of prophetic power or spiritual gifts of any description must be decided. If the person did not teach according to the standard, he was to be rejected. If we relax a constant watchfulness and a free discussion of all practical principles taught, before we are aware of it the faith of the church will be perverted by false teachings, and its life corrupted by sinful practices. "Be sober, be watchful: your adversary the devil, as a roaring lion, walketh about, seeking whom he may devour." (1 Pet. 5 : 8.)

hold fast that which is good;—Lay hold to that which is good and beneficial in its effects. Those who do so "are such as in an honest and good heart, having heard the word, hold it fast, and bring forth fruit with patience." (Luke 8: 15.) [The connection is the same as: "I pray, that your love may abound yet more and more in knowledge and all discernment; so that ye may approve the things that are excellent; that ye may be sincere and void of offence unto the day of Christ; being filled with the fruits of righteousness, which are through Jesus Christ, unto the glory and praise of God." (Phil. 1 : 9-11.)]

22 abstain from every form of evil.—They were not only to abstain from doing evil, but from the "form of evil"—the *likeness* of evil. This accords with: "Let not then your good be evil spoken of." (Rom. 14: 16.) Do not do good in such a way as to make people think you rendered evil purposes. This is frequently done. Some people do many good things in such a way that others think they are actuated by evil motives and sinister designs.

6. THE APOSTLE'S PRAYER FOR THE THESSALONIANS
5 : 23, 24

23 And the God of peace himself sanctify you wholly; and may your spirit

---

23 And the God of peace himself sanctify you wholly;—The object and purpose of God is to build up a community on earth, recognizing him as the only and supreme Ruler that will in all things be governed by his laws and animated by his Spirit. God gives assurance that such a community would bring the highest degree of happiness to every member and

and soul and body be preserved entire, without blame at the ⁰coming of our

⁰Gr. *presence*

---

confer the highest benefit on the world as well as bring the greatest honor to God that is possible to man in the flesh and eternal glory in the future. But few of those who profess to be his children believe this. We by our actions show plainly that we disbelieve it; we refuse to use our time, talent, and means as God directs. What we have belongs to God; he lends it to us here for a time to use for his honor and our good. If we use it wisely and well, as he directs, when we have proved our worthiness, he will give us eternal possessions as our own. The Savior said: "He that is faithful in a very little is faithful also in much: and he that is unrighteous in a very little is unrighteous also in much. If therefore ye have not been faithful in the unrighteous mammon, who will commit to your trust the true riches? And if ye have not been faithful in that which is another's, who will give you that which is your own?" (Luke 16: 10-12.) What we have here is loaned us by the Lord; what will be given to us in the future will be our own forever.

and may your spirit and soul and body be preserved entire, —The body is the fleshly part of man in which the soul or spirit dwells. The Bible makes no distinction between the soul and the spirit. The terms are used interchangeably and refer to the spiritual entity that dwells in the fleshly body and makes that body a man. The two words are used probably five hundred or more times in the Bible. In this instance they are used together, but as meaning the same thing. Paul, to strengthen his saying and to fully cover the ground, often used several words meaning much the same to give force and breadth to his expression. In this same Epistle are two other examples: "Ye are witnesses, and God also, how holily and righteously and unblamably we behaved ourselves toward you that believe." (2: 10.) Here are three words with hardly a distinction in meaning to express the purity of his life and its worthiness to be followed by them. Again: "For what is our hope, or joy, or crown of glorying?" (2: 19.) These words did not refer to distinct things or feelings. Then the lexicons

Lord Jesus Christ. 24 Faithful is he that calleth you, who will also do it.

define soul as *spirit* and spirit as *soul* showing that they are so used by all scholars. The body is the fleshly part of man in which the soul or spirit dwells. Life on earth is the union of the soul or spirit with the material body; the two combined constitute the living being or person as we see and behold him. Death is the separation of the soul, or spirit, from the material body; so this loses its vitality and crumbles into dust.

without blame at the coming of our Lord Jesus Christ.— [He prays that they may be found free of blame at the coming of the Lord, when the saints and their works "shall be made manifest" (1 Cor. 3: 13) before the judgment seat of Christ. Thus they were to be without blame not merely in conduct before men, but in heart before the Lord himself.]

, 24 **Faithful is he that calleth you,**—God had called them into the service of the Lord Jesus Christ through the gospel that had been preached unto them. [In making promises God does not lie or repent of them when made (Rom. 11: 29), but fulfills them all in his own time (1 Tim. 6: 15). Because of his faithfulness believers are encouraged to confess their sins with the promise that "he is faithful and righteous to forgive us our sins, and to cleanse us from all unrighteousness." (1 John 1: 9.)]

who will also do it.—He was faithful and would so sanctify and preserve them blameless unto the coming of Jesus Christ. He promised to keep them only as they walked in his ways. When they did it, he was faithful to make good his promise.

7. PERSONAL INJUNCTIONS AND BENEDICTION
5: 25-28

25 Brethren, pray for us.[7]

[7]Some ancient authorities add *also*

25 **Brethren, pray for us.**—We learn how Paul esteemed prayer by the constancy with which he prayed for others; how earnest he was in asking the prayers of Christians in his own behalf. If an inspired apostle like Paul felt the constant

26 Salute all the brethren with a holy kiss. 27 I adjure you by the Lord
that this epistle be read unto all the [8]brethren.

[8]Many ancient authorities insert *holy*

---

need of the prayers of others, that he might be able to stand,
be steadfast in the truth, and be bold to teach the whole will
of God to man, how much more do Christians of today need
the help and strength that comes through the prayers of others in their behalf!

26 **Salute all the brethren with a holy kiss.**—The kiss was
the common salutation in the East. The kiss was not ordained
by God as a method of salutation. It was found and regulated. The direction was when you greet one another with a
kiss, let it be holy, not a lascivious or lust-exciting kiss.

27 **I adjure you by the Lord that this epistle be read unto
all the brethren.**—Why it was necessary to make this request
is a little strange. Perhaps then as now, some were not
highly esteemed and were neglected, and he wished all, the
least as well as the greatest, to have the benefit of his teaching. [There is no secret code in Christianity, no mystery for
the initiated few. All God's spiritual gifts are intended for all
God's children. Paul had a message from God to deliver (4:
15) to all the saints, and each individual believer was, personally and directly, responsible to God for his own hearing
and understanding of that message, and for his own obedience
to it. There were distracting influences among the saints (2
Thess. 2: 3). Some lightly accepted untested teachings, some
set prophecy altogether at nought (5: 19-22); some impatient
with the disorderly (5: 14); some may have been so overwhelmed with sorrow as to forsake the assembling of the
saints (4: 13-18). To help such the Epistle had been written,
but only those who had heard it read could profit by it. Thus
garbled reports of its contents might be circulated, and the
authority of the apostle claimed for teachings and practices he
had not sanctioned. And if Timothy had reported that some
were already misusing his name, and pretending to have his
authority for their statements, as was certainly the case afterwards (2 Thess. 2: 2), the public reading of what he had written would be the best cure for the mischief, and the best pre-
ventive of its recurrence.]

28 The grace of our Lord Jesus Christ be with you.

---

28 **The grace of our Lord Jesus Christ be with you.**—[This contains all spiritual good that one Christian can wish another. Such grace is with us, when it constantly attends us, when it forms the atmosphere we breathe, the light by which we see, the guiding and sustaining influence of our whole lives.]

COMMENTARY ON
THE SECOND EPISTLE TO THE
THESSALONIANS

CONTENTS

INTRODUCTION TO THE SECOND THESSA-
LONIAN EPISTLE

I. OCCASION AND DESIGN OF THE EPISTLE

The persons to whom this Epistle was written—"the church of the Thessalonians in God our Father and the Lord Jesus Christ." In order to understand it, we must ascertain the condition of the church when it was written. Paul had been compelled to leave the Thessalonian Christians only partially instructed in the gospel of Christ. He had written them an Epistle to correct abuses and to supply what was lacking in their understanding of the gospel. (1 Thess. 3: 10.) The intelligence brought back to Paul by the bearer of the Epistle or through some other channel was the reason why it was written. He thus received a good report of the Thessalonians, and was enabled to express his joy and thankfulness to God that their faith grew exceedingly, and the love of everyone toward each other abounded. (1: 3.) But still the erroneous views concerning the coming of the Lord and the consequent disorders to which he had called attention had rather increased than diminished. The Lord Jesus Christ had ascended to heaven about twenty years before, and had promised to return at an uncertain date, and therefore nothing was more natural than the church in general should have expected an early return.

Various circumstances, both in the church and in the world, heightened the expectation. Such a view of an immediate coming of the Lord had taken possession of the minds of the Thessalonian Christians. Their deceased relatives who, they thought, would lose all the benefits occurring at the Lord's coming, had indeed been assuaged by the former Epistle, but the expectation of the immediate coming of the Lord had grown in strength. They, it would seem, from misapprehending some passages of the first Epistle that the day of Christ's coming was at hand. (2: 2.) Mistaken and enthusiastic men had also nourished this deception by appealing to visions and to the traditionary sayings of the apostle; and it would even appear that an epistle had been forged in the name of the apostle. The church was thrown into a state of wild excitement; an impatient and fanatical longing for the instant when Christ would come seized upon one portion, while fear and consternation at the awfulness of the event overwhelmed another. The consequence was that many of the Thessalonians were neglecting their secular business and living idle and useless lives, conceiving that there was no use of working in a world which was soon to be destroyed or of performing the duties belonging to a state of things which was soon to terminate. Their only duty they felt was to be in readiness for the immediate coming of the Lord.

Accordingly, the design of the apostle in writing the Epistle was to correct the error which the Thessalonians entertained concerning the immediate coming of the Lord, and to correct those abuses to which that error had given rise. The main object of Paul was to warn the Thessalonians against thinking that the day of the Lord was just at hand. He reminds them of his former instructions on this point and tells them that a series of events—the manifestation and destruction of the man of sin—would intervene. "Now we beseech you, brethren, touching the coming of our Lord Jesus Christ, and our gathering together unto him; to the end that ye be not quickly shaken from your mind, nor yet be troubled, either by spirit, or by word, or by epistle as from us, as that the day of the Lord is just at hand." And along with this correction of error was the correction of disorders occasioned by it. There were among the Thessalonians some who walked disorderly, that worked not at all, but were busybodies; those he enjoined to return to their employment, and "that with quietness they work, and eat their own bread." (3: 10-12.)

II. TIME AND PLACE OF WRITING

This Epistle evidently was written at Corinth not long after the first, most likely in the latter part of the year 53.

COMMENTARY ON THE SECOND EPISTLE TO THE THESSALONIANS

SECTION ONE
RETROSPECTIVE VIEW
1: 1-12

1. SALUTATION AND GREETING
1: 1, 2

1 Paul, and Silvanus, and Timothy, unto the church of the Thessalonians in God our Father and the Lord Jesus Christ; 2 Grace to you and peace from God the Father and the Lord Jesus Christ.

---

1 Paul, and Silvanus, and Timothy, unto the church of the Thessalonians in God our Father and the Lord Jesus Christ; 2 Grace to you and peace from God the Father and the Lord Jesus Christ.—This Epistle was written a short time after the first, and as Sylvanus and Timothy were still with him at Corinth, he joins their names with his, because they were well known to the church in Thessalonica.

2. THANKSGIVING FOR THE STEADFASTNESS THEY HAD DISPLAYED UNDER CONTINUAL PERSECUTION
1: 3-12

3 We are bound to give thanks to God always for you, brethren, even as it is meet, for that your faith groweth exceedingly, and the love of each one

---

3 We are bound to give thanks to God always for you, brethren,—[Paul had prayed: "Now may our God and Father himself, and our Lord Jesus, . . . make you to increase and abound in love one toward another, and toward all men, even as we also do toward you; to the end he may establish your hearts unblamable in holiness before our God and Father" (1 Thess. 3: 11-13). Here he acknowledges that his prayers were answered and that he regarded himself as much bound to thank him for answering his prayers as he was to make known to God his requests. In this we have an instance of the value and efficacy of intercessory prayer, and of the aid we may render our brethren by intercessions in their behalf.]

even as it is meet,—[It was right, on the ground of fitness, that labor should be rewarded (1 Tim. 5: 17, 18) and sin pun-

of you all toward one another aboundeth; 4 so that we ourselves glory in you in the churches of God for your [1]patience and faith in all your persecu-

[1]Or, *stedfastness*

---

ished (Luke 23: 15; Rev. 16: 6). It was fitting for Paul to thank God for the preservation and development of the Thessalonian Church, for it was not to be credited to Paul and his fellow laborers, nor to the converts themselves, nor to those who labored among them, but to the goodness and power of God, and to him he gave thanks.]

for that your faith groweth exceedingly,—Faith was the plant that sprang from the seed—the word of God—sown in the heart. Paul says: "I planted, Apollos watered; but God gave the increase." (1 Cor. 3: 6.) Paul first preached at Corinth, Apollos afterwards came and encouraged and exhorted them to continue faithful and persevere in the begun course. This corresponded to watering the plant, and as a result of the seed planted in the heart, and the watering done by Apollos, God gave the increase—the fruit of a holy, earnest, and consecrated life devoted to God. Faith grows from the very first reception of the word of God in the heart to the strong assurance of knowledge gained through a faithful walk with God.

and the love of each one of you all toward one another aboundeth;—As the result of the growth of faith in God, their love toward each other abounded more and more. Faith in God makes man love his fellow man. True love to our fellow man is shown by helpfulness rendered to him. As faith grows the love to one another abounds more and more abundantly. Our willingness and anxiety to do good to others is the measure of our real faith in God. If our love to man is not active and self-sacrificing, our faith in God is weak and lifeless.

4 so that we ourselves glory in you in the churches of God —This improvement in the faith and love of the Thessalonian brethren caused Paul to glory in them to the other churches in the neighborhood of Corinth such as Cenchrea (Rom. 16: 1) or by letter in those farther away. He was possibly thinking of more distant churches—those of Judea and of Syria, with whom he was most likely in correspondence. [It is at all times right and profitable that the vigor and prosperity of one

tions and in the afflictions which ye endure; 5 *which is* a manifest token of
the righteous judgment of God; to the end that ye may be counted worthy of
the kingdom of God, for which ye also suffer: 6 if so be that it is a righteous

church should be known in all, both for their rebuke and for
their encouragement; but it was eminently so in apostolic
times when churches situated amidst a heathen population
must have felt isolated and forlorn.]

for your patience and faith—Their patience, perseverance,
and unfaltering faith in the midst of the persecutions and
troubles that had come upon them (Acts 17: 5-9; 1 Thess. 2:
14-16) shows that they suffered great affliction on account of
their faith in the Lord Jesus Christ. [Faith and patience are
two distinct Christian graces; but the one upholds the other;
patience strengthens faith because it is faith in action; and
faith strengthens patience because faith is the evidence of the
unseen reward of endurance.]

**in all your persecutions and in the afflictions which ye en-
dure;**—Persecution implies active personal enemies and describes their hostile actions toward others; afflictions are the
various kinds of injury to body and mind suffered by those
who are persecuted.

**5 which is a manifest token of the righteous judgment of
God;**—The persecution brought upon them was a clear sign of
the righteous judgment of God that he might test and try
them and prove them worthy to receive the blessings of the
kingdom of God. [Such affliction is viewed not only as a special privilege granted to the believer but as an unmistakable
token of his acceptance with God—that he is to share Christ's
exaltation and glory at his coming.]

**to the end that ye may be counted worthy of the kingdom
of God,**—[Their sufferings served another purpose; they were
not only suggestive of the judgment to come they were also
disciplinary. They are intended to make those who endured
them meet for the inheritance of the saints.]

for which ye also suffer:—Until the power of the gospel
came into their hearts, they were incapable of such endurance.
That they had patiently endured and their faith had not failed
was proof of the new life and an assurance that God would
vindicate himself and them. Thereby all thoughts of ven-

thing with God to recompense affliction to them that afflict you, 7 and to you
that are afflicted rest with us, at the revelation of the Lord Jesus from
heaven with the angels of his power in flaming fire, 8 rendering vengeance to

geance were banished and a solemn sense of submission to
God's will was encouraged.]   It is a blessing to man to try
and to test him and prove his worthiness for the kingdom of
God.

6 **if so be that it is a righteous thing with God to recompense affliction to them that afflict you,**—While God permitted them to suffer persecution as a means of testing and
strengthening their faith and love, he recompensed tribulation
on those who troubled them.   God uses wicked men to try the
faith and love of his servants, to test their worthiness, and
then so orders that these wicked persecutors are punished for
the evil they brought on his servants.   God works in and
through his people and overrules and controls the courses of
the wicked.

7 **and to you that are afflicted rest with us,**—God recompen-
ses evil to the wicked who trouble his children, but will give
to those who suffer evil rest with the chosen apostles of Jesus
Christ.   [Though Paul's absence prevented him sharing their
gifts, he was not therefore exempt from affliction.   (1 Thess.
3: 3, 4, 10, 11.)   The prospect of its early satisfaction had
faded indeed, but their reunion was assured notwithstanding
its delay.   Here he associated himself and them who will be
alive on the earth at that time, and associated himself with
those who would pass away before it.   (2 Cor. 4: 14; 1 Thess.
4: 15.)   The subject immediately before his mind was not the
rest of the saints, but the retribution of God on their persecutor.]

at the revelation of the Lord Jesus from heaven—When the
Lord Jesus shall come from heaven in visible form, it will be a
revelation, a manifestation of the Lord Jesus before unseen.
"Behold, he cometh with the clouds; and every eye shall see
him, and they that pierced him; and all the tribes of the earth
shall mourn over him." (Rev. 1 : 7.)

with the angels of his power—The angels of exalted rank
and glory will accompany him.   Their presence suits the majesty in which "he cometh in the glory of his Father with the

them that know not God, and to them that obey not the ²gospel of our Lord

²Gr. *good tidings:* and so elsewhere. See marginal note on Mt. 4. 23

---

holy angels." (Mark 8: 38.) They are frequently associated with Christ in connection with his redemptive and mediatorial work. They announced his birth (Luke 2: 8-14), resurrection (Matt. 28: 2-6), and return (Acts 1: 10) ; they minister to him after his temptation (Matt. 4: 11) and in Gethsemane (Luke 22: 43) ; they will attend him at his return to judgment (Matt. 16: 27). In that day they will be called upon to worship him. (Heb. 1: 6.)

in flaming fire,—[God is described in the Old Testament as a consuming fire, and especially his coming to judgment is described as a coming in fire. (Ex. 3: 2; Dan. 7: 9, 10.) What is there ascribed to God is here transferred to Christ. (1 Cor. 3: 13.) The additional clause accordingly serves for a further exaltation of the majesty and glory in which Christ will return.]

8 rendering vengeance to them that know not God,—He will send his angels to execute his wrath on all who know not God. [This has reference to the Gentiles who gave way to the gratification of every lust and evil desire. In speaking of heathenism, Paul declares that this ignorance of God was willful, that idolatry was the outcome of ungodliness, and that its wickedness was shown by the horrible depravity of morals it produced. It was, therefore, culpable in the highest degree and merited vengeance, being the ignorance of men who "refused to have God in their knowledge, God gave them up unto a reprobate mind, to do those things which are not fitting; being filled with all unrighteousness, wickedness, covetousness, maliciousness; full of envy, murder, strife, deceit, malignity; whisperers, backbiters, hateful to God, insolent, haughty, boastful, inventors of evil things, disobedient to parents, without understanding, covenant-breakers, without natural affection, unmerciful: who, knowing the ordinance of God, that they that practise such things are worthy of death, not only do the same, but also consent with them that practise them." (Rom. 1: 28-32.) Such is the sentence that Paul pronounces on heathenism in view of its general character and

Jesus: 9 who shall suffer punishment, *even* eternal destruction from the face of the Lord and from the glory of his might, 10 when he shall come to be

---

fruits. In this Paul had before his mind those Gentiles who refused the knowledge of God and showed their hatred toward his children.]

and to them that obey not the gospel of our Lord Jesus:—[These are all, whether Jews or Gentiles, to whom the gospel of Christ is brought and who reject the message. Obedience is faith in practice, the submission of heart and life to the demands of the gospel of Christ. This is what such men refuse. This warning echoes that of Christ concerning all who are brought face to face with the gospel. They are warned: "He that disbelieveth shall be condemned." (Mark 16: 16.) This condemnation takes effect at once, and operates in the present life: "He that believeth on him is not judged: he that believeth not hath been judged already, because he hath not believed on the name of the only begotten Son of God. And this is the judgment, that the light is come into the world, and men loved the darkness rather than the light; for their works were evil." (John 3: 18, 19.) This sentence the Lord Jesus pronounces on those who, with his light shining upon them, refuse him the obedience of faith. The judgment of the last day will be the consummation of this present *actual judgment.*]

9 who shall suffer punishment,—Those whom he comes to punish will be punished with a destruction from the presence of the Lord and the glory of his power that shall be everlasting.

even eternal destruction from the face of the Lord and from the glory of his might,—This is not a destruction of the souls of men, but they will be banished from the presence of the Lord. The bonds that unite them will be destroyed forever. They will never be restored. And away from God, with all the means of help and blessing from God severed, man will be the subject of misery and woe forever. The Scriptures are so clear on this point that it seems that none willing to receive the truth can doubt this. In making the punishment for sin a light matter, we make sin against God a trivial matter and derogate his honor, majesty, holiness, and power. The whole

glorified in his saints, and to be marvelled at in all them that believed (because our testimony unto you was believed) in that day. 11 To which end we also pray always for you, that our God may count you worthy of your calling, and fulfil every ³desire of goodness and *every* work of faith, with

³Gr. *good pleasure of goodness.* Comp. Rom. 10. 1

---

trouble arises over a misconception of the meaning of death. Death does not mean annihilation, but separation of the spirit, the vital principle, from the body. Spiritual death means the separation of the soul and body from God, the vitalizing principle of spiritual life. Eternal death is the final and everlasting separation of soul and body from the presence and glory of God. Thus separated, it is not annihilated. It is subject to perpetual and eternal suffering. Nothing looking toward annihilation is found in the Bible when we rightly use terms. This idea is not found in the Bible. Whence does it come? It comes from a disposition to mitigate rebellion against God, and to find lighter punishment than God has prescribed. Why should this be done? Is man too fearful of sinning against God? Lighten the sin and ameliorate the suffering and will it then make men dread sin and rebellion more? We may well suspect our position and our spirit when we find ourselves excusing sin or ameliorating the woes that come from sin against God.

10 **when he shall come to be glorified in his saints,**—Jesus Christ will come again to take vengeance on his enemies and to receive glory and honor from all those who are redeemed through his blood and saved unto his everlasting kingdom.

and to be marvelled at in all them that believed—All those who believe in and trust him honor and praise him, but when they shall see him, as he comes in the clouds of glory with all his holy angels, to save those who have trusted him, their admiration for him will greatly abound.

(because our testimony unto you was believed) in that day. —He speaks to them of that which will come to believers because they had believed his testimony concerning Jesus. And these promises are theirs.

11 **To which end we also pray always for you, that our God may count you worthy of your calling,**—On account of the superior glory that will come to those who believe in him, Paul

power; 12 that the name of our Lord Jesus may be glorified in you, and ye in him, according to the grace of our God and the Lord Jesus Christ.

---

prayed constantly that God would *count* them worthy of the calling to which he had called them. [In the bestowal of reward, whether for suffering or for service, grace reigns. At best the servant is "unprofitable" (Luke 17: 10), yet because it was in his heart to serve (1 Kings 8: 18), and because he did what he could (Mark 14: 8), using what was at his disposal (2 Cor. 8: 12), according to the opportunity provided (Matt. 25: 15), God will reward him not according to the actual attainment or to the work accomplished, but according to the riches of his grace in Christ. Christians are to be holy, for God is holy (1 Pet. 1: 15); to be perfect, as their "heavenly Father is perfect" (Matt. 5: 48); to be "imitators of God," since they are his "beloved children" (Eph. 5: 1). Thus the expression *worthy* describes the ideal Christian life, the ideal of every spiritually-minded person.]

and fulfil every desire of goodness—[The word rendered "desire of goodness" is that which Paul uses when he says: "My heart's desire and my supplication to God is for them, that they may be saved" (Rom. 10: 1), and is commonly used for *desire,* especially when the desire is a benevolent one. The prayer of Paul is that God would so increase their goodness as to make these desires themselves perfect, irrespective of their results, and would enable them to maintain and perfect that activity and endurance to which faith had prompted them. His mind still dwells on the grand graces—"work of faith and labor of love and patience of hope"—which they had displayed (1 Thess. 1: 3), and for the two graces he prays for completion.]

and every work of faith, with power;—The work was peculiar to their faith, by which it was characterized, inasmuch as it was something begun with energy and held fast with resoluteness, in spite of all obstacles and oppositions.

12 that the name of our Lord Jesus may be glorified in you, —If Christians are thus faithful and worthy, then the name of Christ is glorified in them as his servants. When the servants of God are worthy, and are glorified in it, the Lord is glorified in them.

and ye in him,—When he is glorified all the true and faithful in Christ will be glorified in him. All this will be brought about through the provisions that God's love has made for making men righteous and saving them.

according to the grace of our God and the Lord Jesus Christ.—All the grace of God is developed in, and magnified through, Jesus Christ the Lord and Savior.

SECTION TWO

THE LORD'S COMING TO BE PRECEDED BY THE LAWLESS ONE
2: 1-17

1. WARNING AGAINST SUPPOSING THAT THE DAY OF THE LORD IS NOW PRESENT
2: 1-12

1 Now we beseech you, brethren, ⁴touching the coming of our Lord Jesus Christ, and our gathering together unto him; 2 to the end that ye be not quickly shaken from your mind, nor yet be troubled, either by spirit, or

⁴Gr. *in behalf of*
⁵Gr. *presence*

1 **Now we beseech you, brethren, touching the coming of our Lord Jesus Christ,**—Paul presented in the preceding chapter the coming of the Lord, and the gathering of his people to him, and the judgments visited on the wicked, and the rewards of the righteous. He had taught them in the first Epistle (5: 2) that the day of the Lord should come as a thief in the night when they were not expecting him. It is now clear that some had taught that the day of the Lord would speedily come. Then, as now, the people were easily excited over this question, were excited and unfitted for the faithful performance of everyday duties of Christians. Paul wrote this Epistle to correct the false teaching that had so excited them.

and our gathering together unto him;—[The word translated "gathering together" occurs only once again in the New Testament, where it is used with reference to the assembling of Christians for worship. (Heb. 10: 25.) Here it is used with reference to the assembling of believers to Christ, when he shall be revealed from heaven; it refers not to the raising of the dead, but the gathering together of the saints who are alive.]

2 **to the end that ye be not quickly shaken from your mind, nor yet be troubled,**—They had evidently been excited by false impressions about the nearness of the Lord's coming, and had acted as men who had lost their sense, giving up their ordinary occupations and scandalizing sober-minded people. The word shaken marks that shaken and disquieted state of mind which was due to wild spiritual anticipations. To pre-

by word, or by epistle as from us, as that the day of the Lord is just at hand; 3 let no man beguile you in any wise; for *it will not be*, except the falling away come first, and the man of °sin be revealed, the son of perdition, 4 he that opposeth and exalteth himself against all that is called God or ⁷that is worshipped; so that he sitteth in the ⁸temple of God, setting himself forth

°Many ancient authorities read *lawlessness*
⁷Gr. *an object of worship*. Acts 17. 23
⁸Or, *sanctuary*

---

vent this instability and disorder Paul now again writes to them.

either by spirit, or by word, or by epistle as from us, as that the day of the Lord is just at hand;—That they would not know when he would come was so clearly revealed that none of the things mentioned should move them on the subject. Just as he said: "But though we, or an angel from heaven, should preach unto you any gospel other than that which we preached unto you, let him be anathema." (Gal. 1: 8.) In other words, the truth that none would or could know the time of his coming was so fixed that no one could truthfully say it could be known.

3 let no man beguile you in any wise:—[They were surrounded by many influences tending either to lead them into error and delusion or into unbelief. Whatever device they might adopt—spirit, letter, or whatnot—they were deceivers or deceived; they were warned not to be deceived by them.]

for it will not be, except the falling away come first,—A widespread apostasy from God, on the part of his followers, was to arise within the church. The foundation principle of the falling away is the assumption of the right to change or modify the laws and commandments of God.

and the man of sin be revealed, the son of perdition,—There has been much diversity in the religious world as to what is "the man of sin," "the son of perdition." Most Protestants say the Roman Catholic Church is the man of sin. I doubt if any organization is "the man of sin." A principle was at work that would set aside God's order and establish one of its own in its stead. It leads to ruin and perdition—is called the son of perdition.

4 he that opposeth and exalteth himself against all that is called God or that is worshipped;—This principle under differing circumstances works out different developments and

as God. 5 Remember ye not, that, when I was yet with you, I told you these

organizations. The highest, the most sacred right, and pre-rogative that God has reserved·to himself is the right to make laws for his kingdom and to rule it. This he jealously guards because it lies at the foundation of his claims to be God, and out of this grows all other claims. It requires as great authority to.repeal or change a law as it does to enact it; hence, the power that enacts laws for God's people repeals or changes the laws of God, exalts itself into a rival and an opponent of God.

so that he sitteth in the temple of God, setting himself forth as God.—Whoever or whatever claims the right to legislate for the children of God exalts himself or itself against all that is God and sits in the seat of God. This principle, that claims the right to change the order of God and to legislate for the church of God, is the man of sin. The principle develops different bodies or forms, according to surrounding circumstances. Roman Catholicism, I have no doubt, is one development or outgrowth of this man of sin. But the same principle manifests itself in many different forms in the history of the church.

5 **Remember ye not, that, when I was yet with you, I told you these things?**—The spirit of lawlessness was at work in Paul's day. The principle was just developing itself. It was not a grown man. It was really an unborn babe. It took several hundred years to grow into papacy. All the time back to Paul's day it was that same man of sin in different stages of growth. It was the same person in its essential nature and character from its conception until its complete development in the papacy. It is easy in history to trace it back to its appearance at its birth. Its essential character was that it assumed the right to change and modify the order and appointments of God to legislate for the kingdom of God. Wherever that principle is found, there the mystery of iniquity is. This is its one essential character.

All organizations, institutions, and practices in the church that grow out of the exercise by man or men of this power are developments of the man of sin. Some one body, by pre-eminence in time or power, may be called the "man of sin," but

things? 6 And now ye know that which restraineth, to the end he may
be revealed in his own season. 7 For the mystery of lawlessness doth al-

---

all are of the same family, even though less pronounced in
character. This principle has not confined itself to one church
or to one development, but has made many and varied
growths, each shaped by the conditions and surroundings of
its growth. Whenever or wherever men in the church have
added to, taken from, or changed the laws, institutions, or
order God has ordained, there the man of sin is at work. The
outgrowth of that principle, wherever found, is a development
of the man of sin.

6 **And now ye know that which restraineth, to the end that
he may be revealed in his own season.**—The disposition to
amend and change the appointments of God was at work and
was restrained in its growth by Paul's authority as an apostle
of the Lord; but when he was taken out of the way it had free
course and developed rapidly. It is not difficult to trace its
growth through the succeeding centuries, culminating in hier-
archies for which God's word made no provision. But that
principle is not confined to one or two churches. Its presence
is manifest in a greater or lesser degree in all the churches, in
the changes in the order of worship, in the ordinances of the
church; and in the multiplication of societies and organizations that seem for a time to add to its beauty and activity,
but which in the end, as parasites, sap the life out of the
churches. This principle is manifest especially in the organizations of the churches themselves into societies and ecclesias-
ticisms that first usurp the work of the churches and then control them and come between man and God.

God placed the churches as distinct congregations connected with each other only by the bonds of faith and love.
The office of the congregation is in the ordinances and teachings to bring man into close and constant contact with God
and to cultivate a sense of personal responsibility and nearness to him. This condition will bring out all that is best in
him and stir him to zeal in the service of God. God's service
leads to doing good to man in his name. All added organizations come between and separate man from God. They make
his service a proxy service, which destroys his sense of ac-

ready work: ⁹only *there is* one that restraineth now, until he be taken out of the way. 8 And then shall be revealed the lawless one, whom the Lord ¹⁰Jesus shall ¹¹slay with the breath of his mouth, and bring to nought by the

⁹Or, *only until he that now restraineth be taken &c.*
¹⁰Some ancient authorities omit *Jesus*
¹¹Some ancient authorities read *consume*

countability to God and weakens his zeal and devotion. Obedience to God's order as he gave it builds up his kingdom, and the substitution of a human order destroys it, and changes it into the "man of sin." All efforts to consolidate the churches into one organization for any purpose must be manifestations of this principle, and must result in the turning of the churches from fidelity to God. This was typified in the Jewish people. The consolidation of the people into one nation was rebellion against God, and resulted in their ruin as a people. No power should come between the churches of Christ and God. Any such breaks the sense of responsibility to God, and is the mystery of iniquity that sits in the seat of God, displeases him, and will bring ruin sooner or later to his church.

7 For the mystery of lawlessness doth already work:—The influence is called "the mystery of lawlessness" because it is not open in its work, is not seen, and is of the spirit that sets aside the law of God. It is not regulated by the law, has no law to guide or control it. It was already at work, spreading among the children of God, when this Epistle was written.

only there is one that restraineth now, until he be taken out of the way.—Paul, protesting against the lawless power, maintaining the sole authority of God in the work and worship of the church, insisting that all should give heed to the things they had seen and learned of him, and should follow his instructions closely as he had followed Christ, was the restraining power about to be taken out of the way. This accords fully with Paul's style. (2 Cor. 12: 1-16.)

8 And then shall be revealed the lawless one,—When Paul should be taken out of the way then this spirit of lawlessness would run riotously and carry the great body of Christians and churches into apostasy.

whom the Lord Jesus shall slay with the breath of his mouth,—The breath of his mouth means his word. All this

manifestation of his ⁵coming; 9 *even he,* whose ⁶coming is according to the working of Satan with all ¹²power and signs and lying wonders, 10 and with all deceit of unrighteousness for them that ¹³perish; because they received not the love of the truth, that they might be saved. 11 And for this cause God

¹²Gr. *power and signs and wonders of falsehood*
¹³Or, *are perishing*

power to legislate, make, repeal, change the laws, add to the institutions that God has appointed is of "the man of sin." Taking the Roman Catholic hierarchy as the development of the man of sin, as I am sure it is, it will be seen that this mystery of lawlessness developed into the "man of sin" only after several hundred years' growth. But the principle was at work in the days of Paul and developed into activity soon after he was taken out of the way and grew into the great Romish hierarchy. Can we find the first developments of the man of sin? What it was in its childhood? We should understand this, lest we unconsciously nurse an infant of the same brood into life and vigor.

and bring to nought by the manifestation of his coming;— [That is, as soon as his coming shall be made manifest. The very sight of the advancing King shall carry terror to the heart of his adversary and bring to utter ruin. The vision of him from afar shall be, as it were, instant destruction of his foes.]

9 even he, whose coming is according to the working of Satan with all power and signs and lying wonders,—Satan in the days of miracles wrought all forms and deceptions that unrighteousness could invent to lead to destruction those that obey him. When and where signs and lying wonders were performed, it is difficult to tell. In the age when Christ and the apostles and prophets wrought wonders, the devil and his emissaries did also. There were miracles of evil wrought in the early age of the church by the evil one as there were wrought by Jesus and his disciples. As these miracles of his disciples were said to follow them that believe do follow them as their heritage handed down from the early church, so also these miracles of evil wrought in the days of the early church.

10 and with all deceit of unrighteousness for them that perish; because they received not the love of the truth, that they might be saved.—And this evil comes to the destruction of

sendeth them a working of error, that they should believe a lie: 12 that they

---

those who disobey God, because when they learned the truth they did not receive it in the love of the truth. To receive it in the love of it was to receive it in the heart and obey it in all of its precepts: "For this is the love of God, that we keep his commandments." (1 John 5: 3.) To love the truth is to obey it. To know the truth and not obey it is to "hinder the truth in unrighteousness." (Rom. 1: 18.) There is no more dangerous condition for man than for him to know the truth and refuse to obey it. To do this is to harden the heart and make the condemnation sure.

11 **And for this cause God sendeth them a working of error, that they should believe a lie:**—When one knows the truth and refuses to obey it, he is a fit subject for following any delusion that sweeps over the land. The prophet teaches the same thing: "Yea, they have chosen their own ways, and their soul delighteth in their abominations: I also will choose their delusions, and will bring their fears upon them; because when I called, none did answer; when I spake, they did not hear: but they did that which was evil in mine eyes, and chose that wherein I delighted not." (Isa. 66: 3, 4.) This teaches plainly that when men know the truth, refuse to receive it in the love of it, refuse to obey it, they hold it in unrighteousness, and God sends strong delusions upon them that they should believe a lie. [Of all fatal effects of sin, none looks so dreadfully, none strikes so just an horror into considering minds as that every sinful action a man does naturally disposes him to do anything so ill, that it does not prove a preparative and introduction to the doing of something worse.] The number of men who are willing to work on either side of a question that will pay would be surprising to those not in position to know and who have not become accustomed to such things. It is the discouraging feature about the work of the churches today. So few men are willing to stand to their convictions—nay are willing to have convictions on any subject that will interfere with their worldly success. But truth can never be maintained, save by those who are willing to honor their own convictions, cherish a keen sense of right, are afraid of the least participation in that which is wrong, and

all might be judged who believed not the truth, but had pleasure in un-righteousness.

---

will honor and maintain the truth, let it cost what it may of popularity or private prosperity. Let us, then, drink deeply of the essence of the spirit of Christ. Without it the Christian religion cannot exist.

12 that they all might be judged who believed not the truth, —To know the truth and refuse to obey it is not to believe it with the earnest living faith that God requires and blesses. If a man at heart desires to do the whole will of God, God's will in its fullness will be opened to him that he may do it. God does not cast pearls before swine. When a people desire not to do the will of God, God withdraws the knowledge of himself from them. We may infer that when men wish to do only a part of his will, he permits only partial knowledge of himself to be known. This doubtless explains why so many professed Christians seem never able to see portions of the will of God; they do not desire to do it all. They see only what they wish to do. "Blindness in part" has happened to those people.

but had pleasure in unrighteousness.—Instead of that faith that works by love and obeys God in doing his will, they had pleasure in doing the things that were displeasing to him. [They are credulous of that which falls in with their evil inclination. Wicked men are of wickedness.]

2. RENEWED THANKSGIVING ON THEIR BEHALF AND PRAYER FOR THEIR COMFORT AND HOPE
2: 13-17

13 But we are bound to give thanks to God always for you, brethren beloved of the Lord, for that God chose you [14]from the beginning unto salva-

[14]Many ancient authorities read as *firstfruits*

---

13 But we are bound to give thanks to God always for you, brethren beloved of the Lord,—Paul felt bound to give thanks to God for them because they pursued the opposite course from those who held the truth in unrighteousness.

for that God chose you from the beginning unto salvation —[From what time was it from which these persons were

tion in sanctification of the Spirit and [15]belief of the truth: 14 whereunto he called you through our [16]gospel, to the obtaining of the glory of our Lord

[15]Or, *faith*
[16]Gr. *good tidings:* see ch. 1. 8

chosen? As the choosing was "in sanctification of the Spirit and belief of the truth," it is impossible that the choosing could have preceded the belief of the truth through which it was effected. Then it was the beginning of their spiritual life when they heard the gospel and became obedient to it—the time of their conversion.]

in sanctification of the Spirit and belief of the truth:—All who hear and obey the truth as revealed by the Spirit through the inspired apostles are sanctified by the Spirit, and are God's chosen ones. Those who will not be thus guided refuse to let God sanctify them, for in so doing they reject the means God uses to accomplish that end.

Many think to know the truth is sufficient; but the truth must be so received into the heart that it is warmed into life that it may assimilate the feelings and purposes of the heart to its needs in producing in the heart the new living plant of faith that bears the fruits of love and holiness. The seed that falls into the earth will remain barren and unfruitful unless it so comes into contact with the moisture and warmth of the soil as to excite to activity the germ of life within the seed. Then this aroused principle of life so appropriates to itself the strength and richness of the soil as to produce a new plant that will multiply the seed sown. The word of God is the seed of the kingdom sown in the heart; and when properly cherished, it appropriates all the better qualities to the growth of a spiritual plant that will abundantly multiply the seed sown. The great end, then, is not simply to get the seed sown —the word known—but to get it into the conditions that will energize the life principle and cause it to root and ground itself in the heart and direct and appropriate all the feelings of the heart. This can be done by cherishing the word of God in the heart and seeking to have it permeate our whole being.

14 whereunto he called you through our gospel,—God called all who believed the gospel that he might sanctify and purify and fit them to obtain the glory of the Lord Jesus Christ.

Jesus Christ. 15 So then, brethren, stand fast, and hold the traditions which
ye were taught, whether by word, or by epistle of ours.

to the obtaining of the glory of our Lord Jesus Christ.—
They were called by the gospel to school and fit them to share
the glorious inheritance of the saints in light. [The glory of
the saints will be complete and secure in the completeness of
his glory. "We know that, if he shall be manifested, we shall
be like him; for we shall see him even as he is." (1 John 3:
2.)]

15 **So then, brethren, stand fast,**—Because they had been
called by the gospel to this glorious end, he exhorts them to
stand fast in the faith, and hold to the teaching they had received from him.

and hold the traditions which ye were taught,—Traditions
were handed down from one to another or taught, and is used
in both a good and a bad sense in the Scriptures. The people
were warned against the traditions of the elders which displaced and made void the commandments of God. Jesus said:
"Ye leave the commandment of God, and hold fast the tradition of men." (Mark 7:8.) The traditions that they had been
taught by Paul, by word or letter, were the commandments
which he had given to them.

whether by word, or by epistle of ours.—[Traditions as
used in this passage are the teachings and precepts which the
inspired men taught as the precepts of God, whether they
taught them by the word of mouth or by writing. Paul draws
no distinction between oral and written tradition as was done
later. The worth of tradition lies not in the form, but in the
source and quality of the thing. Paul says: "For I received of
the Lord that which also I delivered unto you, that the Lord
Jesus in the night in which he was betrayed took bread; and
when he had given thanks, he brake it, and said, This is my
body, which is for you: this do in remembrance of me." (1
Cor. 11: 23, 24.) In this he was communicating to the church
by epistle and stamps it with the authority of his spoken
word. The sentence asserts the claim of the true apostolic
teaching as against any who would beguile the church away
from it. "Now I praise you that ye remember me in all

16 Now our Lord Jesus Christ himself, and God our Father who loved us and gave us eternal comfort and good hope through grace, 17 comfort your hearts and establish them in every good work and word.

things, and hold fast the traditions, even as I delivered them to you." (1 Cor. 11:2.)]

16 **Now our Lord Jesus Christ himself, and God our Father who loved us**—Paul commends them to God that they might be by him directly cheered and maintained in the evil day. "Herein is love, not that we loved God, but that he loved us." (1 John 4:10.) "Even when we were dead through our trespasses, made us alive together with Christ . . . and raised us up with him, and made us to sit with him in the heavenly places, in Christ Jesus." (Eph. 2:5, 6.) "Hereby know we love, because he laid down his life for us." (1 John 3:16.)

and gave us eternal comfort and good hope through grace, —Freely, not in discharge of obligation, but without restraint of any kind. Hope here describes the happy anticipation of good. The element of uncertainty with the consequent disappointment, which is the essence of all hope among men of the world, has no place in the hope of the faithful Christian. "Beloved, now are we children of God, and it is not yet made manifest what we shall be. We know that, if he shall be manifested, we shall be like him; for we shall see him even as he is." (1 John 3:2.)

17 **comfort your hearts**—Comfort implies more than the merely external condition of enjoyment, exemption from annoyance, or even relief from affliction; these are later and lesser meanings. To comfort was originally to impart strength, fortitude, cheerful energy, and in the passages in the New Testament, the word should be understood in this sense. When we come thus to understand the word, it invests it with fresh significance.

and establish them in every good work and word.—[Bring your Christian life to maturity and strength. The order is significant; practice should precede precept "that ye may become blameless and harmless, children of God without blemish in the midst of a crooked and perverse generation, among whom ye are seen as lights in the world, holding fortlf the word of life." (Phil. 2:15, 16.) The phrase comprehends the whole Christian conduct, private and public.]

SECTION THREE

HORTATORY
3 : 1-18

1. REQUESTS PRAYERS FOR HIMSELF
3 : 1-5

1 Finally, brethren, pray for us, that the word of the Lord may run and be glorified, even as also *it is* with you; 2 and that we may be delivered from

---

1 **Finally, brethren, pray for us,**—Paul here shows his faith in the efficacy of true and earnest prayers of the Christians. [It was a strength to know that he was remembered by those who loved him in the presence of God. It was no selfish interest that he had in view when he asks a place in their prayers; it was in the interest of the truth with which he was identified. How much a Christian teacher's power, increasing as time goes on, comes from the accumulation of intercession from his spiritual children! Paul left Christians praying for him everywhere. (Rom. 15: 30; 2 Cor. 1: 11; Eph. 6: 18, 19; Col. 4: 3.) In all these cases the request is for active help in his work of evangelizing.]

that the word of the Lord may run—This evidently expresses the desire that they pray that the gospel might not meet with obstruction, but that it might be spread abroad with great rapidity. The gospel would spread rapidly in the world if all the obstructions that men have erected were removed; and he exhorts them to pray for their removal.

and be glorified,—He was anxious that the gospel should not go halting and picking its steps, but like "a strong man to run his course," overlapping all barriers and prejudice and hatred, may meet with no check in its onward course, but spread ever further and wider, from city to city, from country to country, till "the earth shall be full of the knowledge of Jehovah, as the waters cover the sea." (Isa. 11 : 9.)

even as also it is with you;—The word was glorified among them by their receiving it as the word of God and trusting it. (1 Thess. 1: 2-7.) It was glorified by the manifest influence it had on their conduct and by their work of faith and patience of hope.

unreasonable and evil men; for all have not faith. 3 But the Lord is faith-

---

2 and that we may be delivered from unreasonable and evil men;—This clause is an amplification of the words "may run and be glorified." The impediments to the gospel progress were—except when they were overruled for good—such persecutions as these. [When Paul expressly requests the Ephesians (6: 19, 20) and the Colossians (4: 13) to pray that he may have boldness, and when God, on the very occasion of which Paul is now speaking, sees it needful to address him in the words, "Be not afraid, but speak and hold not thy peace: for I am with thee, and no man shall set on thee," we need not scruple to ascribe to him so much apprehension of danger as would prompt him to ask the Thessalonians to pray for his deliverance. The actual circumstances in which Paul was, and what the dangers were, may be learned from Acts 18: 9-17, this Epistle having probably been written during the latter part of Paul's residence in Corinth. It was perhaps in direct answer to the prayers for which Paul here asked that he received the vision of assurance of our Lord, and Gallio was moved to quash so abruptly the proceedings of the Jews.]

for all have not faith.—In this the apostle refers to the Jews who boasted of their faith in the true God, who assumed to themselves the appellation of lovers of wisdom and truth. [But perhaps the Jews were not the most serious enemies of faith. It is not a want of susceptibility of faith in the most desperate class of sinners of which Paul speaks, but of the actual destitution of faith in some to whom the gospel came. And the fact is stated in general terms as something that holds good, as with the force and regularity of a law wherever the gospel is preached. Perhaps these are the most serious enemies of faith. With many their hostility, often bitter in its tone and manifestly anxious to wound, creates a feeling of sorrow and shame rather than of alarm or doubt. They may do less harm that those who, without denying Christ, render him no true service. For these create an atmosphere or indifference to the Lord Jesus Christ and to his service. Unreasonable and wicked men may often escape public notice, while the influence of their characters and lives is wholly hostile to faith. We need, then, to watch, not only against the

ful, who shall establish you, and guard you from ¹the evil *one*. 4 And we
have confidence in the Lord touching you, that ye both do and will do the
things which we command. 5 And the Lord direct your hearts into the love
of God, and into the ²patience of Christ.

¹Or, *evil*
²Or, *stedfastness*

---

open and confessed adversary, but also against the un-
suspected and secret source of danger.]

3 **But the Lord is faithful,**—While we cannot trust men,
God is faithful to his promises and purposes. We can always
trust in him; and when men are unbelieving and perverse and
disposed to do wrong, we can always go to him and always
find in him one in whom we may confide. [We often come to
know, to our deep sorrow and disappointment, that "all have
not faith." We see how they turn away from the truth.
Many who once gave promise of faith and zeal in the cause of
Christ abandon it. At such times how consoling it is to be
able to turn to the Lord who is faithful, and who never fails
his devoted followers.]

who shall establish you,—He will make you firm and steadfast.

and guard you from the evil one.—He will keep you from
all the evil these unbelieving men wish to bring upon you.
[Their safety is insured by the Lord's fidelity, but it requires
their own obedience.]

4 **And we have confidence in the Lord touching you, that ye
both do and will do the things which we command.**—He had
confidence that the Lord would so lead them that they both
then did and would continue to do what he commanded them
to do.

5 **And the Lord direct your hearts into the love of God,**—
The Lord directs the hearts of those who trust and pray the
Lord to direct their hearts. He prays also that their hearts
may be willing to receive and act upon the directions the Lord
gives. These Christians already cherished the love of God in
their hearts more and more into the reception of that love
which moves God. Paul's desire was that they should have
the same love that God had, and unto the patient waiting
under the evil threatened, that marked the course of Christ.

and into the patience of Christ.—Christ was patient under all trials and persecutions. Paul desired that Christians might love as God loved man and be patient under all persecutions as Christ was in his.

2. DIVERS EXHORTATIONS, AUTOGRAPHIC ATTESTATION, AND BENEDICTION
3: 6-18

6 Now we command you, brethren, in the name of our Lord Jesus Christ, that ye·withdraw yourselves from every brother that walketh disorderly, and not after the tradition which ⁸they received of us. 7 For yourselves know how ye ought to imitate us: for we behaved not ourselves disorderly among you; 8 neither did we eat bread for nought at any man's hand, but in labor

⁸Some ancient authorities read *ye*

6 **Now we command you, brethren, in the name of our Lord Jesus Christ,**—To do a thing in the name of the Lord Jesus Christ is to do it for him and as he directs. Do it by his authority; do it as his servant, for his honor and glory.

that ye withdraw yourselves from every brother that walketh disorderly, and not after the tradition which they received of us.—To walk disorderly was to violate any of the teachings they had heard from the apostle. He had given the true teachings of God, and any other walk was disorderly. From these disorderly persons he commands all Christians to withdraw themselves. (Verse 14.) The withdrawing from them meant more than a public announcement of the elders—that "ye withdraw" from them.

7 **For yourselves know how ye ought to imitate us: for we behaved not ourselves disorderly among you;**—Paul endured all the trials and sufferings, but never sought deliverance from any of them. Probably the most intense suffering that he endured was the anxiety and care for the churches; the sympathy he had for the weak, the anxiety for maintaining the truth, and the deep anguish and sorrow he felt over the Christians turning from the truth. I can claim this much in common with Paul, the most oppressive care that comes upon me, the deepest suffering I endure, far above all physical pain, is the anxiety I have to see the children of God stand firm to his truth, the oppressive sorrow that comes to my soul, when I see those who know the truth lightly turn from it and from

and travail, working night and day, that we might not burden any of you: 9 not because we have not the right, but to make ourselves an ensample unto you, that ye should imitate us. 10 For even when we were with you, this we

God to the weak and beggarly institutions and provisions of men. These things certainly being true, the apostles and their associates are examples to all others for all times and all countries as to how the truth of God is to be spread abroad.

8 neither did we eat bread for nought at any man's hand,— When an evil prevailed, Paul was ready to show his condemnation of it by both precept and example. Because of their sin in this direction he was more careful to set them an example of industry that he might not be dependent upon them. That prevented his being an example to others in his labor in spreading the gospel.

but in labor and travail, working night and day, that we might not burden any of you:—This he did lest his influence should be weakened and the gospel hindered. Of his course at Corinth he said: "When I was present with you and was in want, I was not a burden on any man; for the brethren, when they came from Macedonia, supplied the measure of my want; and in everything I kept myself from being burdensome unto you, and so will I keep myself." (2 Cor. 11 : 9.) He certainly intended this to be an example to the preachers as well as to others, and shows that he did not regard his inspiration as placing him on a plane that prevented his being an example to others in his labor of spreading the gospel.

I do not believe he intended this as an example to others, that they were not allowed to accept help in their preaching, for he here asserts his right to receive help and in other passages reproves Christians for not aiding him, and approves them for helping him as a means of securing their own salvation so as to place it beyond doubt that a teacher may receive help and that it is a duty, the neglect of which imperils their salvation, laid on Christians to help him who teaches the word.

9 not because we have not the right,—[Paul had the right of maintenance from the churches among whom he labored, but for the sake of those who became obedient to give them an example of diligent working, and to remove every impediment

commanded you, If any will not work, neither let him eat. 11 For we hear
of some that walk among you disorderly, that work not at all, but are busy-

---

to the progress of the gospel, he often waived his rights. This
he did at Thessalonica (1 Thess. 2: 6, 9); at Corinth (Acts
18: 3; 2 Cor. 11: 9); and at Ephesus (Acts 20: 34); in all these
places he labored for his maintenance as a tentmaker.]

**but to make ourselves an ensample unto you, that ye should
imitate us.**—He says this to encourage them to cultivate a
habit of industry and self-reliance, that he might cast out the
disposition of idleness and begging, which are wholly incompatible with the spirit of Christ.

**10 For even when we were with you, this we commanded
you, If any will not work, neither let him eat.**—There was and
is no obligation resting on a Christian or a church to help or
feed an idle, lazy sponge who is able to work. This is true of
both men and women. The obligation is imperative to help
the helpless. Christ is personified in these. In so doing we
help Christ. But Christ never was personified in an individual, man or woman, able but unwilling to work for a living.
Christ has no sympathy for such people, every true Christian,
like Paul, is unwilling to be a tax, to be a burden upon others
when it is possible to help self. Cases present themselves frequently that are difficult to determine what to do. An able-
bodied, lazy father and husband leaves a worthy and struggling wife and children to suffer. It is impossible to help
them without helping him in his laziness. One course seems
right in this case to relieve the personal and present needs of
the wife and children as far as possible, show a sympathy for
them, and withhold from him, while dealing candidly and
firmly with him. It will work a cure if anything will.

[Paul saw that the gospel was to be propagated chiefly by
its splendid effects on the lives of all classes of society, and he
realized that almost the first duty of the church was to be respected, and so he not only exhorts the individual members
to independence, but he lays down the principle that no eco-
nomic parasite is to be tolerated in the church. This forms
an important complement to the teachings of Jesus.]

11 For we hear of some that walk among you disorderly,—
[This explains how he came to speak upon the topic.

bodies. 12 Now them that are such we command and exhort in the Lord
Jesus Christ, that with quietness they work, and eat their own bread.

Hitherto he has only been giving directions without assigning
any reason for so doing. It was not simply that he heard that
there were such persons at Thessalonica; he knew about
them, who they were and how they were deporting themselves. Further word had reached him since the first Epistle
was written. (1 Thess. 4: 11; 5: 14.) Now he singles out the
offenders and severely censures them.]

that work not at all, but are busybodies.—Busybodies are
busy only with what is not their own business. This is, as a
matter of fact, the moral danger of idleness in those who are
not otherwise vicious. "And withal they learn also to be idle,
going about from house to house; and not only idle, but tattlers also and busybodies, speaking things which they ought
not." (1 Tim. 5: 13.) [Where men are naturally bad, it multiplies temptations and opportunities for sin; Satan finds some
mischief for idle hands to do. But even where it is the good
who are concerned, as in the passage before us, idleness has
its perils. The busybody is a real character, who, having no
steady work to do, which must be done whether liked or dis-
liked, and is therefore lonesome, is very apt to meddle with
other people's affairs; and meddle, too, without thinking it is
meddling. One who is not disciplined and made wise by regular work has no idea of its moral worth and opportunities
nor has he, as a rule, any idea of the moral worthlessness and
vanity of such an existence as his own.]

12 Now them that are such we command—He directs this
command, though indirectly and in the third person, to those
very persons; it was to be expected that all would be present
at the reading of this Epistle (1 Thess. 5: 27), and that all
would be listening to it. The term *command* is a severe word
and is used four times in this chapter. (Verses 4, 6, 10.)

and exhort—This word would break the seeming sternness,
and introduces the grounds on which the appeal was made.

in the Lord Jesus Christ,—When Paul was in Thessalonica
he taught them what their daily life should be in order to
please God; and he exhorted them, as those who abode together in living fellowship with the Lord Jesus Christ, that

13 But ye, brethren, be not weary in well-doing. 14 And if any man obeyeth
not our word by this epistle, note that man, that ye have no company with

now they should more and more strive to excel therein.   (1
Thess. 4: 1.)

that with quietness they work, and eat their own bread.—
Paul had already bidden these mischief-makers to quietly do
their own work and eat their own bread (1 Thess. 4: 11), and
not that of their honest and laborious brethren.   Honesty, industry, attention to one's own business, freedom from tattling,
and mischief-making are cardinal and essential virtues in the
religion of Jesus Christ.   To follow these adds so much to the
happiness of a community.

13 But ye, brethren, be not weary in well-doing.—While
Paul commands all who are able to eat their own bread, be
quiet, and not meddle, he cautions them not to cease to render
assistance to the needy, to do good to all, as the opportunity
affords.   This is in perfect harmony with the foregoing instructions.   Nothing discourages giving to the needy like having the lazy and meddlesome seeking support.

14 And if any man obeyeth not our word by this epistle,—
Paul makes obedience to the things he teaches in this Epistle a
test of discipleship.   He did the same in the first Epistle.   (4:
3-7.)   He did this because he wrote under the inspiration of
the Holy Spirit, and to obey that which was thus taught is to
obey God.

note that man,—The first step was to discriminate between
those who obeyed and those who did not.   The second was to
note him as disobedient.

that ye have no company with him,—Refuse him that social
companionship that would encourage him in the wrong way.
While refusing to regard him as walking as an orderly Christian should, they were yet to admonish him as a brother to return to an orderly walk in the Lord.

to the end that he may be ashamed.—While they were required to keep no company with them, they were not to count
him as an enemy, but to entreat and admonish him as a
brother.   The apostle says: "I wrote unto you not to keep
company, if any man that is named a brother be a fornicator,

him, to the end that he may be ashamed. 15 And *yet* count him not as an enemy, but admonish him as a brother.

16 Now the Lord of peace himself give you peace at all times in all ways. The Lord be with you all.

17 The salutation of me Paul with mine own hand, which is the token in

---

or covetous, or an idolater, or a reviler, or a drunkard, or an extortioner; with such a one no, not to eat." (1 Cor. 5: 11.) Discipline consists in admonishing, warning, and persuading; in separating them for a time from the fellowship of the church, yet continuing to admonish as a brother before the final exclusion comes. Cutting one off is not discipline; it is the end and failure of discipline. The steps taken to save one is the discipline.

15 **And yet count him not as an enemy, but admonish him as a brother.**—[Though deprived of church privileges, and shut out from fellowship with the members of the church, he was not to be counted hopeless. This discipline was to be expected to terminate in his repentance and restoration. And for this end, he was to be admonished as a brother.]

16 **Now the Lord of peace himself give you peace at all times in all ways.**—The Lord of peace signifies not only that he can bestow peace, but also and primarily that it is his own tribute. He has peace because he sees the end from the beginning, and is unassailable in his righteousness and sovereignty. He gives his own peace by enabling men to rely upon him, to accept his will—that will which shall certainly be accomplished—and by lifting them up above anxiety into his own security.

The Lord be with you all.—[The prayer is based upon the promises of the Lord Jesus (Matt. 18: 20; 28: 20), and accords with his name—"and they shall call his name Immanuel; which is, being interpreted, God with us" (Matt. 1: 23), and indeed, just a short while before this Epistle was written Paul had heard the Lord say unto him: "I am with thee, and no man shall set on thee to harm thee" (Acts 18: 10. Thus with the comfort wherewith he himself had been comforted, Paul sought to comfort others. (2 Cor. 1: 4.)]

17 **The salutation of me Paul with mine own hand,**—Paul's letters were usually written by an amanuensis. These last

every epistle; so I write. 18 The grace of our Lord Jesus Christ be with you all.

few verses, that he calls the salutation, or expression of his personal feelings in and for them, were written by his own hand.

which is the token in every epistle: so I write.—This is given in every letter as the token of his love for them.

18 The grace of our Lord Jesus Christ be with you all.—In the Epistle to the Colossians it was: "Grace be with you." In that to the Galatians it was: "The grace of our Lord Jesus Christ be with your spirit, brethren." But it was a solemn invocation of grace which Paul always wrote with his own hand. With this invocation of grace he begins and with this he ends. For the one thing which he held was that all men needed to make them holy and happy here and hereafter is *grace*.

COMMENTARY ON THE FIRST
EPISTLE TO TIMOTHY

CONTENTS

INTRODUCTION TO THE FIRST EPISTLE TO TIMOTHY

I. LIFE OF TIMOTHY

Timothy was a native of Lystra. (Acts 16: 1-3.) He had been carefully instructed in "the sacred writings" by his pious mother, Eunice, and grandmother, Lois, and trained in the knowledge and observance of the same. (2 Tim. 1: 5; 3: 14, 15.) He became obedient to the gospel under the preaching of Paul during his first missionary journey. (1 Tim. 1: 2; 2 Tim. 2: 2.) On the second missionary journey (A.D. 51-54) Timothy, being commended by the brethren that were at Lystra and Iconium, was selected by Paul as his assistant in the work of the Lord, and after his circumcision (Acts 16: 3) was set apart to that work. Thenceforward he remained the beloved and trusted friend and fellow laborer with Paul and companion with him in all the perils and labors and triumphs of his marvelous career. Among the last words of Paul, written just before his death, these were addressed to his true and faithful "child" in the gospel.

Frequent mentions of Timothy are found in Acts of Apostles and Paul's Epistles. From Lystra he accompanied Paul through Asia Minor to Macedonia and assisted in planting the gospel in Philippi (Phil. 2: 22) and probably in Thessalonica. At Berea he was with Paul and probably accompanied him to Athens, thence he was sent back to Thessalonica to assist, to instruct, and strengthen the young congregation there. (1 Thess. 3: 2.) On leaving there he went with Silas to Corinth, where he assisted in the establishment of the gospel, as also in the neighboring cities of Achaia. (Acts 18: 5; 1 Thess. 3: 6.) His name, with that of Silas, is associated with Paul's in 1 Thess. 1: 1; 2 Thess. 2: 1, and his service in that city is mentioned with high commendation.

On Paul's third missionary journey he is again seen with him at Ephesus, and near the close of the three years spent there, he was sent to Macedonia and Achaia on a special mission to the churches in those regions. (Acts 19: 21, 22; 1 Cor. 4: 17; 16: 10, 11.) Returning, he was with Paul in Macedonia

—probably in the autumn of A.D. 57—when the Epistle to the Corinthians was written (2 Cor. 1: 1), and in the following winter he was laboring with Paul at Corinth, when the Epistle to the Romans was written, as he there writes in the salutations sent to the church in Rome (Rom. 16: 21). On Paul's return eastward through Macedonia, Timothy was in the company that preceded him from Philippi and waited for him at Troas. (Acts 20: 4.)

His subsequent course at this time is not indicated. It is not certain whether he accompanied Paul to Jerusalem, and was with him during the two years' imprisonment at Caesarea and the voyage to Rome. But he was with him during his first Roman imprisonment—A.D. 61-63—as he is mentioned with glowing eulogy in some of the Epistles written at that time (Col. 1: 1; Phil. 1: 1; Phile. 1); and Paul speaks of his intention of sending him to Philippi for the comforting of the church there (Phil. 2: 19-23). It was probably at this time that Timothy suffered imprisonment at Rome (Heb. 13: 23), and possibly there in the presence of the imperial court confessed the "good confession in the sight of many witnesses" (1 Tim. 6: 12). After Paul's release from his first imprisonment at Rome—A.D. 63 or 64—Timothy's movements, like those of Paul's, are not certainly known; but in A.D. 65 or 66 he was with Paul at Ephesus, and on Paul's passing into Macedonia, Timothy was left behind to act in Paul's stead during his absence. (1 Tim. 1: 3.) The separation seems to have been deeply sorrowful to Timothy, who trembled in view of the responsibility thus placed upon him. (2 Tim. 1: 4.) At a later period—in the fall of A.D. 67—Paul, then a prisoner at Rome, wrote the second Epistle to Timothy, charging him to hasten his coming to Rome and gave to him his farewell counsels. Beyond this nothing is certainly known concerning Timothy. Whether he reached Rome before Paul's execution, and was present to cheer him in his closing hours, is not known. Tradition says he suffered martyrdom.

The character of Timothy as set forth in the Scriptures is one of rare beauty. There is not an intimation in the divine record that there was ever a failure of his faith. From his call at Lystra to the end of his earthly sojourn there is not an intimation of his swerving from the faith revealed in the gospel, never a shrinking from the post of duty and danger of suffering, and never of failing in fidelity to the trust committed to him or in love and loyalty to Paul.

II. PURPOSE OF THE EPISTLE

After Paul's release from his first Roman imprisonment, he went to Ephesus, where he left Timothy to set in order the things that were lacking. There were two sources of anxiety to the apostle: (1) False teachers had arisen in the church— Jewish in their origin—desiring to be teachers of the law, whose teaching was accompanied by a debased ethical standard and a factious and disorganizing spirit. (2) The other which gave him great concern was the practical administration of the work of the church. The position of Timothy was one of great and delicate responsibility, and it was especially important that his right to act should be fully authenticated by the apostle, and that he be given clear and explicit instructions for his guidance. Paul, therefore, after reaching Macedonia, writes and sends his Epistle to him, which, while adapted for this immediate end, was also especially suited to be an infallible guide for church activity throughout all future ages. The affecting circumstances in which Paul himself was placed carry home to every earnest heart his impassioned eloquence.

III. TIME AND PLACE OF WRITING

This Epistle was written to Timothy in the year 66 or 67 as Paul was passing through Macedonia, possibly at Philippi or Corinth.

COMMENTARY ON THE FIRST EPISTLE TO TIMOTHY

PART FIRST
INTRODUCTORY
1: 1-20

SECTION ONE

REMINDER OF THE PURPOSE FOR WHICH TIMOTHY WAS LEFT AT EPHESUS
1: 1-11

1. ADDRESS AND SALUTATION
1: 1, 2

1 Paul, an apostle of Christ Jesus according to the commandment of God our Saviour, and Christ Jesus our hope; 2 unto Timothy, my true child in faith: Grace, mercy, peace, from God the Father and Christ Jesus our Lord.

1 **Paul, an apostle of Christ Jesus**—Paul begins this Epistle as usual by declaring his apostleship. This Epistle was an affectionate reminder from Paul, "the aged," to Timothy to be steadfast in the faith in the midst of the many dangers to which he would be exposed in the city of Ephesus.

according to the commandment of God our Saviour,—It was a commandment from God to resist the powerful school of false teaching which had arisen in the Ephesian church. So Paul prefaces the Epistle by designating himself as an apostle according to the Holy Spirit who said: "Separate me Barnabas and Saul for the work whereunto I have called them." (Acts 13: 2.) The designation "God our Saviour" fitly describes him in reference to his redeeming love through his Son Jesus Christ.

and Christ Jesus our hope;—Christ Jesus gave hope to man. He died for him, opened the way for him to return to God, and gave him hope of life beyond the grave. (Eph. 2: 12.)

2 unto Timothy, my true child, in faith:—No fleshly relationship existed between the two, but a closer and far dearer connection. Paul had taken him while yet a very young man to be his companion and fellow laborer. (Acts 16: 3.) Of

him, in the Epistle to the Philippian church, he said: "I have
no man likeminded, who will care truly for your state." (2:
20.) On another occasion he said: "Now if Timothy come,
see that he be with you without fear; for he worketh the work
of the Lord, as I also do: let no man therefore despise him."
(1 Cor. 16: 10, 11.) Paul taught him as a son, and Timothy
looked to him as a father in the gospel. The relationship of
father and son was restricted to faith.

**Grace, mercy, peace, from God the Father and Christ Jesus
our Lord.**—Grace is the highest good for the guilty; mercy
for the suffering is grace in action; and peace comes from God
through the mediation of Jesus Christ.

2. CHARGE RESPECTING THE MISUSE OF THE LAW
1: 3-11

3 As I exhorted thee to tarry at Ephesus, when I was going into Macedonia, that thou mightest charge certain men not to teach a different doctrine, 4 neither to give heed to fables and endless genealogies, which minister

**3 As I exhorted thee to tarry at Ephesus, when I was going
into Macedonia,**—When Paul left Ephesus, he left there to restrain certain teachers who taught differently from Paul.

**that thou mightest charge certain men not to teach a differ-
ent doctrine,**—The teachers were doubtless the Judaizers who
insisted that the Gentiles could not be saved unless they were
circumcised and kept the law of Moses.

4 neither to give heed to fables—As a part of this Judaizing
spirit they gave much attention to Jewish fables, imaginary
occurrences, that constituted a part of the traditions of the
elders handed down from generation to generation. The Tar-
gums, the Jewish sacred books written by the rabbis, are
largely composed of these.

and endless genealogies,—The Jews laid much stress upon
their ability to trace a distinct and unbroken genealogical line
to Abraham. This care on this point was instilled by Moses
and others of the prophets. This was done (1) so that the
possessions of the different tribes might be kept in the families; (2) that the Levites might be kept separate who alone
were to minister to sacred things; (3) that the lineage of the
Messiah might be kept clear and distinct. Down to the coming of Jesus these genealogies were correctly kept. Since that

questionings, rather than a ¹dispensation of God which is in faith; *so do I*

¹Or, *stewardship*. See 1 Cor. 9. 17

time they seem to be so involved in confusion that no Jew is able to tell to which tribe he belongs. It is said that all genealogical tables that had hitherto been preserved so carefully were destroyed by Herod the Great because he was an Idumaen, seeking to establish a hereditary rule over the Jews, could not establish a line back to Abraham; and as he could not, he destroyed the advantages that these tables gave the children of Abraham over him.

Whatever personal motives may have actuated him, the destruction of the tables, when the divine purposes of their establishment had ended, must be regarded as providential. They had ended because the land of Canaan would no longer be the home of the children of Israel, the Levitical priesthood had served its purpose in bringing forward its nation to Jesus Christ, the end of the law had come.

The Jewish family as a distinct people of God, the Levitical priesthood, and the genealogy of Jesus, all like the law, were added because of transgression till the promised Messiah should come.

Were the Messiah to come now, as the Jews claim he is yet to come, his lineage could not be set forth. The rabbis say these tables of genealogy are to be restored by the Messiah when he comes. But any table restored by a person who is himself the chief beneficiary of the table would rest under suspicion. The Jews among the Christians, especially among the Judaizers of Paul's day, were given to seeking out these genealogies, as though they were to receive great good from them.

which minister questionings,—These genealogies and fables are held in great aversion because they cause much disputing, wrangling, and strife.

rather than a dispensation of God which is in faith; so do I now.—[In the dispensation of God's love as manifested through faith in Christ is the only way of approach to the mercies of God, while these genealogies were uncertain and produced no faith; it was necessary, therefore, to impress upon all who were seeking salvation in any way other than through faith in Christ that it was vain.]

now. 5 But the end of the charge is love out of a pure heart and a good conscience and faith unfeigned: 6 from which things some having ²swerved

²Gr. *missed the mark.* ch. 6. 21; 2 Tim. 2. 18

5 But the end of the charge is love out of a pure heart and a good conscience and faith unfeigned:—The purpose and end of God's law is that man may be led to do God's will out of a pure heart and with a good conscience and faith unfeigned. It takes all three of these conditions to make service acceptable to God. A man without a pure heart, a good conscience, and faith that is unfeigned cannot do acceptable service to God. Men harden their hearts and sear their consciences by doing what their consciences condemn. A man who thus violates and corrupts his conscience cannot do acceptable services to God. While the good conscience may lead men to violate the will of God, run counter to his teaching, it cannot serve God without it is kept pure. A man's conscience is defiled, blinded, seared by doing what he knows is wrong or refusing to do what he knows is right. There is no more dangerous condition in which a man can place himself than to habitually do what he knows to be wrong or refuse to do what he knows to be right.

Of the same nature is the expression "whatsoever is not of faith is sin." (Rom. 14: 23.) This Scripture is usually applied in a sense differing from the meaning of the apostle. Its use is not one hurtful in its nature, or out of harmony with the Scriptures, and it grows out of the true meaning of the apostle in this text. The meaning clearly is that of doing a thing as an act of worship, in reference to which we have doubts, we condemn ourselves. That is, we cannot violate conscience; if it has doubts, they must be respected. The convictions of our hearts must be honored.

God accepts nothing as worship that is not done heartily with full faith. The inference is clear that one who habitually violates his convictions of right soon loses all sense of right, hardens his heart, and makes his reformation impossible. The old philosopher who averred his ability to move the world, if he only had a fulcrum on which to rest his lever, expressed a universal, necessary truth. In the material world the lightest particle of matter cannot be moved without a fulcrum on

have turned aside unto vain talking; 7 desiring to be teachers of the law, though they understand neither what they say, nor whereof they confidently affirm. 8 But we know that the law is good, if a man use it lawfully, 9 as

---

which to rest the lever that moves it. It is equally true in morals. No movement of our moral sense or action can take place without a moral fulcrum on which to rest the lever of truth which moves it. That fulcrum is the sense of right in human nature. If it is destroyed, there is no starting point to correct man's moral and spiritual errors. Hence, Paul found mercy because he did his evil in ignorant unbelief; his conscience was good, pure, active; his sense of right was keen and sensitive. There is always hope of such men; God has respect for them. But when a man trifles with his convictions, does violence to his conscience, holds the truth in unrighteousness—that is, does not practice what he knows to be right, especially if he practices what he knows to be wrong— he corrupts his own moral nature, destroys his sense of right, and cuts off all possibility of his turning. In many evil ways is this protesting against wrong, yet encouraging the wrong, manifested.

6 **from which things some having swerved have turned aside unto vain talking;**—These words teach that those teachers had once been in the right way, but had not remained in it; indeed, it is clear that these persons, not only had been, but were still reckoned among the members of the Ephesian church, and were engaged in disputations that brought no good to anyone.

7 **desiring to be teachers of the law, though they understand neither what they say, nor whereof they confidently affirm.—** [They coveted the respect and influence which was ever paid to the acknowledged teachers of the law of Moses: but they utterly failed to understand the real meaning of that law. This same class of teachers was in the church at Smyrna, of whom it is said: "I know thy tribulation, and thy poverty (but thou art rich), and the blasphemy of them that say they are Jews, and they are not, but are a synagogue of Satan." (Rev. 2: 9.)] These persons aspired to be teachers of the law of Moses, but they did not see that the law of Moses ended in Christ and was taken out of the way by him.

knowing this, that law is not made for a righteous man, but for the lawless and unruly, for the ungodly and sinners, for the unholy and profane, for ¹murderers of fathers and ¹murderers of mothers, for manslayers, 10 for fornicators, for abusers of themselves with men, for menstealers, for liars, for

¹Or, *smiters*

8 But we know that the law is good,—Paul, while affirming this of those who aspired to teach the law, showed his respect for the law.

if a man use it lawfully,—Those who did not see that the law ended in Christ and was taken out of the way by him understood neither the law nor its aim and end.

9 as knowing this, that law is not made for a righteous man, —The righteous man is one made righteous by faith in Jesus Christ, and does not need the Mosaic law with its earthly penalties to govern him.

but for the lawless and unruly,—These refuse to be bound by any law, and submit to no higher authority.

for the ungodly and sinners,—[These have no reverence for God, and are such as God disapproves; are marred or polluted by sin, separated from God, so as to be openly hostile to him.]

for the unholy and profane,—Those who do not regard that which is sanctified or made holy by God, but profane his most sacred institutions. [Those who are impious or scoffers. One who treats the will of the Lord with contempt, mockery, or scorn.]

for murderers of fathers and murderers of mothers,—Often when the parents become old and burdensome they are killed by their children to be free from the trouble that the care of them imposes on them. [We can conceive nothing superior to this in enormity, and yet such crimes have been committed.]

for manslayers,—Those who commit murder. [A crime against which all nature revolts. This sanctity of human life is founded on the fact that man was made in the image of God.]

10 for fornicators,—Illicit intercourse of unmarried persons; also such intercourse of an unmarried person with a person of the opposite sex, whether married or unmarried.

for abusers of themselves with men,—"Carnal copulation between male persons."—Sodomy.

false swearers, and if there be any other thing contrary to the ²sound ³doctrine; 11 according to the ⁴gospel of the glory of the blessed God, which was committed to my trust.

²Gr. *healthful*
³Or, *teaching*
⁴Gr. *good tidings*. See Mt. 4. 23 marg.

for menstealers,—Those who carry on a traffic in human flesh, or those who steal a person in order to sell him into bondage, or those who buy such stolen men or women, no matter of what color or what country. All these were menstealers, and God classed them with the most flagrant mortals. The guilt of manstealing was incurred essentially by those who purchased those who were thus stolen.

for liars,—They who speak for *truth* for what they know to be false.

for false swearers,—Those who deliberately swear to that which is false, and then prove false to their oath.

and if there be any other thing contrary to the sound doctrine;—The law of Moses with its penalties was given to restrain, check, and punish those guilty of these sins, and not to rule those delivered from sin by faith in Christ Jesus. [*Sound* admirably describes the teaching as Paul conceived it in its complete freedom from any doubt as to right and wrong according to the instruction given to them as he was moved by the Holy Spirit.]

11 according to the gospel of the glory of the blessed God, which was committed to my trust.—The gospel of the Lord Jesus Christ, the standard by which everything is to be tested, and the law of Moses was made for those who do not obey the teachings of the gospel which was committed to Paul, which he had preached.

SECTION TWO

EXPRESSION OF GRATITUDE TO CHRIST WHO HAD ENTRUSTED HIM WITH THE MINISTRY AS A PROOF OF GOD'S LONG-SUFFERING AND AS ENCOURAGING TO OTHERS
1 : 12-17

12 I thank him that ⁵enabled me, *even* Christ Jesus our Lord, for that he counted me faithful, appointing me to *his* service; 13 though I was before a blasphemer, and a persecutor, and injurious; howbeit I obtained mercy because I did it ignorantly in unbelief; 14 and the grace of our Lord abounded

⁵Some ancient authorities read *enableth*

---

12 I thank him that enabled me, even Christ Jesus our Lord,—Christ Jesus selected Paul for fidelity to his conscience, his sincere desire to obey God, and his willingness to die for what he believed to be right. God always respects the man who keeps a good conscience and is true to his convictions.

for that he counted me faithful, appointing me to his service;—God honored Paul's faithfulness to his convictions and readiness to die for what he believed to be the will of God, though in error, rather than the man who believed on him, yet did not confess him because he feared the Pharisees. God knows the man who is true to his own conscience, and for this reason Christ Jesus counted Paul worthy and placed him in the ministry of preaching the gospel to the Gentiles.

13 though I was before a blasphemer, and a persecutor, and injurious:—There was no disposition with Paul to conceal his wrongs—he was open and free to confess them—that he might thereby magnify the mercy and goodness of God. So he says he was a blasphemer. To blaspheme is to speak reproachfully, rail at, revile, and calumniate. Paul sought the destruction of the whole church of God. Luke says: "But Saul, yet breathing threatening and slaughter against the disciples of the Lord, went unto the high priest, and asked of him letters to Damascus unto the synagogues, that if he found any that were of the Way, whether men or women, he might bring them bound to Jerusalem." (Acts 9: 1, 2.) When they were placed on trial, he gave his voice for their death.

exceedingly with faith and love which is in Christ Jesus. 15 Faithful is the saying, and worthy of all acceptation, that Christ Jesus came into the world to save sinners; of whom I am chief: 16 howbeit for this cause I obtained mercy, that in me as chief might Jesus Christ show forth all his longsuffer-

---

howbeit I obtained mercy, because I did it ignorantly in unbelief;—This clearly implies that had he persecuted the church as he did knowing it was the church of God, no pardon for him could be found. This accords exactly with the cases of Judas and Pilate and the mob that crucified Jesus. To commit these sins consciously was to forever bar the gates of mercy to them. To them believing they were serving God or with a good conscience left the way open for repentance and pardon to them. But certainly being true to conscience did not secure salvation, else those who crucified the Lord were in a saved state when they were crucifying him, else Paul was in a saved state while breathing out the threatenings and slaughter against all who called on the name of the Lord Jesus. But Paul, because he "did it ignorantly in unbelief," believing that Jesus was not the Son of God, but that he was an impostor, obtained mercy.

14 and the grace of our Lord abounded exceedingly with faith and love which is in Christ Jesus.—He here expresses his gratitude and joy for the exceeding abundant mercy and grace of God that saved him, which was brought through the faith and love which he had in Christ.

15 Faithful is the saying, and worthy of all acceptation, that Christ Jesus came into the world to save sinners;—To believe and confess that Jesus is the Christ, the Son of the living God, who came into the world to save sinners, is a faithful and true saying, and is worthy of being confessed by all.

of whom I am chief:—Paul speaks of himself as the chief of sinners before God. He had been in captivity, and is showing that the grace of God is sufficient to save the worst of sinners who would accept it in faith and love. He held himself as a sample of mercy as the chief of sinners. He was the chief of sinners not because he had been guilty of conscious, willful sin, but because he had been more active and fierce in his determination to destroy the church of God, believing that by so doing he was rendering service to God.

ing, for an ensample of them that should thereafter believe on him unto eternal life. 17 Now unto the King ⁶eternal, ⁷immortal, invisible, the only God,
be honor and glory for ever and ever. Amen.

⁶Gr. *of the ages.* Comp. Heb. 1. 2; Rev. 15. 3
⁷Gr. *incorruptible*
⁸Gr. *unto the ages of the ages*

---

16 howbeit for this cause I obtained mercy,—Notwithstanding the intensity of his bitterness, and his active zeal in destroying Christians, he had obtained mercy. God had forgiven him, that in him Christ should show forth all his long-
suffering. Christ in him led him to bear the persecutions and
the suffering he had inflicted on others.

**that in me as chief might Jesus Christ show forth all his
longsuffering,**—Paul had been chief of sinners in persecuting
Christ. He now must be chief or first among those who suffer
for him. He labored and suffered for Christ more than all the
other apostles. Of himself he says: "Are they ministers of
Christ? (I speak as one beside himself) I more; in labors
more abundantly, in prisons more abundantly, in stripes above
measure, in deaths oft. Of the Jews five times received I
forty stripes save one. Thrice was I beaten with rods, once
was I stoned, thrice I suffered shipwreck, a night and a day
have I been in the deep; in journeyings often, in perils of riv-
ers, in perils of robbers, in perils from my countrymen, in per-
ils from the Gentiles, in perils in the city, in perils in the wil-
derness, in perils in the sea, in perils among false brethren; in
labor and travail, in watchings often, in hunger and thirst, in
fastings often, in cold and nakedness." (2 Cor. 11: 23-27.)
Paul was of an intense temperament and of the heroic mold
that fitted him to inflict suffering on others, and bear it himself for what he believed to be right. He had inflicted it on
others.

**for an ensample of them that should thereafter believe on
him unto eternal life.**—Jesus chose Paul that in him he might
bear sufferings for him and others. In him God desired to set
forth the pattern of sufferings that men, who should thereafter believe in him to everlasting life, should be willing to bear.
The future world will be peopled with those of the true heroic
spirit, who counted it all joy to suffer for right and uphold the
truth.

17 Now unto the King—Paul esteemed it an honor and a glory to him to be chosen to suffer as Jesus had suffered, thus to be made like Jesus in his sufferings, for it brought the assurance that he would be made like him in immortal glory. So he bursts forth in this ascription of praise to God. God is the King, Ruler of the universe.

eternal,—There is no end to his reign and glory.

immortal,—God is immortal in contrast with the beings of this earth.

invisible,—He is invisible in contrast with visible things of creation.

the only God,—The only true and real God.

be honor and glory for ever and ever.—Let him be honored and glorified unto the age of the ages.

Amen.—This denotes the solemn ascent of the heart to the sentiment conveyed by the foregoing words.

SECTION THREE

REITERATION OF THE CHARGE TO TIMOTHY AND ENFORCEMENT OF IT
1 : 18-20

18 This charge I commit unto thee, my child Timothy, according to the prophecies which led the way to thee, that by them thou mayest war the good warfare; 19 holding faith and a good conscience; which some having

18 **This charge I commit unto thee, my child Timothy,**— The charge is to withstand and correct the errors of the false teachers. (Verse 3). The sum of the charge was that men should put their whole trust in Jesus Christ, who came into the world to save sinners, and who alone was able to lead them into everlasting life. The charge was the last heritage, the priceless treasure which Paul, feeling that for him the end was not far distant, would leave to Timothy. Anxious above measure for the churches in Asia, of which Ephesus was the center, foreseeing that the perils and dangers from within and without would rapidly close round the congregations, and placing his greatest earthly hope on the steadfastness and knowledge of Timothy, he charged him, by the memory of the prophetic utterances which years before had been made concerning him (Acts 17: 1, 2), to hold fast the doctrine which taught men to put their trust in Jesus Christ.

according to the prophecies which led the way to thee,— This was done in accordance with the prophecies which had gone before concerning him. Timothy had a spiritual gift imparted to him by the laying on of the hands of the presbytery. (4: 14.) Paul was doubtless of this presbytery. (2 Tim. 1: 6.)

that by them thou mayest war the good warfare;—According to these prophecies, and through the spiritual gifts bestowed when the prophecies were made, Timothy was to be enabled to war the good warfare for Christ. Paul seems to have been presenting his own sins, his trials, his joy in trials to Timothy, as a means of stirring him up to a true spirit of self-sacrifice and devotion to God.

19 **holding faith and a good conscience;**—As a means to this warfare, he was to hold faith and an abiding trust and confidence in God through Jesus Christ. The faith must be held in

thrust from them made shipwreck concerning the faith: 20 of whom is Hy-
menæus and Alexander; whom I delivered unto Satan, that they might be
taught not to blaspheme.

---

a good conscience. Conscience is the faculty within man that
demands he should do what he believes to be right. His conscience is good, clear, pure when he does what he believes to
be right. He must do this to please God. Not to do what
conscience demands is to hold the truth in unrighteousness.

which some having thrust from them—This is to believe
one thing and practice another. To do so is to act hypocritically.

made shipwreck concerning the faith:—Some had violated
their consciences for wordly ends, and in this way had made
shipwreck of their faith. Faith cannot live unless the soul
obeys the conscience in doing the thing to which faith leads.
Conscience demands that a person do the things which faith
approves. "But wilt thou know, O vain man, that faith apart
from works is barren?" (James 2: 20.)

20 of whom is Hymenaeus and Alexander;—Among those
who had put away from them a good conscience and had
made shipwreck of their faith were Alexander and Hymenaeus, thought to have been among the Judaizing teachers of
Ephesus, who, from worldly motives, did violence to their consciences and, their faith miscarried, blasted all their hopes as
when a ship driven by contrary winds is cast upon the break-
ers and all perish.

whom I delivered unto Satan,—This is generally supposed
to mean he had excluded them from the church, but it has always seemed to me to mean more than this. The church at
Corinth was commanded to deliver the incestuous person to
Satan. (1 Cor. 5: 5.) Many of the early critics, and some of
the later ones, James Macknight among them, hold that Satan
inflicted bodily punishments in the days of the apostles.
Sometimes they cast out demons and delivered from the afflictions of the body. That was to deliver from Satan. To deliver
to Satan was to turn the person over to him that he might inflict bodily disease or punishment upon him. If such was the
case, it ceased with the age of miracles. During that age both
God and Satan exerted wonderful working power. They both

ceased at the same time. One used his power to bless, the other to afflict and punish.

that they might be taught not to blaspheme.—The design was reformation that they might be taught not to blaspheme God, Christ, and his cause by their erroneous and unholy teaching. The discipline at Corinth appears to have proved successful in bringing good results. (2 Cor. 2: 5-8.) In this case it seems to have been otherwise. (2 Tim. 2: 16-18.)

PART SECOND

FORMAL INSTRUCTIONS
2: 1 to 6: 2

SECTION ONE

GENERAL REGULATIONS OF CHURCH LIFE
2: 1 to 3: 16

1. THE PROPER SCOPE OF PUBLIC PRAYER
2: 1-7

1 I exhort therefore, first of all, ⁹that supplications, prayers, intercessions,

⁹Gr. *to make supplications &c.*

---

1 **I exhort therefore, first of all,**—[Timothy was to begin at once to carry out the instruction given by Paul—the charge which bade him teach all men to put their whole trust in the Savior of sinners.]

that supplications,—This word signifies requests for particular benefits, and is a special form of the more general word rendered prayers. (Luke 1: 13; Phil. 1: 4; 2 Tim. 1: 3.)

prayers,—Prayer is for direct and specific blessings as we need them. [Prayer is communion with God. It implies that God is a person able and willing to hear us, who has created the universe and still preserves and governs all his creatures and all their actions. He can produce results by controlling the laws of nature or cooperating with them as readily as a man can; nay, more readily, for he is God. He can influence the hearts and minds of men more readily than even a man can induce his fellow men to action. He has had a plan from the beginning, and he accomplishes this plan both by the manner in which he established the universe and the laws which he set in operation, and also by his constant presence in the universe, upholding it and controlling it. And God requires prayer of all men. To pray to God implies a right relation to him. Acceptable prayer can be offered unto God by the righteous only. The prayer of the wicked is abomination unto him. (Prov. 15: 29; 28: 9.) Only those who have forsaken sin are authorized to draw nigh unto God in prayer.]

thanksgivings, be made for all men; 2 for kings and all that are in high place; that we may lead a tranquil and quiet life in all godliness and gravity. 3 This is good and acceptable in the sight of God our Saviour; 4 who would

---

intercessions,—This word suggests a closer and more intimate communion with God on the part of the one praying. It speaks of drawing near to God, of entering into free, familiar speech with him. Prayer is its most individual, urgent form as in the case of Abraham for Sodom. (Gen. 18: 24-32.) One of the most distinct examples of intercessory prayer is that of the Lord's intercession for Peter. (Luke 22: 31-34.)

thanksgivings,—Thanksgiving should never be absent from any of our devotions; we should never fail in any of our prayers to thank God for mercies received.

be made for all men;—These prayers were to be offered for all men that God would bestow on them that which is for their good—bring them to honor and glorify God.

2 for kings and all that are in high place;—For kings as the supreme rulers of the country and for all them that are under the kings.

that we may lead a tranquil and quiet life in all godliness and gravity.—The end of the prayer was not that the kings and governments of the earth might be built up and strengthened, but that these rulers might so conduct affairs that the people of God might lead a quiet and peaceable life, living a godly and earnest life in all things; that no hindrance might be thrown in the way of Christians living a godly and earnest life in all things, discharging all obligations to God and practicing honesty toward all men. Similar instruction was given to the Jews who were carried away into captivity. "And seek the peace of the city whither I have caused you to be carried away captive, and pray unto Jehovah for it; for in the peace thereof shall ye have peace." (Jer. 29: 7.) This was concerning the wicked city of Babylon, which had carried them captive, and which was doomed to destruction for their sins; yet for the sake of their own peace, they were exhorted to seek the peace of the city. This prayer for its peace does not involve support, active participation its affairs, or even approval of its course. This Epistle was written during the reign of the most wicked of the Roman rulers. It involves no question of

have all men to be saved, and come to the knowledge of the truth. 5 For
there is one God, one mediator also between God and men, *himself* man,
Christ Jesus, 6 who gave himself a ransom for all ; the testimony to be *borne*

approval of them or of the course they may pursue. No matter what the government, this prayer is proper.

**3 This is good and acceptable in the sight of God our Sa-
viour ;**—To please God is the highest motive that can influence a Christian.

4 who would have all men to be saved,—God's good will to
all men is here expressed, and he desires that all should come
to the knowledge of the truth and be saved.

and come to the knowledge of the truth.—There is no intimation that salvation is granted save through the knowledge
of the truth. The truth was revealed by God to guide man
into the way of salvation. Without God's direction man can
never obtain remission of sins and eternal life.

5 For there is one God,—This is stated as a further reason
why Christians should pray for all men. Polytheists could
not pray for all men because they would not pray for their enemies. One who believed in the gods of Rome would not
pray for the Carthaginians. In the very nature of things, a
polytheist could not pray for all men. For the gods of one nation were regarded as enemies of another nation. Whether
there was one God or many gods was the issue between Judaism and polytheism. It had required constant struggle, with
many failures, to keep even the Jews from polytheism. But
after the sore trials during the captivity in Babylon, they were
soundly converted to the belief in one God. Whatever else
may be said against them, it is evident that they were sound
in the belief in one God—Jehovah. But while that is true,
they did not believe he was the God of all men. All others
they regarded as godless. It took Jesus Christ to teach them
that Jehovah is the God of all men. Then the fact that there
is one God who loves all constitutes the reason for those who
love God to pray for all.

one mediator also between God and men,—As we have just
seen, there is one God of all men, so also there is one mediator, and only one, between God and all mankind. A mediator
stands between parties who are at variance, who are so widely

in its own times; 7 whereunto I was appointed a ¹⁰preacher and an apostle
(I speak the truth, I lie not), a teacher of the Gentiles in faith and truth.

¹⁰Gr. *herald*

---

separated that they can communicate only through an inter-
mediary.

himself man, Christ Jesus,—These words emphasize the nature in which Christ acts as mediator. It is in humanity the
nature common to all men, and for that reason all who bear
that nature are eligible to partnership in his mediation. (Heb.
2 : 6-18.) Herein we see how God dignifies man, since it is in
humanity he performs his mediatorial work, and by thus ex-
alting our nature has thus set before all human beings the
possibility of attaining eternal life. [The statement that
"there is one God, one mediator also between God and men,
himself man, Christ Jesus" is in the present tense when Paul
wrote. He was still a man. He did not leave his humanity
behind when he went up on high. As he did not leave his
Godhood above when he came down to earth and became a
man, so he did not leave his manhood on earth when he ascended to heaven. In heaven today the "man, Christ Jesus"
officiates as mediator on our behalf. Realizing this, let us rejoice and give renewed diligence to make our calling and election sure.]

6 **who gave himself a ransom for all;**—Ransom is the price
paid for the redemption of a captive. Man had through sin
sold himself a captive to the evil one. Jesus became mortal,
shed his blood, and died to redeem man from the thraldom of
sin and the bondage of the grave. He died as "the lamb that
hath been slain." (Rev. 13 : 8.)

the testimony to be borne in its own times;—Jesus Christ
was to be manifested in the last days of the Mosaic dispensation or testified in due time when the Lord should appoint.
He came to die and rescue man at the time appointed by God.

7 **whereunto I was appointed a preacher and an apostle**—
The word "preacher" here carries the meaning of an original
herald or proclaimer rather than one who teaches an old truth.
The apostles of Christ were those sent and authorized to
speak in his name, which authority was attested by the power
to work miracles.

(I speak the truth, I lie not),—In parentheses he emphasizes that he speaks the truth in Christ and does not lie. This is said in response to the teaching of the Judaizers who called in question his claims to be an apostle. [These words were uttered in view of the surpassing magnitude of the message with which he was charged—solely to bear a weighty and imposing testimony to the truth of his assertion, which so many were ready and eager to dispute—the assertion that the gospel of Jesus Christ is a message of glad tidings was an offer of salvation, not to a people, but to the whole world.]

a teacher of the Gentiles—This specifies the especial duties of Paul's apostleship with reference to the peculiar fitness which marked him out as the proclaimer of the divine will in respect to this gracious offer of redemption to the Gentiles.

in faith—Paul's own faith in Jesus Christ—the grand motive power of his life and work.

and truth.—[This refers to the well-known facts of the gospel story. Paul carried on his ceaseless labors, *within* gathering fresh and ever fresh strength from the exhaustless spring of his own mighty faith in Jesus Christ.]

2. THE POSITION OF MEN AND WOMEN IN PUBLIC PRAYER
2: 8-15

8 I desire therefore that the men pray in every place, lifting up holy hands, without wrath and ¹¹disputing. 9 In like manner, that women adorn

---

¹¹Or, *doubting*

---

8 I desire therefore that the men pray in every place,—Because he was an apostle to the Gentiles, he declares his wish that in every place, not at Jewish altars only, but that the Gentiles as well as Jews should pray.

lifting up holy hands,—Those leading the prayer did so with outstretched hands. They must be men whose hands were holy—unstained with wrong. [This is a figure for uprightness and purity of life. (Job 17: 9; Psalm 24: 4; James 4: 8.) The church is "an elect race, a royal priesthood, a holy nation, a people for God's own possession" (1 Pet. 2: 9), and no man should attempt to exercise this priestly function whose life and character is not that of an earnest and consecrated Christian.]

themselves in modest apparel, with shamefastness and sobriety; not with braided hair, and gold or pearls or costly raiment; 10 but (which becometh women professing godliness) through good works. 11 Let a woman learn in

---

without wrath and disputing.—Without animosity or bitterness toward other nations or people and without disputing over questions the Holy Spirit has not decided. [These angry feelings can have no place in the heart of one who really prays whether in public or in private.]

9 **In like manner, that women**—He had laid down rules for the men in the public worship; he now gives rules for the women in the congregation who had duties as well as the men.

adorn themselves in modest apparel,—[Their place in public worship was one of quiet attention. Their reverence and adoration must be shown not by thrusting themselves forward with a view to public teaching or public praying, but by being present and taking part silently, avoiding especially in these services anything like conspicuous dress or showy ornaments —anything, in fact, which would be likely to arouse attention or distract the thoughts of others.]

with shamefastness—That which shrinks from overpassing the limits of womanly reserve and modesty as well as dishonor of which would justly attach thereto. [That habitual inner self-government, with its constant rein on all the passions and desires which would hinder the temptation to this from arising or, at all events, from arising in such strength as to overcome the hindrances which shamefastness oppose to it.]

and sobriety;—The well-balanced state of mind arising from habitual self-restraint.

not with braided hair, and gold or pearls or costly raiment; —[The reference is to the then common fashionable custom of interweaving gold, silver, and pearls in the hair, causing it to glisten in the light. Gold or pearls refer to the bracelets, necklaces, anklets, rings and chains, and such things with which women were often laden. The Jews denounced such extravagant ornamentation. (Isa. 3:16-23.)]

10 **but (which becometh women professing godliness) through good works.**—To follow both these negative and positive requirements is church work because it is the work of Christ and must be observed by women if they be faithful

quietness with all subjection. 12 But I permit not a woman to teach nor to have dominion over a man, but to be in quietness. 13 For Adam was first

members of the church. The works a widow must have done to entitle her to the support of the church are: "If she hath brought up children, if she hath used hospitality to strangers, if she hath washed the saints' feet, if she hath relieved the afflicted, if she hath diligently followed every good work. . . . I desire therefore that the younger widows marry, bear children, rule the household, give no occasion to the adversary for reviling." (1 Tim. 5: 10-14.) That is church work. The church has no more important work than bearing children and training them for service to God. Women must do that work. Paul instructs Titus to teach sound doctrine. "That aged women likewise be reverent in demeanor, not slanderers nor enslaved to much wine, teachers of that which is good; that they may train the young women to love their husbands, to love their children, to be sober-minded, chaste, workers at home, kind, being in subjection to their own husbands, that the word of God be not blasphemed." (Tit. 2: 3-5.) A Christian woman is doing church work when she keeps her house well. The word of God is blasphemed when she does not do so, when she fails to love and honor her husband and fails to love her children and train them in the nurture and admonition of the Lord.

11 **Let a woman learn in quietness with all subjection.**—The position of women in public worship is that of a quiet learner in manner and in act, yielding submission in all lawful respects to the position God had placed man as leader of the worship in the public assembly of the church. This is given as the rule "in all the churches of the saints." (1 Cor. 14: 33, 34.)

12 **But I permit not a woman to teach, nor to have dominion over a man, but to be in quietness.**—The point guarded against here is woman's assuming authority over man. It is not wrong for her to teach the word of God, but wrong for her to teach it in a way that assumes authority or superiority over man. (Tit. 2: 5.) This is the only reason given in the Scriptures why it is wrong.

formed, then Eve; 14 and Adam was not beguiled, but the woman being beguiled hath fallen into transgression: 15 but she shall be saved through [12]her
childbearing, if they continue in faith and love and sanctification with sobriety.

[12]Or, *the childbearing*. Comp. Gal. 4. 4

---

13 For Adam was first formed, then Eve;—The reasons for
this teaching are here given, which show the reach or extent
or the principles. Adam had priority in creation. He was the
original human being. Eve was from him and subordinate to
him, and was formed a help suited to him. The argument
here based on priority of creation is much strengthened by the
following statement: "For the man is not of the woman; but
the woman of the man." (1 Cor. 11: 9.) This teaching of
Paul respecting the public position of woman as regards man,
in which he shows that she is to hold a subordinate place, is
based upon no arbitrary human speculation, but upon God's
original order in creation—that divine order which first
created man and after man's creation formed woman as his
helpmeet.

**14 and Adam was not beguiled, but the woman being be-
guiled, hath fallen into transgression:**—Priority in creation
was the ground alleged by Paul as the reason why the woman
was never to exercise authority over man. Paul now refers to
the general basis of his instruction concerning the exclusion of
woman from all public praying and teaching contained in the
preceding verses, Adam and Eve both sinned, but Adam was
not beguiled. He followed Eve into sin with his eyes open.
Eve, on the other hand, was thoroughly deceived. She fell
into Satan's deceit. Both were involved in the sin, but only
Eve allowed herself to be deluded. It would be difficult to find
a more vivid illustration of the essential difference between
the masculine and feminine nature. If there be this distinction between the sexes, that distinction furnishes the basis of
an argument and a reason for the instruction here given. The
catastrophe of Eden is the beacon for all generations when the
sexes repeat the folly of Eve and Adam, and exchange their
distinctive position and functions. So, according to inspired
teaching, she is not to be the leader, but to be in subjection.

15 but she shall be saved through her child-bearing,—Childbearing here embraces not only the act of childbearing, but

the life of caring and training children that the bringing of
them into the world necessitates. This domestic life of child
rearing is placed in contrast with the forward public life in
which she had blundered, and she is told that in this quiet life
women shall be saved.

**if they continue in faith and love and sanctification with so-
briety.**—If they continue in faith in God and love to humanity
and holiness of life, coupled with a modest, retiring behavior.

Sometimes women and men, too, think this is assigning
women to an inferior position. Inferior in the sense that she
is not by nature, physically or morally, suited to public positions or to counteract the rougher elements of the world. But
she is of finer texture physically and morally than man, and is
better fitted (superior to man) for work of nursing, training
children, and keeping home attractive and cheerful. She is
the trainer of children and the companion of man in the home,
becomes the conservator of virtue, morality, and religion and
of all the purifying and elevating influences shed by them.
No more sacred and no higher office did God ever lay on mortals than that he has laid on woman—to bear and train children and subjects for his everlasting kingdom. The woman
who neglects the duties she owes her children and her home
for the public life that God has created for man leaves her
work, her character, and her mission.

3. QUALIFICATIONS OF ELDERS* AND DEACONS
3: 1-13

Timothy was to take the place of Paul the apostle in teaching, instructing, and guiding the churches in perfecting themselves, and in doing the work for which they were planted.
The bishops or overseers were to do the work which their
names indicated. Bishop or overseer was the name applied in
Greek and Roman countries to the same work or office indicated among the Jews by the words elders or presbyters.
They were to take the oversight of the congregations and
teach, guide, and direct all the performances of the duties that
fell to them. He here speaks of the importance and sanctity

---

* For discussion on appointment of elders and their duties, see appendix
on page 305.

1 [13]Faithful is the saying, If a man seeketh the office of a [14]bishop, he desireth a good work. 2 The [14]bishop therefore must be without reproach, the husband of one wife, temperate, sober-minded, orderly, given to hospitality, apt to teach; 3 [15]no brawler, no striker; but gentle, not contentious, no

[13]Some connect the words *Faithful is the saying* with the preceding paragraph
[14]Or, *overseer*
[15]Or, *not quarrelsome over wine*

of the work and character of the persons fitted to perform the work.

1 Faithful is the saying, If a man seeketh the office of a bishop, he desireth a good work.—This saying would indicate that the work had been so highly esteemed that it had already grown into a saying, "The man who desired the overseeing desired a good work." No more important and no better work exists among the people of God. Paul instructed to "take heed unto yourselves, and to all the flock, in which the Holy Spirit hath made you bishops, to feed the church of the Lord which he purchased with his own blood." (Acts 20: 28.)

2 The bishop therefore must be without reproach,—The elders and deacons must be men whose character is unimpeachable, who stand high in public estimation, known for their pure life and spotless integrity. Not only must the believers reverence the character of the elders and deacons of a congregation, but those not members. In other words, they should be men of unimpeachable character.

the husband of one wife,—Paul, seemingly at least, required the bishop to have a wife. He at all events encouraged it. In later years the idea grew up that there was more holiness in celibacy, and the Roman Catholic Church forbids its bishops to marry. When Paul required they forbid. Nowhere do the Scriptures teach that there is more holiness in the unmarried state than in the married. [All the directions concerning marriage in the New Testament are based on the idea of the union of one man to one woman.]

temperate,—Watchful over himself in restraining the appetites and passions, using all in moderation so as to blend all the faculties to the highest degree of activity.

sober-minded,—Not excitable or passionate, but self-restrained. [Having or proceeding from a realization of the importance and earnestness of life; not flighty or flippant.]

lover of money; 4 one that ruleth well his own house, having *his* children in subjection with all gravity; 5 (but if a man knoweth not how to rule his own house, how shall he take care of the church of God?) 6 not a novice,

---

orderly,—Of good behavior, kind, considerate, and orderly in deportment. [Not only must he be wise and self-restrained in himself, but his outward bearing must in all respects correspond to his inner life.]

given to hospitality,—Entertaining strangers is frequently impressed as a Christian virtue. The elders should possess all Christian virtues in a high degree so he will be an example to the flock—teach by example as well as by precept.

apt to teach;—His work is to teach and lead others in the right way. In order to do this he must know the truth, then by kind and faithful example lead the flock in the way the Lord would have it go. It is very important that elders should have aptitude for teaching privately as well as publicly. (2 Tim. 2: 24-26.) It requires patience and perseverence in teaching others who are out of the way.

3 **no brawler,**—[The margin says "not quarrelsome over wine."] No more dangerous and hurtful practice is known to man than the use of strong drink. An elder must set a good example in all things.

no striker;—Ungoverned in temper, ready to resent insult or wrong, real or imaginary, quarrelsome, or ready to fight.

but gentle;—Not bitter and impatient, but kind in manners even to the froward and unpleasant.

not contentious,—This does not mean that one is not to stand and contend for the truth, but many are ready to contend over unimportant matters. Such always live in foment and strife. Even truth and right should not be maintained in a contentious spirit.

no lover of money;—not willing to use wrong means to obtain money, not anxious for sudden riches.

4 **one that ruleth well his own house,**—He who knows how to train children and lead them in the right way—in a kind and gentle manner so as to make worthy men and women of them—exercising the qualities given here for the bishop. The

lest being puffed up he fall into the ¹condemnation of the devil. 7 Moreover
he must have good testimony from them that are without; lest he fall into
reproach and the snare of the devil. 8 Deacons in like manner *must be*

¹Gr. *judgment*

same qualities are needed for the proper training of a family
that are needed for the training of a congregation.

having his children in subjection with all gravity;—He is to
train his children to be grave and sober in manner and to respect him and to honor God.

5 **(but if a man knoweth not how to rule his own house,
how shall he take care of the church of God?)**—His rule or
management of his family is the evidence of his ability to rule
the church. If a man cannot manage his own children whom
he has reared, and whom he always has under his care, how
can he manage the church of God?

6 **not a novice, lest being puffed up he fall into the condemnation of the devil.**—Not a new convert, lest he become proud
and self important and fall into the traps the devil lays for
men.

7 **Moreover he must have good testimony from them that
are without;**—He must so conduct himself as to have the respect and commendation of those without. Sometimes the enemies of the religion of Christ or even those who become personally offended will speak evil of good men on account of
their fidelity to right and to truth. But when a man lives a
just and upright life among people, there is seen in bad men a
sense of justice that makes them give due credit for it. If a
man is just and upright in his walk and kind and merciful to
the needy, without ostentation or display, the wicked world
will give him credit for it.

lest he fall into reproach and the snare of the devil.—The
man who has the reputation for dishonesty and untruthfulness
and for love of money is not fit for an elder of the church of
God. [Those who once knew him among other associations
living a very different life would be only too ready to attack
the blameless of the congregation through the stained and
scarred reputation of such an elder. The temptation to fall
away and deny the Lord in such a case would be overwhelming. The man might be in earnest, might wish to lead a new

grave, not double-tongued, not given to much wine, not greedy of filthy

and better life, but the risk that one with such connections, with memories of old days, would of necessity run, would be very great. Weakened and disheartened, such an elder would be likely to fall an easy prey into some snare skillfully laid by the devil, and, by his fall, cause a terrible and damaging injury to the church. For these weighty reasons Paul charged Timothy to be very watchful when the elders were chosen to choose only those who in their former days had preserved their good name stainless and their character unscarred.]

8 **Deacons**—Deacons are servants, helpers. It is generally believed that the seven appointed at Jerusalem (Acts 6: 3) to see that the destitute Grecian widows were not overlooked in the daily distribution was the beginning of the order of deacons. Their work then is to look after the poor and distribute the contributions of the church among them properly. They became helpers to the bishops or elders in their work, and the needs of the service to be performed seemed to regulate the number appointed. Feeding the poor with the contributions of the church is just as spiritual as preaching the gospel. If they attend to all the temporal interests of the church, according to the directions of the Spirit, they do an extended spiritual work.

in like manner must be grave,—The reverent decorum, the quiet gravity, which never interferes with innocent childlike happiness is especially to be looked for in a deacon [who ought to show an example of everyday Christian life].

not double-tongued,—Truthful, not talking two ways to suit the company he is in. [Such a grave fault would soon injure his influence, and would inflict a deadly wound on his spiritual life.]

not given to much wine,—The use of strong drink is entirely incompatible with a fully developed Christian character. The character given for the elders is that of the most complete and best-rounded Christian. Every Christian is bound to seek, in his spiritual growth, to develop the character portrayed for the elder. This will lead every Christian to entirely refrain from the use of strong drink.

not greedy of filthy lucre ;—The deacons, like the elders, are

lucre; 9 holding the mystery of the faith in a pure conscience. 10 And let these also first be proved; then let them serve as deacons, if they be blameless. 11 Women in like manner *must* be grave, not slanderers, temperate,

not to be lovers of money. They must not follow callings that will work evil to others or to be so anxious for it that they neglect their duties as Christians in order to obtain it. Deacons are required to develop the same character as bishops.

9 **holding the mystery of the faith**—The mystery means those truths which could only be known to a man by direct revelations, truths which could not be reached by any process of reasoning from natural observation.

in a pure conscience.—A pure conscience is one that has not been corrupted by being misused and abased by being violated or perverted. A man perverts and corrupts his conscience by doing what he believes to be wrong, seeing the truth and violating convictions of right. A man may have a pure conscience and do wrong, but he must do what he believes is right or he corrupts his conscience. A man must take hold of the great truths of the Bible with a good and pure conscience.

10 **And let these also first be proved; then let them serve as deacons, if they be blameless.**—Deacons must not be young converts or inexperienced men. They must have had time for study and practice of God's word. These deacons or helpers in ministry and managing the church of God and its work, until by service they have proven their intelligence and fidelity and steadfastness in the work of God, must have shown their fidelity in doing the work so as to be held blameless by the disciples of Christ.

11 **Women in like manner must be grave,**—They who serve the church in looking after the wants of women can perform for women that which men are unsuited to do. They can do much in the sickroom and in needy families that man cannot do. All Christian women should be of serious and earnest deportment, not light-minded and frivolous, but cheerful, hopeful, and earnest.

not slanderers,—They are not to circulate false reports or be given to gossip injurious to others.

temperate,—To be calm and collected in spirit, dispassionate, circumspect.

faithful in all things. 12 Let deacons be husbands of one wife, ruling *their* children and their own houses well. 13 For they that have served well as deacons gain to themselves a good standing, and great boldness in the faith which is in Christ Jesus.

faithful in all things.—Moderate and true and faithful in all they say or do. It may mean be faithful in using the means entrusted to them, to be distributed among the needy and giving to those in need impartially according to their needs. [From their position they would become the depositories of many household secrets; to those confiding in them in moments of trouble they must be true; scrupulously faithful in the instructions they would be often called on to give in the course of their ministrations.]

12 Let deacons be husbands of one wife,—As was said of the bishops and be faithful to her.

ruling their children and their own houses well.—They, like the bishops, are to show their ability to care for the church by having shown ability in caring for their own families.

13 For they that have served well as deacons gain to themselves a good stand,—The services of the deacons in looking after and caring for the needy and afflicted, relieving their temporal needs, teaching them the way of the Lord, gain for themselves a good understanding and skill as teachers of the word of God.

and great boldness in the faith which is in Christ Jesus.—The Scriptures do not contemplate a man going among the sick and afflicted administering to their necessities without teaching them the word of God, admonishing them as to their duties and so gaining strength as a Christian, and giving him courage and boldness in teaching the word of God. Through service of the deaconship a man grows into the qualifications and fitness for the work of the elder.

4. THE CHARACTER OF THE CHURCH AND ITS HEAD
3: 14-16

14 These things write I unto thee, hoping to come unto thee shortly; 15

14 These things write I unto thee,—This has reference to the foregoing instructions, especially to those relating to the qualifications of elders and deacons.

but if I tarry long, that thou mayest know ²how men ought to behave themselves in the house of God, which is the church of the living God, the pillar

²Or, *how thou oughtest to behave thyself*

hoping to come unto thee shortly;—Although he hopes to
be with Timothy again, he nevertheless will not allow matters
of such gravity to await his return to Ephesus. For this hope
may be frustrated.

15 but if I tarry long,—Paul, feeling that dangers were
pressing closer upon him every day and that the hoped-for
visit to Ephesus might never be accomplished, wrote the foregoing solemn directions.

**that thou mayest know how men ought to behave them-
selves**—These words refer not to Timothy alone, but to Timothy and his fellow workers in the church, concerning whom
such particular directions had just been given.

in the house of God,—The spiritual house, the temple made
without hands. The local assembly with its bishops and deacons is the house of God in which God through the Spirit
dwells.

which is the church of the living God,—A living God dwells
in a living temple. It is built of living spiritual stones—men
and women.

the pillar and ground of the truth.—The church is the foundation and support of the truth. God has given the truth to
the world and has established the church for the upbuilding,
maintaining, practicing that truth in its purity in the world.
Its duty is to do it by precept and example. In precept it pro-
claims the truth just as God gave it. Changed or modified it
ceases to be truth or the truth. It compromises nothing. Its
divine mission is to bear that truth in its divine purity to the
world. It must present to the world what the truth is when
practiced. The church, fulfilling its mission, is an exhibition
of a body of people such as the world would be if it was what
God desires it to be. He proposes to convert the world by
showing to the world in the example of the church how much
better it would be if it, like the church, would live by the
truth or be governed by God.

[In the first picture the church is presented as a vast assembly with the living God dwelling in its midst. In this it is

and ²ground of the truth. 16 And without controversy great is the mystery of godliness;

⁴He who was manifested in the flesh,
Justified in the spirit,
Seen of angels,
Preached among the ⁵nations,
Believed on in the world,
Received up in glory

---

²Or, *stay*
⁴The word *God,* in place of *He who,* rests on no sufficient ancient evidence. Some ancient authorities read *which*
⁵Or, *Gentiles*

---

represented as a massive pillar, holding up and displaying before men and angels the truth—the gospel. In the first picture the thought of a great company gathered together in the midst of which God dwells is prominent; in the second, the thought of the gospel as 'the power of God unto salvation to every one that believeth" comes to the front, and the church of God is no longer viewed as a company of separate individuals, but as one massive foundation pillar supporting and displaying the glories of redemption.]

16 **And without controversy great is the mystery**—It is a revelation of truth originally hidden from man's knowledge, to which man by his own unaided reason and abilities would never be able to find the way—a communication by God to men of truth which they could not have discovered for themselves.

of godliness;—The Word, taking on him humanity and living, suffering, dying, rising, and reigning in humanity, is for human beings the source of godliness. In it are all possible motives to holy living. It is this great fact, fully apprehended and believed in the soul, which breaks the power of sin and quickens to a new life of holiness. The all-potent revelation of the gospel is Christ as the God-man, and from it, as received in the soul, comes all true godliness. For it is written: "Like as he who called you is holy, be ye yourselves also holy in all manner of living; because it is written, Ye shall be holy; for I am holy." (1 Pet. 1 : 15, 16.)

He who was manifested in the flesh,—Jesus was God in the flesh, manifesting or showing to the world the true example of what God in the flesh would do and what he would not. He showed this because he desired man to be like him. So he came in the flesh to give the pattern to which he wished man while in the flesh to conform.

Justified in the spirit,—Jesus had the Spirit without measure. Through the Spirit he worked miracles, showed that God was with him, justified his claims to be the Son of God; by this Spirit he was sustained and upheld in his sufferings; by the same Spirit he was raised from the dead and carried to the home of God.

Seen of angels,—The Son of man in his humiliation revealed himself as the Son of God, and at every step in his earthly manifestation the angels saw in him the eternal God. They announced his advent, they ministered to his wants, they announced his resurrection and attended him in his glorified humanity.

Preached among the nations,—He was proclaimed as the Savior of men, in whom alone they had standing before God and everlasting blessedness. He was proclaimed without respect to national distinction, to social condition, or culture; with respect simply to the fact all were sinners and in need of salvation. It was impressive to the early church to witness the proclamation of a world-wide salvation.

Believed on in the world,—The proof that Jesus rose from the dead and is the Son of God were so irresistible that many among the Gentile nations believed on him.

Received up in glory.—A convoy of angels received him and escorted him to the throne of God, where he was crowned Lord of lords and King of kings. These were the great truths concealed from the world, which the angels desired to look into, which have been made known unto men for their obedience of faith, and constitute the gospel of Jesus Christ.

SECTION TWO

PERSONAL INSTRUCTION TO TIMOTHY
4: 1 to 6: 2

1. APOSTASY FORETOLD
4: 1-5

1 But the Spirit saith expressly, that in later times some shall fall away from the faith, giving heed to seducing spirits and doctrines of demons, 2

---

1 **But the Spirit saith expressly,**—There are two kinds of revelations made by the Spirit as presented in the Bible; one was a revelation to an individual for his obedience, the other a revelation by inspiration to enable those inspired to work miracles and teach others. The prophets and apostles were subjects of this latter inspiration. Connected with the knowledge to be revealed was the ability to work miracles to prove that the message was from God. This species of inspiration, miraculous in character, was confined to the apostolic age of the church, and continued in force only until the full revelation of God to man was made and confirmed by testimonies that no one can gainsay. This inspiration was effected by God's Spirit taking possession of the human body, using the human tongue and through it speaking to the world. God's Spirit on the day of Pentecost took possession of the tongues of the apostles and gave the very words then spoken. (Acts 2: 4, 14-36, 40.) The Spirit used the apostles' organs of speech, through which to make known to the world his message. Sometimes the Spirit spoke without the intervention of man's tongue. (Acts 8: 29.) He spoke in an audible voice on the occasion of the baptism of Jesus. (Matt. 3: 17.)

that in later times some shall fall away from the faith,—From the time at which he was writing and forward in all periods of the church, men have apostatized from the faith.

giving heed to seducing spirits—Spirits that so beguile them as to lead them from the truth. Every spirit that teaches that man can in any manner set aside the law and appointment of God, or substitute man's devices for the order of God, is a seducing spirit that turns man from the truth.

and doctrines of demons,—Demons are the evil spirits. The means the devil used to beguile Eve was to convince her that

through the hypocrisy of men that speak lies, [6]branded in their own conscience as with a hot iron; 3 forbidding to marry, *and commanding* to ab-

[6]Or, *seared*

another way was better than that which God had directed,
and thus he beguiled her and led her to follow what seemed
best to her rather than to give heed to God's directions.

2 through the hypocrisy of men that speak lies,—These seducing spirits speak lies, pretending to lead them into the way
that will bless them. No greater hypocrisy was ever shown
than that by Satan when persuading Eve to believe that to eat
the fruit would bring good to her, when he knew it would
bring her and the world into subjection to him, and that the
wages of sin is death. These demons work through evil men
who hypocritically speak lies to accomplish their wicked designs.

branded in their own conscience as with a hot iron;—These
men have become hardened and insensible to all feelings of
justice and right. To live in neglect of a known duty or violation of a principle of right is to demoralize the spiritual man,
weaken his moral character, and sear his conscience. This
unfits man for the higher duties of life and gradually fits him
for a life of sin and wrongdoing. Habitual violation of the
sense of right educates a man for doing what is wrong. An
occasional outburst, a great wrong repented of is not so fatal
in its tendency, not so hardening in its influence on the heart
and character of men as a continual violation of the principles
of right in what are regarded as small matters. Peter, under
the impulse of fear, could deny his Master and repent of it,
and yet have a better conscience and a truer character than
Judas Iscariot, who, during the time he carried the bag for the
disciples, was doubtless guilty of petty peculations and pilfer-
ings continually. The man who cherishes some private or secret sin, which he thinks is petty and unimportant, is gradually hardening his heart and fitting himself for a total breakdown of his moral character that will develop itself in permanent open sinfulness and degradation. The conscience should
be kept good and tender; the heart pure.

3 forbidding to marry,—Some of the errors into which they
lead men are here enumerated. Now and then men may be

stain from meats, which God created to be received with thanksgiving by
them that believe and know the truth. 4 For every creature of God is good,
and nothing is to be rejected, if it be received with thanksgiving: 5 for it is
sanctified through the word of God and prayer.

---

found like Paul who can live lives of virtue and purity without marriage and develop themselves more faithfully in the
service of the gospel; but usually to hinder a man from marriage is to lead to a life of sin and uncleanness. The univer-
sality of marriage is an indication of a high state of virtue and
civilization.

**and commanding to abstain from meats, which God created
to be received with thanksgiving**—God created meats for man
and they will administer to his good if they are received with
thanksgiving.

by them that believe and know the truth.—By those who
understand how properly to use them.

4 For every creature of God is good,—This refers to all the
appointments and gifts of God—marriage and meats. God
created all things on earth for man (Gen. 1: 28, 29), and everything properly used for the purpose for which he created
them will bring good to man.

and nothing is to be rejected,—It is not the part of wisdom
to reject or refuse what God does not reject.

if it be received with thanksgiving:—God's appointments
and gifts are to be received with thanksgiving and used as
God directs that they should be used.

5 for it is sanctified through the word of God and prayer.—
but all these blessings given by God should be received with
prayer that we might use them as God directs and that we
may be blessed in the use of them. This is an indication of
how we should pray in all things, as we give thanks to God
for our food that we may be blessed in its use and be guided
by God in using it. So we should receive all blessings and favors. [Thus all food is sanctified, not only by the thanksgiving before partaking of it, which too often degenerates into a
mere form of words—into lip service of the most heartless
form. The sanctification to which reference is made is the
constant habit of looking to God as the giver of every good
and perfect gift.]

2. WITH REGARD TO HIS OWN TEACHING AND CONDUCT
4: 6-16

6 If thou put the brethren in mind of these things, thou shalt be a good minister of Christ Jesus, nourished in the words of the faith, and of the good doctrine which thou hast followed *until now*: 7 but refuse profane and old wives' fables. And exercise thyself unto godliness: 8 for bodily exercise is

---

6 **If thou put the brethren in mind of these things,**—"These things" refer to all the things mentioned in verses 1-5. Timothy as a. teacher was to warn the brethren against the teachings of these seducing spirits, to admonish them to receive all the gifts and favors of God with prayer and thanksgiving, and to teach them to receive them in prayer and use them according to the will of God.

thou shalt be a good minister of Christ Jesus,—In doing this he himself would be nourished and built up in the words of the faith and of the good doctrine unto which he had attained or had learned. These evils and dangers were coming upon them, and Paul wished them to be warned of it that they guard against them.

nourished in the words of the faith,—From early youth he had been carefully trained in the truths of the Old Testament. (2 Tim. 1: 5; 3: 15.) Paul had trained him in the gospel (2 Tim. 3: 16) and now instructs him to continue this training by guarding the church against the doctrine of false teachers.

and of the good doctrine which thou hast followed until now:—[He had been faithfully taught, and with good understanding of it had diligently followed it.]

7 **but refuse profane and old wives' fables.**—These may refer to the Jewish traditions that were handed down and are now found in the Talmud. Many absurd and ridiculous things and fables and tales are told as a part of their religious instruction. The heathen worship also adounds in many ridiculous and absurd tales of cures performed and wonders wrought.

And exercise thyself unto godliness:—As the athlete trains his body so do you with strenuous effort train yourself in true piety in your heart and life. A man needs to school himself to the restraint of his passions, lusts, and worldly ambitions, and

profitable for a little; but godliness is profitable for all things, having promise of the life which now is, and of that which is to come. 9 Faithful is the
saying, and worthy of all acceptation. 10 For to this end we labor and
strive, because we have our hope set on the living God, who is the Saviour
of all men, specially of them that believe. 11 These things command and

⁷Or, *for little*

---

to the use of his spiritual faculties and powers that he may
practice godliness.

8 for bodily exercise is profitable for a little;—The exercise
or training of the body to fit it for skill in the athletic games
from the Christian viewpoint had but little profit. Any skill
or success merely in earthly affairs was of but little value
compared with the spiritual and eternal interests. The rewards and honors gained are unsatisfactory and short lived.

but godliness is profitable for all things,—[Godliness is not
merely an inward holiness, but an operative, active piety,
which, springing from an intense love for God, manifests itself in love for his creatures. This godliness transfigures and
illumines with its divine radiance all busy, active life, every
condition, every rank in all ages. This surely is that to which
every faithful child of God should seek to attain.]

**having promise of the life which now is, and of that which
is to come.**—A life according to the laws of God has the promise of protection, help, and the blessings of God in this life,
and then all the blessings and powers of the throne of God in
the world to come.

9 Faithful is the saying, and worthy of all acceptation.—
Paul emphasizes that this truth is a faithful saying and worthy of a full and hearty acceptance by all. It will bring good
to all who follow this instruction.

10 For to this end we labor and strive,—He explains that
the practice and exercise in godliness that led him to toil and
labor and suffer reproach for the cause of God would fit him
for the glories of the eternal world.

because we have our hope set on the living God,—He did it
because he trusted that the living God would bring blessings
both in this world and in that which is to come.

**who is the Saviour of all men, specially of them that be-
lieve**—The law of the Lord meets all the contingencies possi-

teach. 12 Let no man despise thy youth; but be thou an ensample to them that believe, in word, in manner of life, in love, in faith, in purity. 13 Till I

ble to arise in life. It meets every special case that arises, and in its working reaches every case as fully as God can reach it by special law or interference. God is always present in his laws. What is done through these laws, God does. Those who believe come more fully into harmony with his laws than those who believe not, and so they receive blessings of God more fully than others do. The answer to prayer requires no departure from this principle. The blessings of God flow through his laws to those who are in the proper state and condition. Tap the channel through which they flow and receive just such blessings as you are fitted to receive. God is personally present in all his laws to bless those who comply with them in spirit and in truth, and to curse those who refuse to comply with them. God is all-wise and all-powerful. He sees the end from the beginning. Eternity, past and future, is an everlasting present to him, and he provides for all contingencies that may arise in the onward march of his forces. Not a sparrow falls to the ground without a father's care and the hairs of our head are numbered. Because we fail to see and understand how the laws of the spiritual and material world interlace and harmonize with each other, all composing parts of one harmonious whole, we are not to conclude that they are not such. God is in all his works.

11 **These things command and teach.**—These truths that God is the Savior of all, desires that none should perish, but that all should repent and live, and that it is man's highest duty to trust and obey God.

12 **Let no man despise thy youth;**—This would indicate that Timothy was quite a young man at the time this was written. The Romans divided life into childhood up to eighteen years, youth up to forty-four, and old age up to death. But Paul's language would imply that he was of an age that he would be liable to youthful indiscretions and follies.

but be thou an ensample to them that believe,—[An example in reference to the firmness with which he embraced the gospel, the fidelity with which he adhered to it in trials, and

come, give heed to reading, to exhortation, to teaching. 14 Neglect not the

the zeal which he showed in spreading it abroad. He exhorts him to so live as to be a model or pattern after which the devotion of others should be molded.]

in word,—This has reference to teaching the word of God, but particularly to his words in social intercourse.

in manner of life,—In conduct, in deportment, in behavior. This certainly is of the deepest importance. [The words of men placed in such a position should ever be true and generous, helpful and encouraging.]

in love—In love to God and man which shows itself in honoring God and doing good to man.

in faith,—Faithful in all things, faithful in teaching the will of God, and being an example of fidelity in keeping its requirements.

in purity.—He should be pure, holy, clean in thought, in life, and actions. Young preachers and all young men need to take these admonitions to heart and be guided by them.

13 **Till I come, give heed to reading,**—Paul expected to give him more instruction when he would come to see him. Till then he exhorts him to give attendance to reading the Scriptures of the Old Testament. Books were not then plentiful, and the Old Testament foretold the coming of the Messiah. He was to study and use them in his teaching. Philip's beginning at the prophecy of Isaiah and preaching Jesus (Acts 8: 26-40) is a sample of much of the preaching of this early age. It was showing that these Scriptures foretold the coming of Jesus and how he came in fulfillment of them. This reading was to be done in private to instruct and improve himself, and in public to improve and benefit others.

to exhortation,—On these Scriptures exhortations to obedience and faithful living were to be based.

to teaching.—He was to study the teachings of these Scriptures concerning Jesus and teach these to others that they should practically apply them to their own lives. The Old Testament must still be studied and taught, for it was typical of the New Testament. In the Old Testament we have the example of God applying his law to the conditions of life as

gift that is in thee, which was given thee by prophecy, with the laying on of the hands of the presbytery. 15 Be diligent in these things; give thyself wholly to them; that thy progress may be manifest unto all. 16 Take heed

they would arise. From these we are to learn how he will apply the spiritual and eternal laws given in the New Testament.

14 **Neglect not the gift that is in thee,**—This was a spiritual gift qualifying him for the work to which he had been called. Before the completion of revelation spiritual gifts were given to qualify for the work of converting sinners and teaching saints till the completed will of God was fully made known. The gift seems to have been bestowed upon him by the laying on of the hands of the presbytery, Paul joining them in it. And by or through his hands the gift was bestowed, for he says: "For which cause I put thee in remembrance that thou stir up the gift of God, which is in thee through the laying on of my hands." (2 Tim. 1:6.) This was possibly done by the elders at Lystra, for he says: "This charge I commit unto thee, my child Timothy, according to the prophecies which led the way to thee, that by them thou mayest war the good warfare." (1 Tim. 1:18.)

which was given thee by prophecy, with the laying on of the hands of the presbytery.—A prophecy at the time of his conversion or at some period had been made concerning him, to which reference is made in these two passages. I infer that these spiritual gifts needed to be used, not neglected. To be stirred up lest they should be lost through disuse. This is in accordance with the order of God. The talent used multiplies; disused, it is taken from the possessor and is lost. The apostles, including Judas, were gifted before the death of Jesus. They used these gifts for a time and rejoiced in them. In the later months of the Savior's ministry, as the dark clouds overshadowed his pathway they seemed to lose faith, ceased to work, and they lost their gifts. Only with the renewal of their faith did the gifts again appear.

15 **Be diligent in these things;**—Timothy was to give his whole time and attention to the study of the Scriptures and the cultivation and use of the gifts and graces bestowed on him.

to thyself, and to thy teaching. Continue in these things; for in doing this
thou shalt save both thyself and them that hear thee.

---

give thyself wholly to them;—He was not to divide his attention with worldy aims and callings. [He was to devote his
whole being, in every faculty of body and mind, to the attainment of that which had been made possible by the gift which
had been bestowed upon him.]

that thy progress may be manifest unto all.—By this diligence in study and in the gifts bestowed, his improvement
would be apparent to all. [There must be no standing still,
no resting content with the knowledge already acquired, no
being satisfied with the present attainments in the spiritual
life; there must be a restless striving after the acquirement of
new stores of knowledge ever deeper and more accurate; there
must be a ceaseless endeavor to attain to a higher degree of
eminence in the spiritual life; and the result of these efforts
will be manifest to all.]

16 **Take heed to thyself, and to thy teaching.**—He was to be
careful as to his life and conduct, watchful and faithful in the
use of the gifts bestowed, and continue in that which he had
received from Paul.

**Continue in these things; for in doing this thou shalt save
both thyself and them that hear thee.**—Timothy could save
himself only by faithfully teaching the word of truth delivered
to him through the Holy Spirit. He could save others only by
teaching the word which God had given him to teach. In
striving to save others, he would really be striving to save
himself.

3. WITH REGARD TO HIS DEALING WITH CLASSES OF PEOPLE
5: 1 to 6: 2

(1) CONCERNING WIDOWS
5: 1-16

1 Rebuke not an elder, but exhort him as a father; the younger men as

---

1 **Rebuke not an elder, but exhort him as a father;**—Paul
here instructs Timothy how to treat the different ages and
classes of people. The term elder sometimes denotes an over-

brethren: 2 the elder women as mothers; the younger as sisters, in all purity. 3 Honor widows that are widows indeed. 4 But if any widow hath
children or grandchildren, let them learn first to show piety towards their
own family, and to requite their parents: for this is acceptable in the sight of

seer of the church, but here it means those advanced in age,
for it is put in contrast with the elderly women, the younger
men, and the younger women. He admonishes Timothy not
to rebuke or speak harshly to the aged men; but, if they commit wrong instead of reproving them in a censorious manner,
entreat kindly or beseech them to turn from the wrong as a
son would his father.

the younger men as brethren:—Treat the younger as a man
would his brother. Do it in and from love.

2 the elder women as mothers;—Treat the elderly women
with respect and affection as one would his own mother.

the younger as sisters, in all purity.—As a brother would
his own sisters. The younger women must be treated by him
in all purity. Let no impure thought or practice be cherished
in your association with them. [What miserable scandals
would have been avoided in all ages if this had been constantly remembered? If Timothy was thus advised, let others
consider what sort of conduct is required of them that they
should give no ground of suspicion, no shadow or pretext to
those who wish to calumniate.]

3 Honor widows—The word honor contains the idea not
only of respect, consideration, but also in such a connection as
this, that of temporal support. It suggests that such relief is
not to be dealt to them as paupers, in a manner so as to de-
grade them, but as to Christians whom the church holds in
honor, and to whom it thus shows honor. Care for widows
was a marked feature of the Old Testament (Ex. 22: 22-24;
Deut. 24: 17-19), and in the apostolic churches it was very
early made a prominent duty (Acts 6: 12).

that are widows indeed.—Those who are destitute and truly
desolate, without children or relatives to whom they can look
for help. Widows in this condition are widows indeed and
need the help and support of the church.

4 But if any widow hath children or grandchildren, let them
learn first to show piety towards their own family,—They

God. 5 Now she that is a widow indeed, and desolate, hath her hope set on God, and continueth in supplications and prayers night and day. 6 But she that giveth herself to pleasure is dead while she liveth. 7 These things also command, that they may be without reproach. 8 But if any provideth not for his own, and specially his own household, he hath denied the faith, and is

should learn first to care for their helpless and destitute mother or grandmother, and even if they are not destitute, this piety demands kindness, gentleness, patience, and love toward their own family.

and to requite their parents:—Repay with love and tender regard the parents in their helpless old age for all the love, patience, sleepless care they took for you in your helpless infancy. None can ever know the intensity of a mother's love for her child, her constant self-denying life to help the child she has borne. Now a child should remember this and return it in kindness and love when the mother grows old.

for this is acceptable in the sight of God.—What we render in kindness and love to our parents, God accepts as service to him.

5 Now she that is a widow indeed, and desolate,—She that is destitute, helpless, without children, or other relatives on whom she could depend for support is a widow indeed.

hath her hope set on God,—She has no one to whom to look but God.

and continueth in supplications and prayers night and day. —Her lack of others on whom to depend leads her to feel her dependence upon God, and makes her constantly come with supplications and prayers to God for help night and day.

6 But she that giveth herself to pleasure is dead while she liveth.—In contrast with her who feels her bereaved condition and draws near to God, the widow who lives for pleasure is dead. [Her frivolous, selfish, sensual existence is not true life; it fills none of life's true ends; and, as to any real value to herself or to others, she is practically dead. While alive in the flesh, she has no real life in the Spirit.]

7 These things also command, that they may be without reproach.—Give these teachings in charge of the whole church that they may be without blame in providing for "widows indeed," and not pampering idleness in those able to take care of themselves.

worse than an unbeliever. 9 Let none be enrolled as a widow under three-score years old, *having been* the wife of one man, 10 well reported of for good works; if she hath brought up children, if she hath used hospitality to

8 But if any provideth not for his own, and specially his own household,—If any child or grandchild provides not for his own widowed mother or grandmother, especially those who live with him, he is guilty of a crime in the sight of God.

he hath denied the faith,—So heinous is the crime that he denies the faith in so doing. To grossly violate the will of God is to deny the faith, and a failure to provide is such a violation.

and is worse than an unbeliever.—Many of the godless heathens, recognized the duty of caring for their parents, and for Christians not to do it is worse than an unbeliever. By some it is interpreted to mean if a man does not provide for his own family. But this is to introduce a wholly foreign subject in the connection and to do violence to the context.

9 Let none be enrolled as a widow under threescore years old,—[This did not necessarily preclude aid to widows who were younger and were in need; but these were the ones who were to be enrolled in the class whom the church maintained in comfort and in honor.]

having been the wife of one man,—[The fatal facility and the lax state of morality in the pagan world, and even in this country, must be taken into account when we seek to illustrate and explain the directions to Christians. She must not be a bigamist, or an adulteress, or one who had indulged in the prevalent custom of divorce, but had been faithful and true to her marriage vow.]

10 well reported of for good works;—Who has been faithful in performing good works so that she has a good report for them. [The Lord Jesus had first used the phrase and taught how "good works" of his disciples (Matt. 5: 16), as they were evidences of his own mission (John 10: 32, 33.) It denotes all kinds of good actions as distinguished from sentimentality—feeding the hungry, clothing the naked, and visiting the sick are good works. (Matt. 25: 35, 36.)]

if she hath brought up children,—To bring up children faithful to God is implied. The church has no more important

strangers, if she hath washed the saints' feet, if she hath relieved the afflicted,
if she hath diligently followed every good work. 11 But younger widows
refuse: for when they have waxed wanton against Christ, they desire to

work than bearing children and training them for service to
God. [She must be well known as one who loves children,
and would be ready and willing gladly to discharge any duties
to children who might be entrusted to her charge.]

if she hath used hospitality to strangers,—Entertaining
strangers has always been esteemed a virtue among the servants of God. "Forget not to show love unto strangers: for
thereby some have entertained angels unawares." (Heb. 13:
2.) The strangers to be entertained are those without means
to care for themselves.

if she hath washed the saints' feet,—Feet were washed at
the end of a footsore journey, and was an act of hospitality to
strangers. This had from the beginning been regarded as an
act of hospitality and kindness. Abraham entertained strangers and offered them water to wash their feet. (Gen. 18: 4.)
Jesus set his disciples the example that they should go beyond the hospitality of the ancients in love and condescen-
sion; they should wash the feet of their brethren. Jesus
washed the disciples' feet and told them that they "also ought
to wash one another's feet." (John 13: 14.) In the passage
before us Paul classes it as a good work with bringing up
children and visiting the sick. It is nowhere regarded as a
church ordinance. Pious and godly women did it for their
brethren who came to them.

if she hath relieved the afflicted,—[Not merely, or even
chiefly, by gifts, but by all kindly and sisterly encouragement,
ever ready to mourn, deeming none too low or degraded for
her kindness, none out of reach of her sisterly help and counsel, implying the visitation of the distressed in their homes.]

if she hath diligently followed every good work.—Every
work that administered good to needy and suffering men and
women. Women who have through life so conducted themselves as to be well reported of for such works are to be
honored and supported by the church.

11 But younger widows refuse:—Do not take into the number to be honored or supported widows younger than three-
score.

marry; 12 having condemnation, because they have rejected their first
¹pledge. 13 And withal they learn also *to be* idle, going about from house to
house; and not only idle, but tattlers also and busybodies, speaking things

¹Gr. *faith*

for when they have waxed wanton against Christ,—Those
younger than sixty are liable to grow wanton or wax lustful
against Christ. [The word *wanton* implies indulging in desires in spirit and conduct in opposition to Christ. It is to
surrender oneself to a carnal and luxurious course of life as
antagonistic to the claims and calling of Christ.]

they desire to marry;—"The flesh lusteth against the
Spirit." (Gal. 5: 17.) He does not condemn their marrying,
but encourages it. (Verse 14.) The point the apostle makes
is that the younger widows would cultivate idle habits and excite wanton and lascivious feeling that would lead them to
give up faith in and obedience to Christ and they would seek
marriage.

12 having condemnation,—They would fall under condemnation. [Those who give up the work which for their Master's sake they have undertaken, expose themselves to a
searching judgment, which will thoroughly sift the reasons
that induced them to forsake the begun toil, and that, if the
reasons be not satisfactory, will be unfavorable, and will
surely involve condemnation.]

because they have rejected their first pledge.—This seems
to carry with it the idea that the coming into the number that
are supported by the church take on themselves pledges of
fidelity and self-consecration to God and his cause. Younger
women in wantonness of the flesh give up their feeling of
self-consecration and seek to gratify their feelings in marriage. They take a step away from Christ. A backward step
from Christ is a fearful step. Christians ought to daily grow
in grace and in the knowledge of the truth, and this will daily
draw them nearer and nearer to God. The first step away
from God is the fatal one.

13 And withal they learn also to be idle, going about from
house to house;—That giving way to the feelings of the flesh
shows itself in a disposition to wander from house to house.

and not only idle, but tattlers also and busybodies, speaking

which they ought not. 14 I desire therefore that the younger ²*widows*
marry, bear children, rule the household, give no occasion to the adversary
for reviling: 15 for already some are turned aside after Satan. 16 If any

²Or, *women*

---

things which they ought not.—This leads to idle and mischievous gossip and vicious talking. Friendly intercourse and
kindly offices of friendship are good; especially is it good to
care for the sick and to help the needy, but too much and constant visiting and going from place to place are not good either for the visited or the visitor.

14 **I desire therefore that the younger widows marry,**—It is
better that the younger widows should marry than that they
should be taken into the number of those cared for by the
church. Marriage and a home of her own to look after and
care for are needed to develop the better nature and call out
the true abilities and qualities of women.

bear children, rule the household,—They fulfill their true
destiny, call into their noblest qualities, and develop the highest type and character of true womanhood in marrying, bearing children, and training souls for immortality, and making
good homes as conservatories of virtue, morality, and godliness. No holier trust was ever committed to mortals than
this.

give no occasion to the adversary for reviling:—In failing
to do these things they give occasion to the adversary of
Christ to speak reproachfully of his cause and people. Paul
said that the elderly women should be instructed to "train the
young women to love their husbands, to love their children, to
be sober-minded, chaste, workers at home, kind, being in subjection to their own husbands, that the word of God be not
blasphemed." (Tit. 2: 4, 5.) Reproach and blasphemy of the
word of God is brought in by Christian woman failing to keep
a clean and comfortable home. These may seem to be small
things, but to God nothing is small. These seemingly small
things are often most far-reaching and widespread in their influence for good or evil.

15 **for already some are turned aside after Satan.**—Some
had already forsaken God and turned aside to follow Satan.
And he warns them against the influences that lead in that direction.

woman that believeth hath widows, let her relieve them, and let not the church be burdened; that it may relieve them that are widows indeed.

16 **If any woman that believeth hath widows, let her relieve them, and let not the church be burdened; that it may relieve them that are widows indeed.**—The apostle here gives the general direction, if any woman have a widowed mother or grandmother, let her relieve them, take care of them, and let not the church be charged with their support that it may relieve widows that have no one to support them. This applies to men as well as women. (See verse 8.) Paul here, as the Scriptures everywhere do, recognizes that men and women able to work should have some proper calling at which they should labor industrially to make a living for themselves and to support those who by the ties of nature are dependent upon them. It is the duty of the church of God to require all to work and discharge the duties they owe to their families and kindred.

(2) CONCERNING ELDERS
5: 17-25

17 Let the elders that rule well be counted worthy of double honor, espe-

17 **Let the elders that rule well**—The apostle having concluded the direction as to the support of widows comes to the treatment of the elders. The elders here, as the connection plainly shows, refers to those who had the oversight of the congregation. They were selected by looking out those who had the qualifications set forth. (3:1-7.) How they were selected gives the trouble. Luke gives an example of selecting persons to work in the church. The apostles were the teachers and the leaders. They directed the disciples: "Look ye out therefore, brethren, from among you seven men of good report, full of the Spirit and of wisdom, whom we may appoint over this business. . . . And they chose Stephen, a man full of faith and of the Holy Spirit, and Philip, and Prochorus, and Nicanor, and Timon, and Parmenas, and Nicolaus. . . . whom they set before the apostles." (Acts 6: 3-6.) The expression, "Look ye out," carries the thought of diligent inquiry and private consultation to reach the agreement. This is not nominating and electing by votes. Nothing of this

cially those who labor in the word and in teaching. 18 For the scripture

kind is found in the Scriptures. This excites division, party
spirit, and strife, while the scriptural order seeks union, harmony, and agreement. They were to inquire among themselves who was most suited according to the qualifications
given by God. When the agreement was reached, the apostles apointed them to the work. A faithful preacher present
or anyone capable of conducting public affairs might do this
for the congregation now. When the selection has been
made, it is their duty to take the oversight of the congregation, direct its affairs in its public meetings, and to look after
the lives of the members and see that all engage in the work
for which they are fitted. This takes time and attention.
They are the overseers and teachers of the churches and individual members. They are to teach the word of God.

be counted worthy of double honor,—They are entitled to
the respect and honor of the members of the church and are
entitled to support while in the work. The idea of doing
God's work for money or for the wages it brings is adhorring
to this Scripture teaching. That idea destroys it as God's
work. A man that preaches for the money he gets is not approved of God and will never receive reward from God.
While this is true, the man who labors for good must live, and
when he devotes his time to the service, it is the duty of the
people of God to support him. This applies to labor of any
kind in the church. The elders who devote their time to the
service of God through the church must be supported. The
honor bestowed on them is not only respectful treatment and
deference, but support.

especially those who labor in the word and in teaching.—
Those who do their duty well, preaching the word privately
and publicly, are worthy of a double portion of honor and support. The elders of a church are always spoken of in the
plural, showing that a plurality of elders for each congregation was contemplated. It also shows that some elders labored in word and doctrine—devoted their time to preaching
and teaching—while others did not. All gave attention to the
interests of the church and looked after the welfare of the

saith, [3]Thou shalt not muzzle the ox when he treadeth out the corn. And The laborer is worthy of his hire. 19 Against an elder receive not an accusation, except at *the mouth of* two or three witnesses. 20 Them that sin

[3]Dt. 25. 4

members. Some did it in a private way, others devoted their time to teaching and preaching. These were entitled to double honor.

18 For the scripture saith, Thou shalt not muzzle the ox when he treadeth out the corn.—This is given as an illustration of the relation the elder who labors sustains to the church. The ox does not tread out the corn for the sake of what he eats but how he is used to do that work; it is right that he should enjoy the fruits of his work so as to eat of the corn while he treads it out.

And, The laborer is worthy of his hire.—This does not mean that he is to labor for the sake of the money, but while laboring he is worthy of his support. Jesus in sending out his apostles quoted it: "The laborer is worthy of his food." (Matt. 10: 10.) Worthy of a support to enable him to do the work.

19 Against an elder receive not an accusation, except at the mouth of two or three witnesses.—No accusation of wrong or ill-doing is to be entertained against an elder, save before two or three witnesses. It seems that Timothy as the inspired representative of the apostles was forbidden to entertain an accusation, which indicates that accusations against elders would come before him. Under the idea that young men as evangelists are the successors in the office of Timothy and Titus, the idea prevails to some extent that any youth doing the work of an evangelist may try and dispose of elders, and lord it over the heritage of God. Timothy and Titus as inspired men were the representatives of the apostles of God until the canon of revelation was perfected. None occupy such position before God or such relations to the church now as did these men. The fellow elders as the rulers of the church might bear such accusations regulated by the scriptural teachings on the subject or wise and prudent men might be chosen to make such investigations as are needed and might act for the church. The elders are not to do all the

reprove in the sight of all, that the rest also may be in fear. 21 I charge
thee in the sight of God, and Christ Jesus, and the elect angels, that thou
observe these things without ⁴prejudice, doing nothing by partiality. 22 Lay

⁴Or, *preference*

work, but to see that it is done by those who are competent to
do it.

20 Them that sin reprove in the sight of all,—When the
accusations have been properly made and the elders found
guilty of sin, reprove them in the sight of all. When we cover
up sins in the church, we corrupt the morality and virtue of
the church and destroy its efficacy to honor God or to save
men. Evil teachers and evil men must be exposed and purged
out of the church or the church becomes corrupt and a synagogue of Satan instead of a church of Jesus Christ. And what
or who is injured by exposing evil teaching or evil men? No
truth can be injured by the exposure of falsehood. The greatest injury that can be inflicted on truth is to yoke it with
falsehood. God cannot be honored by covering up evil and
cherishing false teachers or evil men in the church. To do
this is to honor the devil and his servants equally with God
and his servants. It cannot help good men to keep evil men
in association with them. It corrupts their goodness, destroys
their influence for good, injures bad men themselves, and
countenances them as though they were good. The weakness
of the churches is: they cherish falsehood and evil among
them. They cannot be strong either with God or man while so
doing. To expose error and bad men is to proclaim to the
world that they seek truth, purity, holiness, and godlikeness.

that the rest also may be in fear.—That others may fear to
sin. He is a particular character, occupies a higher position,
and his punishment for wrong must be rendered accordingly
that the warning may spread over the whole congregation,
and thus others also may fear.

**21 I charge thee in the sight of God, and Christ Jesus, and
the elect angels, that thou observe these things without prejudice, doing nothing by partiality.**—God is no respecter of persons and holds to stricter accountability those who have the
best opportunities and occupy the higher places and demands
that his servants shall be guided by the same principles of

hands hastily on no man, neither be partaker of other men's sins: keep thyself pure. 23 Be no longer a drinker of water, but use a little wine
for thy stomach's sake and thine often infirmities. 24 Some men's sins are

right and justice. It takes courage to do this. But in the
doing of the more difficult duties, God bestows the highest
blessings. So he solemnly charges Timothy that he discharge
these duties without favor or partiality.

22 Lay hands hastily on no man,—This verse has given rise
to much diversity of thought. Some consider it to mean to
lay hands on no man, to ordain him as an elder hastily, or
without due trial and proof of his fitness. But there is nothing in the context that refers to ordaining elders. To throw
in a highly figurative expression on the subject without any
connecting links to show its meaning is unnatural and harsh,
and would lead to great doubt as to the meaning. Others
maintain that it refers to laying violent hands on a man. This
would indicate that Paul did not think it would be wrong for
Timothy to deliberately and with due consideration strike a
man for wrongdoing. This is so contrary to the whole teaching of Christ and the apostles to be inadmissible. He is
speaking of the accusation and trial of elders, and it seems to
me that the connection leaves but one possible construction—
do not hastily lay hands on an elder to draw him up for trial.
Since elders are presumed to be good, true, and faithful men
proved by experience, let no accusation be brought against
them hastily.

neither be partaker of other men's sins: keep thyself pure.
—Do not become partakers of the sins of other men by per-
mitting them to bring hasty and unjust accusations against
elders, but keep thyself pure from all sinful complications.

23 Be no longer a drinker of water,—Paul now gives Timothy some personal directions. Timothy refrained from the use
of wine and strong drink. This should be a significant lesson
to us. That was an age of wine drinking, yet Timothy refrained from its use even when sick, as a matter of Christian
purity, and a good example to others.

**but use a little wine for thy stomach's sake and thine often
infirmities.**—He tells him not to go to an extreme in refusing
wine as a medicine. Drink no longer water alone, but for the

evident, going before unto judgment; and some men also they follow after.
25 In like manner also ⁵there are good works that are evident; and such as
are otherwise cannot be hid.

⁵Gr. *the works that are good are evident*

sake of his stomach, which doubtless was weak, and for his
often infirmities, use a little wine. Many have quoted this instruction of Paul to justify the use of wine as a beverage. It
does no such thing, but the reverse. Timothy, a model and
true Christian, a young man trained from childhood in the
knowledge of the Scriptures, refuses to use wine at all, even in
sickness. Paul tells him to use a little wine for his illness. He
encourages its use for no other purpose. Paul laid down the
principles that ought to govern all Christians: "Wherefore, if
meat causeth my brother to stumble, I will eat no flesh for evermore, that I cause not my brother to stumble." (1 Cor. 8:
13.) And again: "It is good not to eat flesh, nor to drink
wine, nor to do anything whereby thy brother stumbleth."
(Rom. 14: 21.)

24 **Some men's sins are evident, going before unto judgment;**—[The wrongdoing of some men is of an open character, seen without any inquiry or proof that is no trouble to ascertain and decide upon as to the discipline necessary for their
good.]

and some men also they follow after.—[In the case of some
their wrongs are secret, hard to find out, and hard to decide as
to what ought to be done for their good, and the good of the
cause of Christ.]

25 **In like manner also there are good works that are evident;**—[The same is true of the good deeds of some; they are
of so public a character that everyone around them sees and
knows them.]

and such as are otherwise cannot be hid.—[Those not good
cannot be permanently concealed.]

(3) Concerning Servants
6: 1, 2

1 Let as many as are ⁶servants under the yoke count their own masters

⁶Gr. *bondservants*

1 **Let as many as are servants under the yoke**—[Human
slavery was one of the most perplexing questions the gospel

worthy of all honor, that the name of God and the doctrine be not blasphemed. 2 And they that have believing masters, let them not despise them,

of Jesus Christ had to face. It was common to all peoples and nations, and entered into all grades and ranks of society. In the old world war and commerce were equally responsible for its existence. To attempt to eradicate it by preaching against it as hateful to God and degrading to man would have produced rebellion and revolution in its darkest and most violent form. Christ did not propose to break up such relations by violence. He recognized the relationship, regulated it, and put in operation principles that in their workings would so mold public sentiment as to break down all evil relations and sinful institutions.] A very grievous type of slavery existed throughout all the countries of Asia and Europe at the time of the introduction of the Christian religion. The relation of both masters and servants was recognized by the apostles. Here Paul is instructing Timothy how he should teach servants to conduct themselves toward their masters. Under the yoke means in slavery.

count their own masters worthy of all honor,—They were not to think for a moment that Christianity was to interfere with the existing social relations and put master and slave on an equality on earth, but they were to show respect and honor to their own masters.

that the name of God and the doctrine be not blasphemed. —That no reproach be brought upon the name of God whom the servants worshipped. On the other hand, the fidelity of the Christian servants in the discharge of all the duties laid on him by the master should commend his religion to his master.

2 And they that have believing masters, let them not despise them,—Here he recognizes that believers could be masters. In the spiritual kingdom they were one in Jesus Christ, brethren invested with equal rights; [and the slave might conclude that this destroyed the earthly relation of master and slave. But this spiritual relationship though, it must influence and modify the civil relationship, did not dissolve it. In civil relation they were still master and slave, and a Christian is forbidden to cease to honor and be obedient to the civil relation.]

because they are brethren; but let them serve them the rather, because they
that ⁷partake of the benefit are believing and beloved. These things teach
and exhort.

⁷Or, *lay hold of*

---

because they are brethren;—The slave would think because
his master was a Christian he ought to set him free because he
was his brother, and if he did not he would condemn or despise him.

**but let them serve them the rather, because they that par-
take of the benefit are believing and beloved.**—On the other
hand, let the service be more cheerful because they are brethren who partake of the benefits of service. Paul impresses
that they ought to prefer to work for a Christian master because a brother was helped by their labors.

These things teach and exhort.—It is likely that disturb-
ances had taken place over these questions. On such questions it would be easy to arouse deep feelings in slaves. From
the severity of the denunciation in the next verse of those who
teach differently, we may justly conclude that evil-disposed
persons had been teaching differently and arousing discontent
and a rebellious spirit.

SECTION THREE

CONCLUSION
6: 3-21

1. WARNINGS AGAINST DISPUTATIONS AND COVETOUSNESS
6: 3-10

3 If any man teacheth a different doctrine, and consenteth not to ⁸sound words, *even* the words of our Lord Jesus Christ, and to the doctrine which is according to godliness; 4 he is puffed up, knowing nothing, but ⁹doting about

⁸Gr. *healthful*
⁹Gr. *sick*

---

3 If any man teacheth a different doctrine,—The form of statement here used is general, but it comprehends all teaching contrary to that of the inspired apostle. It is quite probable that among other heretical doctrines adapted to embitter different classes of society against each other and excite a social revolution, was human slavery. It is evident that such teaching, while it wholly ignored the spiritual significance and value of the gospel, was in high degree dangerous where a great portion of the population were slaves. It could result only in revolution. Hence, the importance of the instruction to slaves to be in obedience to their masters. While he nowhere affirms the rightfulness of the relation of master and slave, in all his epistles he instructs slaves to be in obedience to their masters.

and consenteth not to sound words, even the words of our Lord Jesus Christ,—This reference must be to the general tenor of the teaching of the Lord Jesus Christ, which was to interfere with no relation regulated by the government. [Here he was in all probability referring to such sayings of the Lord as: "Then saith he unto them, Render therefore unto Caesar the things that are Caesar's; and unto God the things that are God's." (Matt. 22: 21.) "Resist not him that is evil: but whosoever smiteth thee on thy right cheek, turn to him the other also." (Matt. 5: 39.) But the false teachers, who were the bitterest enemies of the truth would not consent to "sound words," though they were the words of the Lord Jesus Christ.]

and to the doctrine which is according to godliness;—Such a state of insubordination and discontent as they would produce would be a great hindrance to the progress of the gospel.

questionings and disputes of words, whereof cometh envy, strife, railings, evil
surmisings, 5 wranglings of men corrupted in mind and bereft of the truth,

---

4 **he is puffed up, knowing nothing,**—He is self-conceited,
thinks his reasons above the teachings of the Lord and the
apostles. All such really know nothing as they should know.
They do not know that God in his workings does not suddenly break these relations, but he lays down principles that
work out results gradually and gently through changing the
heart and molding and directing the feelings and purposes.
God, in other words, works results through the heart, changes
the outward acts and relations first by changing the heart and
feelings. Hence he breaks and changes no relation by sudden
and violent means.

but doting about questionings and disputes of words,—They
had such a morbid fondness for questionings and disputings
over untaught questions and words that it amounted to a disease. These men deal with subtle, useless, and unpractical
questions, which have no practical bearing on ordinary life,
and only tend to stir up strife and useless discussion, and to
make men discontented and rebellious.

whereof cometh envy,—Envy is uneasiness, pain, mortification, or discontent, excited by another's prosperity, or by his
superior knowledge, or possessions.

strife,—Angry contention, hostile struggling, fighting, the
disposition to be quarrelsome and contentious, the feeling
which seeks to irritate. It is not strife for truth and right, but
simply for its own sake.

railings,—Harsh and abusive language toward those who
will not concede a point—a common effect of disputes and
more commonly of disputes about small and unimportant matters than of those which are of magnitude.

evil surmisings,—Evil surmisings are the imaginings of evils
or wrongs of others without clear testimony. This seems to
grow out of the depravity of the flesh and shows itself in the
disposition to attribute evil motives to the acts of others.
This disposition is very prevalent among men, even among
Christians. This habit is here placed in bad association, and
is a warning to all who could please God that it should be sed-

supposing that godliness is a way of gain. 6 But godliness with contentment
is great gain: 7 for we brought nothing into the world, for neither can we

---

ulously avoided. The habit arises from a bitter, jealous
spirit toward others; it is really the reflection of the evil heart
of him who cultivates the spirit, and usually indicates that he
is actuated by evil motives in what he does, and that he
judges others by his own spirit.

5 **wranglings of men**—These words close the long catalogue
of the fruits of the teaching of the false teachers of the faith in
Christ and point out that the wranglings engendered by these
useless and unhappy controversies would be no mere temporary difficulties, but would indefinitely prolong their destructive work.

corrupted in mind—[They corrupted the word of God, and
thus prepared the way for the debasement of their own mind,
leading in turn to that pride and ignorance which were their
most distinguishing qualities.]

and bereft of the truth,—[This indicates that the truth was
once theirs. They had corrupted the word of God, and thus
prepared the way for the debasement of their own mind, leading in turn to that pride and ignorance which were their most
distinguishing qualities. The truth was theirs once, but they
forfeited it by their unfaithfulness and corruption.]

supposing that godliness is a way of gain.—[They did not
preach contentment to the slaves or induce them to acquiesce
with patience in their hard lot, but rather persuaded them to
use religion as a means of worldly betterment. Such counsel
would have disorganizing, disintegrating effects upon society.
But it was, besides, a degradation of the doctrine of Christ.
Godliness was not designed to be a lucrative business or to be
followed only so far as it subserved the promotion of worldly
interests. Simon Magus and such men as made "merchan-
dise" of the gospel are examples of this class. Such persons
would be "teaching things which they ought not, for filthy lucre's sake." (Tit. 1:11.)]

6 **But godliness with contentment is great gain:**—Contentment pertains not to the place or condition, but to the heart.
Being contented in our lot is great gain. It is a precious trea-

carry anything out; 8 but having food and covering [10]we shall be therewith content. 9 But they that are minded to be rich fall into a temptation and a snare and many foolish and hurtful lusts, such as drown men in destruction and perdition. 10 For the love of money is a root of all [1]kinds of evil:

[10]Or, *in these we shall have enough*
[1]Gr. *evils*

sure that brings much joy in this world, and then an unfailing treasure in the world to come. It is great gain to learn to be content without riches or earthly treasures. [In this concise and weighty sentence Paul expresses both these main ideas that godliness makes us content, and to be content is the highest good.]

7 **for we brought nothing into the world, for neither can we carry anything out;**—Every earthly possession is only meant for this life—for the period between the hour of birth and death—then we should only be concerned about what we can wisely use in our journey through life. To burden ourselves with more is to hinder our usefulness and our true enjoyment of life and our opportunities for doing good for others and for improving ourselves.

8 **but having food and covering we shall be therewith content.**—What we eat and what we wear is all the material good we get out of riches. [What else may be granted should be received with thanksgiving. Still it is not absolutely necessary, and the earnest and devout Christian will be satisfied when his actual needs are supplied.]

9 **But they that are minded to be rich fall into a temptation and a snare and many foolish and hurtful lusts,**—The eagerness for riches brings temptation to sin. They are led into a snare of Satan. The effort to gain riches and enjoy them excites many hurtful lusts, which burden the heart, destroys the better aspirations and desires of the spirit, and makes one a sordid and selfish being.

such as drown men in destruction and perdition.—There is no truth more plainly taught on the pages of inspiration than all unjust means—or means gained when we make anxiety for money the chief end of our labors—bring ruin, poverty, and shame upon men and their families. The longer it remains in the family the deeper the ruin it works, the more highly it exalts them the deeper in shame it drags them down. Every dol-

which some reaching after have been led astray from the faith, and have pierced themselves through with many sorrows.

lar brought into a family by dishonest and unjust means is a curse, a poverty breeder to that family. [The gratification of desires, whether these desires are centered in the lower animal passions or in the pursuit of yet baser and more selfish passions, still invariably leads to the destruction of the poor, frail human body first. This premature breaking up of the earthly tabernacle is the herald and precursor of the final perdition of the immortal soul.]

10 **For the love of money is a root of all kinds of evil:**—An inordinate desire of earthly things or of what belongs to our neighbor. Covetousness is a vice that becomes stronger in old age when other vices are weakened; it can never be satisfied; it renders men the abhorrence of God, cruel, oppressive, and unjust toward neighbors; and betrays the man into sins and miseries unnumbered.

which some reaching after have been led astray from the faith,—Some had been so deceived as to depart from the faith or living according to the requirements of God. [The one who covets gold longs for opportunities in which his love of money finds a field for exercise.]

and have pierced themselves through with many sorrows. —They have overwhelmed themselves with many sorrows and afflictions. [The reference here is most likely to the many pains, agonies, troubles attending money seeking, the pangs of conscience, the miseries of unsatisfied greed, and the conscious failure of attaining life's best end.]

2. FIGHT THE GOOD FIGHT OF FAITH
6: 11-16

11 But thou, O man of God, flee these things; and follow after righteous-

11 **But thou, O man of God,**—"Man of God" is one devoted to the service of God. It frequently in the Old Testament means the prophets inspired of God and sent to teach the people, but under the new covenant the name is extended to all faithful men in the Lord Jesus Christ. (2 Tim. 3: 17.)

ness, godliness, faith, love, ²patience, meekness. 12 Fight the good fight of
the faith, lay hold on the life eternal, whereunto thou wast called, and didst

---

²Or, *stedfastness*

---

flee these things;—Paul gives Timothy and all teachers of
the religion of the Lord Jesus Christ the warning to flee from
the love of money, and get far away from such desires and all
the evils and dangers it brings.

and follow after righteousness,—The apostle says: "Be not
overcome of evil, but overcome evil with good. (Rom. 12:
21.) The "man of God" fleeing from all covetous longings for
money must follow after righteousness, shape his inner life
after "the law of the Spirit of life in Christ Jesus," which
makes "free from the law of sin and of death." (Rom. 8: 2.)

godliness,—Godliness gives contentment with food, raiment, and what at present we enjoy.

faith,—Faith in God and Christ assures of a better and more
abiding substance reserved in heaven for us. (1 Pet. 1: 3-12.)

love,—Love is manifested in doing good to our fellow men,
and the divine law tells us that it is the only way we can do it,
hence "love therefore is the fulfillment of the law." (Rom.
13: 10.)

patience,—[Patience is that state of mind and heart that enables one to face difficulties and obstacles that make him willing to toil and suffer adversity in order to maintain his loyalty to God.]

meekness.—Meekness suppresses our wrath and indignation
against those who are injurious to us and takes away from us
that which is our own—submission to the divine will.

12 Fight the good fight of the faith,—Faith in God calls
man to a vigorous fight with evil in his own soul that he
against the influences of the flesh may keep the faith, and then
it summons him to maintain the faith in the world. The
Christian teacher especially had to maintain that truth against
the fierce opposition of the world, and before the world both
in precept and example of what faith in Christ will make of a
man.

lay hold on the life eternal,—He was to do the things required to gain eternal life. In fighting "the good fight of the

confess the good confession in the sight of many witnesses. 13 I charge thee
in the sight of God, who ⁹giveth life to all things, and of Christ Jesus, who
before Pontius Pilate witnessed the good confession; 14 that thou keep the
commandment, without spot, without reproach, until the appearing of our

⁹Or, *preserveth all things alive*

---

faith" a man lays hold on eternal life because faith leads him
to do the things that fit him for eternal life.

whereunto thou wast called,—Unto the attainment of eternal life Timothy had been called.

**and didst confess the good confession in the sight of many
witnesses.**—Timothy was brought before the rulers, was imprisoned for confessing and not denying that Jesus is the
Christ. Of him it is said: "Know ye that our brother Timothy hath been set at liberty; with whom, if he come shortly, I
will see you." (Heb. 13: 23.) Certainly the greater probability is that his confession took place when he was on trial
for his life. The special merit in the confession was in making it in the face of danger and even death.

13 I charge thee in the sight of God,—He cautions him to
remember that God witnesses and will hold him to strict account if he fails to meet the responsibility thus taken upon
himself.

who giveth life to all things,—God is the source of all life,
and from him all life comes. "In him was life; and the life
was the light of men." (John 1: 4.)

**and of Christ Jesus, who before Pontius Pilate witnessed
the good confession;**—This confession of Jesus Christ was
made when he was on trial for his life before Pontius Pilate.
The special merit in the confession was in making it in the
face of danger and death—an occasion similar to that in which
he warned the twelve to confess and not to deny him. Paul
says: "Because if thou shalt confess with thy mouth Jesus as
Lord, and shalt believe in thy heart that God raised him from
the dead, thou shalt be saved: for with the heart man believeth unto righteousness; and with the mouth confession is
made unto salvation." (Rom. 10: 9, 10.) This was addressed
to Christians, not concerning the plan of entering into the
church and having their sins pardoned, but of the course that
would lead to eternal life. Faith in God and the courage to

Lord Jesus Christ: 15 which in [4]its own times he shall show, who is the blessed and only Potentate, the King of [5]kings, and Lord of [6]lords; 16 who

[4]Or, *his*
[5]Gr. *them that reign as kings*
[6]Gr. *them that rule as lords*

confess Christ is just as essential to salvation at every step through life down to death itself as they are at the beginning.

14 that thou keep the commandment, without spot, without reproach,—Here Paul specifies what the charge was that he was commanding in such earnest, solemn language to Timothy. The commandment was the teaching of Jesus Christ, the gospel message, that was to be proclaimed in all its fullness; and that it might be done effectually it was needful that Timothy should be without flaw—should live the life he preached. The false teachers of whom he had been speaking (well known to Timothy) by their lives had dishonored the glorious commandment which they professed to love and teach.

until the appearing of our Lord Jesus Christ:—The coming of the Lord was of all events the goal which all were to keep in view. Death is regarded as the coming of the Son of man to those who die. It might mean until death. If kept till then, it will be kept till the coming of the Lord to judge the world.

15 which in its own times he shall show,—At the time appointed by the Father—Jesus will show forth his coming to the world (Matt. 24: 27-31)—the time which the Father has appointed by his own authority (Acts 1: 7) and said to be known only to him (Mark 13: 32). But the Father's time is Christ's own time. The Father and the Son both have part in the glorious manifestation of his coming. [The plural *times* is suggestive of successive manifestations and fulfillments in the kingdom of God of the predicted manifestations. It is possible, therefore, to include in these *times* the Lord's coming to Christians individually to take them to the home prepared for them. (John 14: 3.)]

who is the blessed and only Potentate,—A potentate is one possessing power, a governor or ruler. Jesus said to his disciples after his resurrection from the dead: "All authority hath been given unto me in heaven and on earth." (Matt. 28: 18.) And "he must reign, till he hath put all his enemies under his

only hath immortality, dwelling in light unapproachable; whom no man hath seen, nor can see: to whom *be* honor and power eternal. Amen.

---

feet. The last enemy that shall be abolished is death. . . . But when he saith, All things are put in subjection, it is evident that he is excepted who did subject all things unto him. And when all things have been subjected unto him, then shall the Son also himself be subjected to him that did subject all things unto him, that God may be all in all." (1 Cor. 15: 25-28.) And because Jesus is the only Ruler, there is no other name under heaven whereby men must be saved.

the King of kings, and Lord of lords;—The King over all kings, the Ruler of all rulers of whatever name or power.

16 who only hath immortality,—Immortality means freedom from death, from suffering, from decay. Jesus Christ in the bosom of the Father only hath immortality with God. He alone can impart it to others. "For as the Father hath life in himself, even so gave he to the Son also to have life in himself." (John 5: 26.) "For as the Father raiseth the dead and giveth them life, even so the Son also giveth life to whom he will." (John 5: 21.) Jesus has supreme rule until he puts down all rule and authority and power, and has rescued the earth from the dominion of death, then he will surrender the world rescued from the rule of sin and death up to God the Father that he may be all and in all.

dwelling in light unapproachable;—The Lord Jesus Christ in the bosom of the Father is as inaccessible as God himself. None can see him and all beings in heaven and on earth must give him glory and honor and yield to his supreme and eternal power.

whom no man hath seen, nor can see:—The light of Jesus is blinding to all who approach him in mortal frame. We shall in the future see him as he is in immortal brightness and then we shall be transformed into his likeness.

to whom be honor and power eternal.—To whom—as alone within himself is worthy and to whom they properly belong—let honor and eternal power be ascribed.

Amen.—This word marks the close of the doxology.

3. CHARGE TO THE RICH
6: 17-19

17 Charge them that are rich in this present [7]world, that they be not highminded, nor have their hopes set on the uncertainty of riches, but on God, who giveth us richly all things to enjoy; 18 that they do good, that they be rich in good works, that they be ready to distribute, [8]willing to com-

[7]Or, age
[8]Or, ready to sympathize

17 **Charge them that are rich in this present world, that they be not highminded, nor have their hope set on the uncertainty of riches,**—Paul had already given fearful warning against anxiety for riches and the improper means of obtaining them. Here he gives an earnest and solemn lesson as to how those who possessed riches should use them. He tells Timothy to charge them to be not uplifted with pride on account of riches—that riches are uncertain. They take wings and fly away; they do not bring the happiness they promise. One must not trust them for true good.

but on God, who giveth us richly all things to enjoy;—No more distinct promise of earthly good was ever made to Jews than this promise to Christians. The same promise is made distinctly to the faithful Christians at Philippi: "And my God shall supply every need of yours according to his riches in glory." (Phil. 4: 19.) Some erroneously claim that under the law of Moses temporal blessings alone were promised, and under the law of Christ only spiritual blessings. Under Christ the promise of temporal blessings has not been withdrawn. They are as great as under Judaism, but under Christ the spiritual blessings have been added. Hence, Christ says: "I say unto you, There is no man that hath left house, or brethren, or sisters, or mother, or father, or children, or lands, for my sake, and for the gospel's sake, but he shall receive a hundredfold now in this time, . . . and in the world to come eternal life." (Mark 10: 29, 30.)

18 **that they do good, that they be rich in good works,**— These words seem to point to the highest enjoyment procurable by those rich—the luxury of doing good, of helping others to be happy, the only enjoyment that never fails.

that they be ready to distribute, willing to communicate;—

municate; 19 laying up in store for themselves a good foundation against the time to come, that they may lay hold on the life which is *life* indeed.

Free to come into fellowship with those at work for Christ by aiding them.

19 laying up in store for themselves a good foundation against the time to come,—The foundation of their hope for eternal life is that through faith in Jesus Christ they have used their riches in doing good to the poor. When they do it through faith in Jesus Christ, they will use it in his name as he directs. Riches impose a fearful responsibility on man. They tempt him to do wrong. There is great temptation to lift him up with pride. The world flatters and fawns upon him because of his riches. The churches do it, give him the chief seats, and give him power and influence as a member of the church because of his money. The care of his riches takes his time and attention and tempts him to forget God and the duties he owes to him. Riches, when used humbly and faithfully in the name of Jesus Christ to honor God and to do good to man, are wings to lift him heavenward. Hoarded, gloried in, used to exalt in the world and gratify his fleshly appetites and desires, they are as a leaden weight around his neck to drag him down to ruin.

that they may lay hold on the life which is life indeed.—The right use of riches lays a foundation from which the rich may lay hold on the life eternal.

4. FINAL CHARGE TO TIMOTHY AND BENEDICTION
6: 20, 21

20 O Timothy, guard [9]that which is committed unto *thee,* turning away from the profane babblings and oppositions of the knowledge which is falsely so called; 21 which some professing have [1] erred concerning the faith.
   Grace be with you.

[9]Gr. *the deposit*
[10]Gr. *missed the mark*

20 O Timothy, guard that which is committed unto thee,— This is an affectionate and earnest appeal to Timothy to guard the work committed to him. Do not alter, add too, or take from it. Be faithful in keeping and teaching it. That is the only thing that could help him or his hearers.

turning away from the profane babblings and oppositions of the knowledge which is falsely so called ;—Turn away from these useless talks and subjects that bring no profit. Too much attention given to errors may, and often does, lead into errors. As a rule, men who become hobby riders are not benefited by discussion, and frequently others are injured by such. When a man exalts one truth above another truth of the Bible, and teaches that to the neglect of other truths, he does evil and not good. But, as a rule, the best treatment is not to yield to him, not to argue with him, but press forward the work of God.

21 which some professing have erred concerning the faith. —When men turn aside in any way from adherence to the plain truth as taught, they make shipwreck of their faith and go into apostasy.

Grace be with you.—These words, no doubt addressed to Timothy, are a gracious, peaceful ending to the Epistle.

COMMENTARY ON THE SECOND
EPISTLE TO TIMOTHY

CONTENTS

INTRODUCTION TO THE SECOND EPISTLE TO TIMOTHY

I. TIME AND PLACE OF WRITING

The internal evidence of the Epistle points to Rome as the place where it was written. It is generally believed that the following refers to Nero: "But the Lord stood by me, and strengthened me; that through me the message might be fully proclaimed, and that all the Gentiles might hear: and I was delivered out of the mouth of the lion" (4: 17), as indicating the place where he was at the time. The seat of judgment, the presence of the emperor, the concourse of the Gentiles, the names of the persons sending salutations, and the expressions of the near approach of death (4: 7, 8) leave little doubt that Paul was now in Rome, and, if so, this certainly was the last of the three Epistles. This Epistle differs wholly from the first, caused by different circumstances. Its main purpose was to encourage Timothy under the new danger which had come upon the church through the persecution by Nero and Paul's imprisonment under a capital charge. By his own example of faith and constancy, by cogent reasonings and exhortations, and by the strongest Christian motives, Paul strives to comfort and sustain Timothy under the trying and perilous circumstances in which he was placed, and adds some prophetic warnings concerning coming heresies and directions as to how Timothy was to meet them. A brief statement of the present conditions of affairs at Rime was a pressing entreaty twice repeated to hasten to him. (4: 9, 21) A.D. 68.

II. PURPOSE OF THE EPISTLE

After his first trial Paul was remanded to prison. The occasion of writing seems to have been his deep concern about Timothy. He was anxious that he should come to him at Rome, bringing with him Mark, at as early date as possible. (1: 4; 4: 11.) But Paul was uncertain about his own condition—whether he should live to see him or be executed before his arrival. He sends to him, therefore, not merely a message to come, but an Epistle full of fatherly exhortations and instructions applicable to his present circumstances. And these seem to have been much needed. Many of Paul's friends had forsaken him (1: 15; 4: 10), and Timothy needed much encouragement. The Epistle, therefore, was calculated, in some measure, to apply what Paul by word of mouth would, if he were permitted to speak face to face, still more fervently urge upon him. And thus we possess an Epistle most important for the church in all ages. The affecting circumstances in which Paul himself was placed carry home to every devout heart his earnest and impassioned eloquence.

After his first trial, nothing is certainly known concerning him. But that he was executed by the sword is the constant tradition of antiquity and would agree with the fact of his Roman citizenship which would exempt him from death by torture. Of his last trial and death there is tradition, but no history.

COMMENTARY ON THE SECOND EPISTLE TO TIMOTHY

SECTION ONE

PERSONAL APPEAL FOR LOYALTY TO THE GOSPEL
1: 1 to 2: 13

1. APOSTOLIC GREETING
1: 1, 2

1 Paul, an apostle of Christ Jesus through the will of God, according to the promise of the life which is in Christ Jesus, 2 to Timothy, my beloved child: Grace, mercy, peace, from God the Father and Christ Jesus our Lord.

---

1 Paul, an apostle of Christ Jesus through the will of God, —Apart from any work or merit of his own, God chose him for the work, and it was that sovereign will which chose him as an apostle, which guided him through his eventful life, and which brought him to the prison in Rome.

according to the promise of the life which is in Christ Jesus, —This indicates the object or intention of his appointment as an apostle, which was to make known, to publish abroad, the promise of eternal life. He was evidently under the expectation of death at the time of writing.

2 to Timothy, my beloved child:—He had tender affection for Timothy whom he had taught the faith in Christ, and who had proved himself worthy of his confidence and affection.

Grace, mercy, peace,—There is invoked grace on him as unworthy, mercy on him as exposed to suffering, peace on him as the result of his being graciously dealt with.

from God the Father and Christ Jesus our Lord.—It is the fatherly feeling in God—that which is highest in his nature and with which redemption originated—that he made his appeal for saving blessings to rest on Timothy. Christ is the dispenser of the blessings in the Father's house, of which there is enough for all.

2. THANKSGIVING FOR TIMOTHY'S PAST AND EXHORTATION THAT HE MAY BE ZEALOUS AND WILLING, LIKE PAUL, TO SUFFER FOR THE GOSPEL
1: 3-14

3 I thank God, whom I serve from my forefathers in a pure conscience, how unceasing is my remembrance of thee in my supplications, night and day 4 longing to see thee, remembering thy tears, that I may be filled with ¹joy;

¹Or, *joy in being reminded*

3, 4 I thank God,—[Notwithstanding the fact that the meaning is somewhat obscured by the parentheses (verse 5), it seems clear that the expression of thanksgiving was for his remembrance of the "unfeigned faith" of Timothy, and his grandmother Lois, and his mother Eunice.]

whom I serve from my forefathers—Paul had served God from childhood, having been trained to do so by his parents. He had been earnest, zealous, and faithful in rendering service to God as he believed was right.

in a pure conscience,—Not only did he worship the same God as his fathers, but, like them, he worshiped in a pure conscience. In becoming a Christian he did not, as his enemies charged, depart from the God of Israel, the God of his forefathers; on the other hand, he, in accepting Christ, was moved by the faith of all the godly Israelites, while those in rejecting him had apostatized from the faith. In his defense before Felix he said: "But this I confess unto thee, that after the Way which they call a sect, so serve I the God of our fathers, believing all things which are according to the law, and which are written in the prophets; having hope toward God, which these also themselves look for, that there shall be a resurrection both of the just and unjust. Herein I also exercise myself to have a conscience void of offence toward God and men always." (Acts 24: 14-16; see also Rom. 4: 12; 9: 31-33; 10: 1-5; 2 Cor. 11: 22; Phil. 3: 5.)

how unceasing is my remembrance of thee in my supplications, night and day longing to see thee,—Paul was now old; his end was at hand; he earnestly desired to see Timothy, to whom he was so much attached, and who had been his companion and helper in his imprisonment.

remembering thy tears,—These tears were probably shed

5 having been reminded of the unfeigned faith that is in thee; which dwelt first in thy grandmother Lois, and thy mother Eunice; and, I am persuaded, in thee also. 6 For which cause I put thee in remembrance that thou ²stir up the gift of God, which is in thee through the laying on of my hands. 7 For

²Gr. *stir into flame*

when he was arrested and sent to Rome and incarcerated in prison. [It is likely that the clouds of danger which were gathering quickly around Paul toward the close of his career had impressed him with a foreboding of coming evil, and had invested the last parting with Timothy with circumstances of unusual solemnity. Paul had affected others besides Timothy with the same great love of the truth, and the great danger threatening it so that tears were shed by strong men when he bade them farewell. (Acts 20: 37, 38.)]

that I may be filled with joy;—[Paul's perpetual remembrance of Timothy in prayer was prompted by warm affection for him, which led to a constant longing to see him that in the reunion he would be filled with joy; and it would be intensified as he recalled the tears of Timothy at their parting.]

5 having been reminded of the unfeigned faith that is in thee; which dwelt first in thy grandmother Lois, and thy mother Eunice;—This faith is not only handed down from parent to child through the teaching and training that is done to the child, but also in the qualities of heart and mind that are transmitted that lead to sincere and unaffected faith. It is probable that both the mother and grandmother had believed in Christ, but this language might be used in reference to those who sincerely worshipped God under the Jewish dispensation and waited for the coming Savior as did Simeon and Anna. (Luke 2: 33-38.) Paul makes no mention of the father, though Luke says, "his father was a Greek." (Acts 16: 1.)

and, I am persuaded, in thee also.—[This is an expression of confidence in the sincerity and reality of Timothy's faith. Of him he said: "I have no man likeminded, who will care truly for your state." (Phil. 2: 20.)]

6 For which cause I put thee in remembrance—With these words Paul introduces an exhortation which is further elaborated in the whole chapter and founded in different motives.

God gave us not a spirit of fearfulness; but of power and love and
¹discipline. 8 Be not ashamed therefore of the testimony of our Lord, nor of

¹Gr. *sobering*

Just because Paul knew that the faith of the mother and
grandmother of Timothy dwelt in him also, he has the candor
to address his exhortation to him.

that thou stir up the gift of God,—Devotion to God here is
compared to a flame and the image is one that is obvious
when we speak of causing it to blaze or burn more brightly.
The exhortation to Timothy is to use the means God had
given him to keep the flame brightly glowing. The agency of
man himself is essential to keep devotion to the Lord ever
warm and active. However rich the gifts God had bestowed
upon us, they do not grow of their own accord, but grow and
increase in strength through the constant and diligent use of
them.

which is in thee through the laying on of my hands.—This
gift seems to have been bestowed upon Timothy by the laying
on of the hands of the presbytery, Paul joining them in it, and
by or through his hands, the gift was bestowed. (1 Tim. 4:4.)
This gift might be allowed through neglect to be withdrawn
or would grow and increase in strength through the constant
and diligent use of it. The law of Moses properly understood
led up to love. From the beginning point in the gospel fear is
swallowed up in love.

7 For God gave us not a spirit of fearfulness;—The spirit of
fear and love are here contrasted. "There is no fear in love:
but perfect love casteth out fear, because fear hath punishment." (1 John 4: 18.) Fear was the leading principle in the
law of Moses, love in that of Jesus Christ. This is a grave reminder to Christians of every age and degree that all coward-
ice, all dread of danger, all shrinking from doing one's duty
for fear of man's displeasure, proceeds not from the Spirit of
God.

but of power and love and discipline.—The Spirit which
Paul had bestowed upon Timothy gave power to work miracles and led to love toward God and man. A sound mind or
judgment enlightened by the Spirit of God then and now is
the only real sound and enlightened judgment. The man who

me his prisoner: but suffer hardship with the ²gospel according to the power
of God; 9 who saved us, and called us with a holy calling, not according to

²Gr. *good tidings:* and so elsewhere. See marginal note on Mt. 4. 23

accepts Christ and is led by him is a wise man, however ignorant or unlearned he may be in the eyes of the world. The
man who rejects Jesus is a fool no matter how learned or wise
or honored in the world's esteem. To accept Christ is the
only true wisdom that leads to true love.

8 **Be not ashamed therefore of the testimony of our Lord,**—
The gospel embraces the testimony of Christ. Paul said: "I
am not ashamed of the gospel: for it is the power of God unto
salvation to every one that believeth; to the Jew first, and also
to the Greek." (Rom 1: 16.) Man might be ashamed of one
who died on a cross, but of one who died to save man and
conquered death and burst asunder the bonds of the grave,
none should be ashamed. [This testimony of which Timothy
was not to be ashamed certainly includes the sufferings and
shame of Jesus. In these sufferings, before a mocking, scornful world, must Timothy glory; but the "testimony" includes
the sufferings and shame of Christ. In these before scornful
men must Timothy, as an example to the suffering Christians,
rather glory, but the testimony includes much more than what
relates only to the sufferings of the Lord Jesus. The Christian, instead of being ashamed "of the testimony of our Lord,"
must, before the sinful, persecuting world, show fearlessly
that its hopes and its promises are his most precious treasures.]

nor of me his prisoner:—This does not imply that Timothy
had been ashamed of Paul as a prisoner, but the exhortation is
intended to brace him up amid dangers and to encourage him
to be a partaker with Paul of the afflictions of the gospel.
There is no evidence that Timothy had shown a lack of faith
and courage; but with the defection of many whom he had
trusted, and the near approach of Paul's death, it was natural
for him to encourage Timothy to stand steadfast in the faith.

**but suffer hardship with the gospel according to the power
of God;**—Our sufferings with and for Christ work out for us
an exceeding and eternal weight of glory. Paul, in love for
his son Timothy, desired that he might suffer with Christ, for

our works, but according to his own purpose and grace, which was given us
in Christ Jesus ³before times eternal, 10 but hath now been manifested by the
appearing of our Saviour Christ Jesus, who abolished death, and brought life
and ⁴immortality to light through the ²gospel, 11 whereunto I was appointed

³Or, *long ages ago*
⁴Gr. *incorruption.* See Rom. 2. 7

that would work the highest good for him in the world to
come. Paul gloried in his sufferings, sorrows, and self-denials.
Every Christian should arm himself with the same spirit and
seek as a true and faithful follower of Christ to suffer with
him.

9 who saved us, and called us with a holy calling,—The assurance that we shall not so suffer is that God has saved us
from our sins and iniquities and has called us to a pure and
holy life here and a life of glory hereafter.

not according to our works,—This holy calling is not on account of our works or deserts, nor is the reward reached by or
through works of our own.

but according to his own purpose and grace,—God purposes
on account of his own love to man to call him to this holy
calling and heavenly end in and through Jesus Christ.

which was given us in Christ Jesus before times eternal,—
This calling of man to a higher calling through Christ Jesus
was the determined will of God before the present order of affairs began—from all eternity. [With such a salvation and
holy calling, we should not be ashamed of the gospel nor
shrink from sufferings and hardships on its account.]

**10 but hath now been manifested by the appearing of our
Savior Christ Jesus,**—While it was purposed to be developed
through Christ before the world began, it is now open to the
world through the appearance of Jesus Christ as the Savior.
[The "appearing" here includes not only the birth, but the
whole manifestation of Christ on earth, including his death
and resurrection.]

**who abolished death, and brought life and immortality to
light**—Jesus overcame death, conquered it, and in his work
put in operation the influences that will finally destroy or
abolish it. [The death thus abolished has a far more extended
meaning than the separation of the soul and body that we call

a ⁵preacher, and an apostle, and a teacher. 12 For which cause I suffer also
these things: yet I am not ashamed; for I know him whom I have believed,

⁵Gr. *herald*

---

death. It signifies that awful punishment of sin which is best
described as the exact opposite to "eternal life." The death
with which we are acquainted by sad experience here is only
the forerunner of the death eternal. Already to the faithful believer in Jesus Christ this death of the body counts for nothing; the time will come when it will even exist no more.
Christ has deprived it of its power. (1 Cor. 15: 26, 55; Heb.
2: 14.) It is no longer an enemy to be dreaded, but a friend to
be welcomed.]

through the gospel,—While these intimations and allusions
to eternal life were made, neither it nor the conditions on
which it could be enjoyed were ever clearly made known to
the world until it was brought to light through the gospel.

11 whereunto I was appointed a preacher,—A preacher is a
herald or first proclaimer as distinct from teacher. In the
Scripture the term preacher or herald or original proclaimer is
used in a different sense from the word teacher of its principles.

and an apostle,—The person and work of the Son of God
had to be declared publicly, heralded in fact, and this was the
first duty of an apostle, as one sent to proclaim Jesus to be a
Prince and a Savior.

and a teacher.—[Having persuaded men to accept the
teaching of Jesus, and having baptized them into the name of
the Father and of the Son and of the Holy Spirit, he was to
teach them all that Jesus had commanded—all the beauties of
the Christian life.]

12 For which cause I suffer also these things:—Because he
was chosen of God as his apostle and a teacher of the Gentiles, he suffered these things. When the Lord sent him, he
said: "He is a chosen vessel unto me, to bear my name before
the Gentiles and kings, and the children of Israel: for I will
show him how many things he must suffer for my name's
sake." (Acts 9: 15, 16.) Paul said to the Ephesian elders:
"And now, behold, I go bound in the spirit unto Jerusalem,
not knowing the things that shall befall me there: save that

and I am persuaded that he is able to guard ⁹that which I have committed

⁹Or, *that which he hath committed unto me.* Gr. *my deposit*

the Holy Spirit testifieth unto me in every city saying that
bonds and afflictions abide me." (Acts 20: 22, 23.) When he
wrote this Epistle he was a prisoner aᵗ Rome, anticipating, if
not then lying under sentence of, death. The sufferings to
which he refers are set forth more specifically in the following
words: "I say again, Let no man think me foolish; but if ye
do, yet as foolish receive me. that I also may glory a
little. . . . Seeing that many glory after the flesh, I will glory
also. For ye bear with the foolish gladly, being wise yourselves. For ye bear with a man, if he bringeth you into bondage, if he devoureth you, if he taketh you captive, if he exalteth himself, if he smiteth you on the face. I speak by way of
disparagement, as though we had been weak. Yet wherein-
soever any is bold (I speak in foolishness) I am bold also.
Are they Hebrews? so am I. Are they Israelites? so am I.
Are they the seed of Abraham? so am I. Are they ministers
of Christ? (I speak as one beside himself) I more; in labors
more abundantly, in prisons more abundantly, in stripes above
measure, in deaths oft. Of the Jews five times received I
forty stripes save one. Thrice was I beaten with rods, once
was I stoned, thrice I suffered shipwreck, a night and a day
have I been in the deep; in journeyings often, in perils of riv-
ers, in perils of robbers, in perils from my countrymen, in per-
ils from the Gentiles, in perils in the city, in perils in the wil-
derness, in perils in the sea, in perils among false brethren; in
labor and travail, in watchings often, in hunger and thirst, in
fastings often, in cold and nakedness. Besides those things
that are without, there is that which presseth upon me daily,
anxiety for all the churches. Who is weak, and I am not
weak? who is caused to stumble, and I burn not? If I must
needs glory, I will glory of the things that concern my weakness. The God and Father of the Lord Jesus, he who is
blessed for evermore knoweth that I lie not." (2 Cor. 11: 16-
31.)

yet I am not ashamed;—Notwithstanding all these humiliating afflictions brought .ipon him, he was not ashamed because he suffered them for the sake of Jesus Christ. He, like

unto him against that day. 13 Hold the pattern of ⁷sound words which thou
hast heard from me, in faith and love which is in Christ Jesus. 14 ⁸That
good thing which was committed unto *thee* guard through the Holy Spirit
which dwelleth in us.

⁷Gr. *healthful*
⁸Gr. *The good deposit*

Peter and John, felt so honored that he rejoiced that he was
"counted worthy to suffer dishonor for the Name." (Acts 5:
41.)

for I know him whom I have believed,—Notwithstanding
all the humiliating punishments brought on him, Paul was not
ashamed of it all. The ground of his confidence, even in the
hour of extreme peril, was his perfect trust in the faithfulness
of the Lord Jesus Christ.

**and I am persuaded that he is able to guard that which I
have committed unto him**—Paul had committed his soul, his
eternal well-being, unto God.

against that day.—Paul was well persuaded that God could
keep his soul until that day when everyone would receive according to the deeds done in the body.

**13 Hold the pattern of sound words which thou hast heard
from me,**—Paul had taught Timothy the truths of salvation in
certain words, and lest the meaning should be perverted the
very form of words that he had heard of him should be used.
None can be too careful in stating the truths of the Scriptures
in the language of the inspired writers. When men cannot
convey their thoughts in the words of the Scripture, it is generally because they do not hold sound doctrine.

in faith and love which is in Christ Jesus.—These truths are
to be held in faith which is to be enjoyed in Christ.

14 That good thing which was committed unto thee—This
is an exhortation to guard the wholesome words spoken
through inspired men, which was extremely necessary before
the teaching of the apostles and evangelists were committed
to writing, in which the full gospel is expressed in the words
of the Holy Spirit. These inspired writings are in our hands,
and we ought to preserve them pure without any change.

guard through the Holy Spirit which dwelleth in us.—The
Holy Spirit dwelled in the apostles and in Timothy also, and
by him they were enabled to understand the teaching and
they were through him to keep it.

3. DESERTERS AND LOYAL FRIENDS
1: 15-18

15 This thou knowest, that all that are in Asia turned away from me; of whom are Phygelus and Hermogenes. 16 The Lord grant mercy unto the house of Onesiphorus: for he oft refreshed me, and was not ashamed of my

---

15 This thou knowest that all that are in Asia turned away from me;—The defection to which reference is here made was from Paul and his interests. It extended to those Asiatics who at one time had been attached to him, and whose attachments had been put to the test when in Rome during his imprisonment. It was to have been expected of them that they would have found their way to Paul's prison; but, as if they put it to themselves whether they would go or not, they chose to treat him as if he were a perfect stranger to them. In the real character of their action it was turning their back on the imprisoned apostle.

of whom are Phygelus and Hermogenes.—These seem to have been leaders of those turning away from Paul. We know nothing of them save what is here said. [It has been their destiny to be handed down to posterity as men who acted an unworthy part toward the most noble man of all time in his extremity. They did not know that such an evil immortality was to attach to their names.]

16 The Lord grant mercy unto the house of Onesiphorus:— In contrast with the course of Phygelus and Hermogenes, he now presents as an incentive to Timothy the noble conduct of Onesiphorus, a resident of Ephesus.

for he oft refreshed me,—Here he recalls the many good offices which he had performed at Ephesus, of which Timothy from his personal knowledge would know better than Paul or anyone else could tell him. He often refreshed Paul, no doubt entertained him in his home when he was weary, worn, and persecuted—a real home of refuge and an asylum for rest and encouragement.

and was not ashamed of my chain;—This most likely indicates that Paul, in this imprisonment, as in the first Roman imprisonment, was bound to a soldier by a chain. Many who admired and honored him in his prosperity, and in the days of

chain; 17 but, when he was in Rome, he sought me diligently, and found me
18 (the Lord grant unto him to find mercy of the Lord in that day) ; and in
how many things he ministered at Ephesus, thou knowest very well.

his success, forsook him when he was a prisoner wearing a
chain.

**17 but, when he was in Rome, he sought me diligently, and
found me**—Among so many prisoners in Rome, gathered
from all parts of the empire, it was a difficult task to find him.
This shows that he did not fare so well as in the first imprisonment.

**18 (the Lord grant unto him to find mercy of the Lord in
that day) ;**—Paul passes over the interval between death and
the judgment. It is on "that day" when all shall appear before
the Judge of all the earth, and when all the deeds done in the
body shall be recompensed by the righteous Judge.

**and in how many things he ministered at Ephesus, thou
knowest very well.**—These services rendered to Paul at Ephesus are placed side by side with those things he had done for
him at Rome, but as they are mentioned after, they perhaps
refer to kind offices undertaken for him by Onesiphorus after
his return from Rome to Ephesus; but in general to the service
he had done in the service of Christ there, of which Timothy
from his residence there had even better knowledge than Paul
himself. What Onesiphorus had done for Paul at Rome was,
therefore, only one instance in a life marked throughout by
deeds of self-sacrificing faith and love—the expression of the
general kindness and beneficence of his conduct in the service
of the Master.

4. RENEWED APPEAL TO TRANSMIT TO OTHERS THE GOSPEL, EVEN AT THE COST OF SUFFERING
2: 1-13

1 Thou therefore, my child, be strengthened in the grace that is in Christ

1 Thou therefore, my child, be strengthened—In view of the
course of the individuals just mentioned, take warning on the
one hand by the defection of all that are in Asia, and as encouraged on the other hand, by the faith and courage of Paul,
and the fidelity of Onesiphorus, be strengthened that you may

Jesus. 2 And the things which thou hast heard from me among many witnesses, the same commit thou to faithful men, who shall be able to teach

be faithful, "for God gave us not a spirit of fearfulness, but of
power." (2:7.)

in the grace—Grace is the spiritual atmosphere, in which
the Christian soul exists, and from which, as a vitalizing principle, the soul derives its strength. He is to find strength to
be filled with power for work and conflict by drawing it from
the grace of Christ, the quickening, empowering element, in
which a Christian lives. "But grow in the grace and knowledge of our Lord and Saviour Jesus Christ." (2 Pet. 3:18.)

that is in Christ Jesus.—The grace which is only in Christ,
and which he imparts to all who are in living union with him,
as the vine imparts the life and fruit-bearing power to the
branches abiding in it. (John 15:4, 5.)

2 And the things which thou hast heard from me among
many witnesses,—The things heard were the fundamental
truths of the gospel. Timothy had frequently listened to Paul
preaching to the many to whom he had proclaimed the gospel.

the same commit thou to faithful men,—Not to men merely
"believers" in Jesus Christ, but the faithful men here denotes
loyal, trustworthy men, who, under no temptation, would betray the charge committed to them, but who, with ability,
would teach it to others.

who shall be able to teach others also.—[Not only must the
teachers of the doctrine of Christ to whom Timothy was given
the commission of teaching be trustworthy men, they must
also possess knowledge and the ability to communicate the
knowledge to others. Although the divine help was to be
prayed for and expected in this and all other sacred works, yet
it is noticeable how Paul directs that no ordinary human
means of securing success must be neglected. Paul's last
charge in these Epistles directed that only those shall be selected as teachers of the truth as revealed through the inspired men of God whose abilities were such as fitted them for
the discharge of their duties. The words of Paul here point to
the duty of the teacher, not only himself to keep unchanged
and safe the oracles of God as taught by the apostles, but to
hand down the same unimpaired and safe to other hands.]

others also. 3 [9]Suffer hardship with *me*, as a good soldier of Christ Jesus.
4 No soldier on service entangleth himself in the affairs of *this* life; that he
may please him who enrolled him as a soldier. 5 And if also a man contend

[9]Or, *Take thy part in suffering hardship, as &c.*

3 Suffer hardship with me, as a good soldier of Christ Jesus.

—To suffer hardness is to bear persecution, deny oneself, and
labor for the salvation of others. God carries his children
through a discipline of hardness to try and strengthen their
faith and develop the worthy elements of their character.
[Here is a volume of tenderness and yearning confidence of a
father's claims to loyal imitation. Take your share in enduring hardness. Take up my mantle. Paul bids Timothy come
with him, come after him, be one with all who war the good
warfare. Though strange it may seem to come, he craved the
right of this to nerve him for his last crowning effort.]

**4 No soldier on service entangleth himself in the affairs of
this life;**—No one who serves as a soldier entangles himself
with the affairs of life that he may serve faithfully the government which has called him out as a soldier. So Christians
should not be so entangled with the affairs of life that they
cannot render faithful service to the Lord Jesus Christ who
called them to be soldiers of the kingdom of heaven. Such
soldiers are under discipline and must render implicit obedience to the laws of their Captain.

that he may please him who enrolled him as a soldier.—[In
applying this figure to the Christian we are not to infer that
he is forbidden to use secular calling as a means of support;
but he is to avoid absorption in it or complications in connection with it, such as may divert him in spirit from his high
calling in Christ. It is not a secular occupation, but entangle-
ment in it, which is forbidden. Paul wrought in an earthly
occupation, but his whole soul was absorbed in the one work
of pleasing the Lord; the secular was incidental, only a means
to a higher end. So should it be with every earnest, faithful
Christian paramount and above any earthly consideration. It
is necessary, too, and most desirable that every Christian
should ever be above all reproach of covetousness. He is to
have a "single eye" in his work as a Christian and all things
are to be set apart as means to that end.]

in the games, he is not crowned, except he have contended lawfully. 6 The
husbandman that laboreth must be the first to partake of the fruits. 7 Consid-

---

5 **And if also a man contend in the games, he is not
crowned, except he have contended lawfully.**—In these games
rewards were offered to him who could obtain the master.
But in the effort he must conform to the laws regulating the
game or he could not receive the chaplet. So in striving for
the crown that the Lord shall give "to all them that have
loved his appearing (4: 8), it will not be bestowed unless he
who strives is governed by the law of God in the effort to
obtain it. In other words, no man can gain the crown except through complying with the laws of God. [These words
extend to all Christians, and they warn us, not against engaging in secular callings, but against so entangling ourselves in
them that they hinder the growth and development into the
likeness of Christ.]

6 **The husbandman that laboreth must be the first to partake of the fruits.**—The husbandman must labor according to
the laws of nature for the production of food, and then he who
labors must first receive the benefit and fruits of that labor.
In the spiritual world men must labor according to the will of
God, and he who labors must first partake of the blessings. [It
is the enduring, patient, self-sacrificing toil that is rewarded
in the affairs of common life. The man who endures hardness, whether as soldier, athlete, or tiller of the ground, wins
the reward, and as in the world so in the service of God. The
teaching in the triple picture that Paul draws is not every soldier wins his commander's applause, but only the one who devotes himself heart and soul to the conflict; not every athlete
wins the prize, but only he who trains with anxious, painful
care; not every toiler of the soil gathers the earth's fruits, but
only the patient toiler. So must it be in the life of the Christian. It is not enough to say, "Behold what manner of love
the Father hath bestowed upon us, that we should be called
children of God," but we should be so earnest and diligent in
the effort to grow into the likeness of the Lord Jesus Christ
that we can say, *"And such we are."* (1 John 3: 1.)]

er what I say; for the Lord shall give thee understanding in all things. 8
Remember Jesus Christ, risen from the dead, of the seed of David, according

7 **Consider what I say;**—[Think of the condition of the soldier, and of the principles on which he is enlisted; think of the
aspirant for the crown in the Grecian games; think of the
farmer patiently toiling in the prospect of the distant harvest;
and then go to work with a similar spirit. These things are
worth attention. When the Christian thinks of his hardships,
of his struggles against the evil world, of his arduous and discouraging toil, let him think of the soldier, of the man who
struggles for the world's honors, and the patient farmer and
be content. How patiently they bear all, and yet for inferior
rewards.]

for the Lord shall give thee understanding in all things.—
Enable Timothy to see the force of these considerations and to
apply them to his case. Such are after the discouragements of
the Christian. So prone are we to despondency that we need
the help of the Lord to enable us to apply these most obvious
considerations and to derive support from the plain and simple truths and promises.

8 **Remember Jesus Christ,**—[Timothy was to remember,
was ever to bear in mind, two great facts. They are to be the
foundation stones of his life's work. Remembering these in
the hour of his greatest trouble, he was never to be cast down,
but ever to take fresh courage. The two parts he was to remember were: that Jesus Christ, for whose sake he suffered,
like Timothy and Paul, was born of flesh and blood and yet he
was risen from the dead. Surely in the hour of his weakness
such a thought would be sufficient to inspire him with comfort
and courage. Two facts, then, the resurrection and incarnation of the Lord, are ever to be in the mind of Timothy.]

risen from the dead,—The resurrection would always be reminding him of his Lord's victory over death and of his present glory.

of the seed of David,—[The thought of Jesus being born "of
the seed of David" would impress on his mind that the risen
and glorified Lord Jesus sprang, too, like himself, from mortal
flesh and blood. The reason of the incarnation being ex-

to my ¹⁰gospel: 9 wherein I suffer hardship unto bonds, as a malefactor; but the word of God is not bound.   10 Therefore I endure all things for the

¹⁰See marginal note on ch. 1. 8

pressed in this special manner, born "of the seed of David," was to include another truth.   The "risen from the dead" was not only born of flesh and blood, but belonged to the very race specified in those so revered by Timothy and the chosen race from which should spring the Messiah: "Behold, the days come, saith Jehovah, that I will raise unto David a righteous Branch, and he shall reign as king and deal wisely, and shall execute justice and righteousness in the land.   In his days Judah shall be saved, and Israel shall dwell safely: and this is his name whereby he shall be called: Jehovah our righteousness."   (Jer. 23: 5, 6.)   No doubt Paul's purpose was to raise the fainting and much-tried Timothy in this hour of discouragement, and to supply a ground of confidence to the yet unborn Christians, who, in their day, would be as Timothy was when Paul pressed these thoughts on his beloved son in the faith; but in the background, in all probability, there lay another purpose.   These great comforting truths were to be maintained and taught in the presence of those false teachers who were ever ready to explain away or even to deny then as now the beginning and the end of the life of the Son of God and his ministry on earth, his incarnation, and his resurrection.]

according to my gospel:—The great truth as preached by Paul was that Jesus Christ rose from the dead.   He was the first fruits that gave assurance of the resurrection of all men as the full harvest.

9 wherein I suffer hardship unto bonds, as a malefactor;— In and for the gospel he suffered trouble, arrest, imprisonment, and affliction as though he had been an evildoer.   Had he been a thief, a murderer, or a disturber of the peace, he would have suffered the same punishment that he did suffer.

but the word of God is not bound.—He was imprisoned, deprived of his freedom, bound, but rejoiced that the word of God was not bound and could not be.   No chain or prison wall can bind the word of God. [The words have a wide range

of meaning. His hands were manacled, but his tongue was
free, and with it he could speak the word of God. Apart from
any action of his own that word was working actively outside
his prison walls. There was no ground for fear that its course
was over.]

10 **Therefore I endure all things**—Paul endured all things in
order that the word of God might be widely spread and dis-
seminated; he as a faithful soldier at his post bore up with
quiet, patient courage against suffering, and he did it for the
elect's sake; that is, for those whom, in his infinite mercy, God
has been pleased to choose as his people, for those who in his
unfathomable love are yet to be brought into the one fold.

for the elect's sake,—From this it is clearly shown that Paul
was speaking of a class, and not as individuals as such. This
is no way intimates that God by any direct power elected
them; but had chosen to elect a certain class, and left it to
everyone to make himself of that class. It is said of that class
that they were elect "according to the foreknowledge of God
the Father, in sanctification of the Spirit, unto obedience and
sprinkling of the blood of Jesus Christ." (1 Pet. 1: 2.) One
who does not show his election by obeying God may be sure
that he will never be elected to anything beyond obedience.
So obedience is the prerequisite to all other higher election.
There is not a word in this to discourage a man from seeking
to make his calling and election sure or to give him assurance
of salvation save in obedience to the will of God. There is no
doubt but there is a certain election taught in the Bible. In
the passage before us it is clearly taught, as well as in some
others. Jesus said: "And other sheep I have, which are not of
this fold: them also I must bring, and they shall hear my
voice; and they shall become one flock, one shepherd." (John
10: 16.) In this he recognizes that he had a flock that were
not then following him as the Shepherd. At Corinth the Lord
said unto Paul: "Be not afraid, but speak and hold not thy
peace: for I am with thee, and no man shall set on thee to
harm thee: for I have much people in this city." (Acts 18: 9,
10.) They had not yet believed, but God called them his peo-

with eternal glory. 11 Faithful is the ¹¹saying: For if we died with him, we
shall also live with him: 12 if we endure, we shall also reign with him: if we

¹¹Or, saying: for if &c.

ple. The meaning of both passages is that they were a number of persons of that frame of mind and disposition of heart
that when they heard the gospel they would believe and obey
it.

that they also may obtain the salvation which is in Christ
Jesus with eternal glory.—This was said before they were
converted and shows that those willing to receive the gospel
when they hear it are regarded as elect. It is possible that
Paul had this class in view and for the sake of those who
would receive it when they heard it, and he was willing to endure all things for this class, whether Jews or Gentiles, that
they might hear the gospel, and through it obtain the salvation which is in Christ Jesus with eternal glory.

11 Faithful is the saying: For if we died with him, we shall
also live with him:—It is a true saying, if we be dead with
Christ to the world, we shall also be alive with him spiritually. [Faith in Christ united us with him in his death (Rom.
6: 1-13; Col. 3: 3; 1 Pet. 2: 24); but this union with him involves, not only a new relation to him, whereby through his
death we have justification with God, but also a true and real
fellowship with him in the spirit and objects of his death, so
that in our present life we know "the power of his resurrection, and the fellowship of his sufferings, becoming conformed
unto his death." (Phil. 3: 10.) Here also a fellowship with
Christ is set forth which is complete fellowship of life, and
consequently also a fellowship of fortune, not barely of
thought and feeling. This spiritual death with him with its
consequent "fellowship of his sufferings," and readiness to
suffer, if need be, bodily death with him, is the sure pledge of
life with him, not only present spiritual life (Rom. 6: 8), but
also the future resurrection life. The necessary result of sharing his death now is the eternal sharing of his life.]

12 if we endure,—It is frequently impressed in the Scriptures that if one would reign with him there, he must suffer
with him here. To suffer with him is to suffer for the truth,

shall deny him, he also will deny us : 13 if we are faithless, he abideth faithful ; for he cannot deny himself.

for the redemption of man as he suffered. To refuse to suffer
with and for him is to deny him. When we deny him before
men, he will deny us before his Father and the holy angels.

we shall also reign with him :—The union with him in suffering, by enduring hardship and death for him, insures ultimate exultation with him. How must this glorious truth, be-
lievingly apprehended, have thrilled the souls of martyrs of
Christ in the days of persecution! But it does not come to
them only. Every Christian is under obligation to die with
Christ through the mortification of his own pleasures and desires, and to put to death his former sins through the martyrdom of the flesh.

if we shall deny him, he also will deny us :—[Perhaps this is
an illusion to the Lord's own words : "But whosoever shall
deny me before men, him will I also deny before my Father
who is in heaven" (Matt. 10 : 33), to which also is added :
"But there arose false prophets also among the people, as
among you also there shall be false teachers, who shall privily
bring in destructive heresies, denying even the Master that
bought them, bringing upon themselves swift destruction." (2
Pet. 2 : 1). Also : "For there are certain men crept in privily,
even they who were of old written of beforehand unto this
condemnation, ungodly men, turning the grace of our God
into lasciviousness, and denying our only Master and Lord,
Jesus Christ." (Jude 4.)]

13 **if we are faithless, he abideth faithful; for he cannot
deny himself.**—If we are not true to our faith in him, yet he
abideth faithful to himself. He cannot be untrue to himself or
be untrue to his teachings. He must be true to them, and they
will condemn everyone not true to him.

SECTION TWO

THE MINISTERS OF GOD AND FALSE TEACHERS
2: 14 to 4: 8

1. HE DISSUADES FROM UNPROFITABLE DISCUSSION
2: 14-26

14 Of these things put them in remembrance, charging *them* in the sight of [12]the Lord, that they strive not about words, to no profit, to the subverting of them that hear. 15 Give diligence to present thyself approved unto God, a

[12]Many ancient authorities read *God*

14 **Of these things put them in remembrance,**—Paul has been urging Timothy to be strong in endurance, to bear trouble and suffering with brave patience. He now charges him respecting the special work he has to do; and first he deals with his duties as a teacher of truth brought face to face with teachers of error.

charging them in the sight of the Lord,—This is a very earnest, solemn thought for every public teacher and one calculated now as then to deepen the life of every proclaimer of the gospel. There was a grave danger that such empty profitless disputes about words and expressions, which, we know, occupied the attention of many of the so-called teachers at Ephesus would end in distracting the minds of the members of the church who would naturally take their tone in matters connected with their religious life from their teachers, and thus words would soon come to be substituted for acts in the lives of men and women called by the name of Christ. See 1 Tim. 6: 4 where these "disputes of words" are mentioned among the special characteristics of the false teachers.

that they strive not about words, to no profit,—It is almost universally regarded that this refers to the Judaizing teachers, but it refers equally to every and all questions not taught in the Scriptures. All things not so taught are without profit to man, and the introduction of them produces strife.

to the subverting of them that hear.—[Not only are such arguments and disputes useless and profitless, but they are positively mischievous. In the history of Christianity, Paul's repeated warning respecting the danger of these disputes about words and expressions has been sadly verified. Such

workman that needeth not to be ashamed, ¹³handling aright the word of truth. 16 But shun profane babblings: for they will proceed further in un-

¹³Or, *holding a straight course in the word of truth.* Or, *rightly dividing the word of truth*

contentions unsettle the mind, shake the faith, and distract from real, earnest, and patient work for Christ.]

15 **Give diligence to present thyself approved unto God,**— The study of the word of God that he might understand and obey it was the way to show himself approved of God. When God approved he would be with and bless and strengthen him. Jesus Christ was the specially appointed of God who was approved because it was his meat to do his Father's will. All who, like Jesus, have no other will save the will of the Father, are approved of God. If he stands approved of God, he will have no cause of shame, no matter who disapproves. David says: "Oh that my ways were established to observe thy statutes! Then shall I not be put to shame, when I have respect unto all thy commandments." (Psalm 119: 5, 6.) If one will learn and keep the commandments of God, he will never have cause for shame. Being approved implies being tried and proved as precious metals are proved before they are accepted as genuine. Of such it is said: "Blessed is the man that endureth temptation; for when he hath been approved, he shall receive the crown of life, which the Lord promised to them that love him." (James 1: 12.)

a workman that needeth not to be ashamed,—[This indicates that ceaseless, serious, earnest zeal, which was one of his chief characteristic traits. And certainly if the proposed standard is to be reached or seriously aimed at, an abundance of zeal will be required. The end proposed is that of presenting himself to God in such a way as to secure his approval without fear of incurring the reproach of being a workman who had shirked his responsibility.]

handling aright the word of truth.—The Scriptures were addressed to different classes of persons as any who will study them will learn. A proper regard for these divisions is needed to avoid confusion. It is probable that Paul here warned Timothy to distinguish properly between the things addressed to those under the law of Moses and those not under it. He

godliness, 17 and their word will ¹⁴eat as doth a gangrene: of whom is Hy-

¹⁴Or, *spread*

---

draws the distinction by saying: "Now we know that what things soever the law saith, it speaketh to them that are under the law; that every mouth may be stopped, and all the world may be brought under the judgment of God: because by the works of the law shall no flesh be justified in his sight; for through the law cometh the knowledge of sin." (Rom. 3: 19, 20.) It would be wrong to apply the law of circumcision to those not under the law of Moses. So there are different classes under the Christian law. Care must be had that the Scriptures be applied to those addressed. For example: "Repent ye, and be baptized every one of you in the name of Jesus Christ unto the remission of your sins." (Acts 2: 38.) If this language were applied to those in Christ who sin, it would require one every time he sinned to be baptized. This would be misleading and cause confusion. Study is required to understand the different classes and divisions, to rightly apply it. Clinging to what is taught, avoiding that not taught, is very necessary in the application of the Scriptures.

16 **But shun profane babblings:**—Everything not commanded by God in the Scriptures may safely be placed under this head. It refers to the questions brought in then, that diverted from the word of God, caused division and strife. This was to be shunned.

for they will proceed further in ungodliness,—[Cherishing them will lead to more and more ungodliness. The addition of one thing not required of God leads to another. Their teaching is of a kind that will spread rapidly, and it is deadly in its effects.]

17 **and their word will eat as doth a gangrene:**—Gangrene poisons the whole frame and quickly becomes fatal. So does the introduction of things not taught by God—the doctrines of men. These doctrines spread rapidly, corrupt the whole church till spiritual death ensues to the church of God. [Error is a diffusive poison rapidly spreading through the whole body and tending to vital decay and ultimate destruction.]

menæus and Philetus; 18 men who concerning the truth have [15]erred, saying that [16]the resurrection is past already, and overthrow the faith of some.

[15]Gr. *missed the mark.* 1 Tim. 1. 6
[16]Some ancient authorities read *a resurrection*

of whom is Hymenaeus and Philetus;—[Of these false
teachers nothing is known beyond the mention of Hymenaeus,
who, regardless of the severe action which had been taken
against him, was apparently still continuing in his error. (1
Tim. 1: 20.) Their names were simply given as examples of
the teachers of errors to which Paul was referring—fearless
leaders, most likely, in their cheerless, destructive school of
doctrine.]

**18 men who concerning the truth have erred, saying that
the resurrection is past already, and overthrow the faith of
some.**—[In the absence of clearer evidence, it cannot be said
with certainty what their error was, but the words apparently
point to Paul's words in Rom. 6: 3, 4 and Col. 2: 12, where he
says, "Having been buried with him in baptism, wherein ye
were also raised with him through faith in the working of
God, who raised him from the dead." If so, they may have
taught that "raised with him" in baptism was the true resurrection and come to the conclusion that the resurrection
was already past. In reaching such a conclusion they made a
fatal mistake, for the resurrection of the body, grounded
upon the Lord's own words, is one of the cardinal doctrines of
the gospel, as the following clearly shows: "Marvel not at
this: for the hour cometh, in which all that are im the tombs
shall hear his voice, and shall come forth; they that have done
good, unto the resurrection of life; and they that have done
evil, unto the resurrection of judgment." (John 5: 28, 29.)
Upon this Paul delighted to dwell, as in his words before
Felix: "But this I confess unto thee, that after the Way which
they call a sect, so serve I the God of our fathers, believing all
things which are according to the law, and which are written
in the prophets; having hope toward God, which these also
themselves look for, that there shall be a resurrection both of
the just and unjust. Herein I also exercise myself to have a
conscience void of offence toward God and men always."
(Acts 24: 14-16.) With this resurrection of the body, Paul,

19 Howbeit the firm foundation of God standeth, having this seal, ¹The Lord knoweth them that are his: and, ²Let every one that nameth the name of the Lord depart from unrighteousness.   20 Now in a great house there are not

¹Num. 16. 5?
²Is. 26. 13?

---

guided by the Holy Spirit, taught men that the future state of rewards and punishments was intimately bound up; the soul will be clothed with a body of glory or with a body of shame, according to the deeds done in the body.   These men opposed their own idealism to the strong and healthy teaching of the Holy Spirit through Paul.]

19 **Howbeit the firm foundation of God standeth, having this seal,**—Great and good men may turn from the truth, may make shipwreck of their own souls and may lead others down to ruin, yet the foundation of God remains steadfast and sure. God's faithfulness to himself, to his promises, to them that trust him as the foundation of all hope of good here and hereafter stands sure and the seal is given.

The Lord knoweth them that are his:—Those who trust him he will never forsake.   Of this class, Jesus Christ said: "My sheep hear my voice, and I know them, and they follow me: and I give unto them eternal life; and they shall never perish, and no one shall snatch them out of my hand." (John 10 : 27, 28.)

and, Let every one that nameth the name of the Lord depart from unrighteousness.—Let everyone who takes the name of the Christ upon him be careful to depart from iniquity.   We believe in Christ, are consecrated to him through faith, in baptism take his name upon us and should be careful to depart from all unrighteousness; therefore, believers must separate themselves from all iniquity, injustice, and wrong. [The words, "nameth the name of the Lord," must be understood in the sense that no man can confess that he believes with all his heart that Jesus is the Christ the Son of the living God and deliberately practice unrighteousness.   The two things are utterly incompatible—incapable of existing together.   Unrighteousness here includes the teaching of false teachers as their teachings led away from the truth and resulted in an evil and lax way of life.]

only vessels of gold and of silver, but also of wood and of earth; and some
unto honor, and some unto dishonor. 21 If a man therefore purge himself

20 **Now in a great house there are not only vessels of gold
and of silver, but also of wood and of earth;**—Paul carries out
here the idea of a house of which God's promises are the foundation by which he means thus to intimate, for the encouragement of the fainthearted believers, that the heresies and back-
sliding of many professing Christians does not affect God's
covenant and promises to true and faithful believers: for as:
"in a great house" there are not only "vessels of gold and of
silver, but also of wood and of earth," so in the church there
are not only true Christians found, but persons who are not,
whose hypocrisy and iniquity are overruled to fulfill his righteous purposes. Such being the case, "let every one that nameth the name" of Christ depart from iniquity if he desires to
attain the resurrection of the just. This he must do. There
are bad as well as good characters in the church as in a large
house there are various kinds of vessels, yet it is only by
cleansing himself from all iniquity that he can be fit for his
Lord and Master's service here and his reward hereafter.

and some unto honor, and some unto dishonor.—[But this
is by no means all. A vessel once made by the artificer cannot change itself. It cannot become any other material than
of that of which it was originally made. But Paul here repre-
sents vessels as changing themselves. This is absolutely incompatible with the idea that God has made a certain number
of persons to be saved and a certain number to be lost. It is,
on the contrary, the most surprising assertion of the freedom
of the human will in Scripture: for a man is not only supposed
to be able, but is responsible for changing himself from that
which is typified by an earthen vessel into that which is typified by a golden one. Hymenaeus and Philetus had fallen
from being golden vessels into earthen ones, but if they repented they might become gold or silver ones; that is, if they
purged themselves from the error in question and abstained
from them who held it. By the fact that a man has once
fallen into this pernicious error, he is not condemned forever,
but by cleaning himself and becoming sanctified meet for the

from these, he shall be a vessel unto honor, sanctified, meet for the master's
use, prepared unto every good work. 22 But flee youthful lusts, and follow
after righteousness, faith, love, peace, with them that call on the Lord out of

---

Master's use "prepared unto every good work."]

**21 If a man therefore purge himself from these, he shall be
a vessel unto honor,**—God uses only such as are fitted for his
use. The reason God does not use more persons, or use them
more effectively, is because they are unfitted for his use.

**sanctified, meet for the master's use, prepared unto every
good work.**—When fitted for his use, he is prepared for every
good work. Man's duty is to so live as to fit himself for the
service of God, and then God will direct him and use him.

22 But flee youthful lusts,—Timothy was at this time about
thirty-six years old. Lusts and passions are strong in youth.
He must fight with and conquer those lusts, passions, and desires which are more peculiarly tempting to those who are
still in the meridian of life. These youthful lusts are by no
means to be limited to those varied and fatal excesses in sensual passion, but to all the irregular desires and propensities
belonging to earlier life as self-conceit, pride, ambition, love of
applause; any impetuous passions to which the warmth of the
age is prone.

[This is not to be interpreted of lusts properly so called,
such a sense being foreign to the context, and to the character
of the person addressed; and the abstinence elsewhere ascribed to Timothy excludes the idea of sensuality. It would
seem that Paul meant to denote those vehement, impetuous,
and headstrong passions mostly found in young men, but
which are sometimes found in middle age, which Timothy had
nearly reached, and accordingly against which Paul here cautions him and through him other preachers of the gospel, both
young and middle aged, as well as Timothy. Now when we
consider that it was rashness, vanity, and rage for controversy
and novelty that hurried Hymenaeus and Philetus into those
baneful errors, against which Paul here cautions Timothy, the
suitableness of the present admonition will be very apparent.]

and follow after righteousness,—To restrain the sins of
youth and cultivate righteousness and holiness is to lay the

a pure heart. 23 But foolish and ignorant questionings refuse, knowing that they gender strifes. 24 And the Lord's ³servant must not strive, but be gen-

³Gr. *bondservant*

---

foundation in youth for resisting the sins of the middle and old age. He was to avoid youthful lust on the one hand, and on the other to follow after righteousness, doing right with God's law as the standard of living.

faith,—Fidelity in all the relations to God and man. Fidelity is the practice of faith.

love,—Live is the doing good to all through discharging the duties God has laid upon man.

peace,—The peace that comes of doing the will of God; peace with all that are at peace with God.

with them that call on the Lord out of a pure heart.—[To call upon is to invoke his aid. To call upon the name of Jesus Christ our Lord is to invoke his aid as the Christ, the Messiah predicted by the prophets, and as our almighty and sovereign possessor and ruler. It is in that sense that Jesus is Lord. All authority in heaven and on earth was committed unto him (Matt. 28: 18) after he died and rose again that he might be the Lord of the dead and the living; that is, that he might acquire that peculiar right of possession in his people which arises from his having purchased them with his own blood (Acts 20: 28). To call upon the name of Jesus as Lord is therefore to worship him. It looks to him for that help which God only can give. All Christians, therefore, are worshipers of Christ and every sincere worshiper is a true Christian. The phrase expresses not so much an individual act of invocation as an habitual state of mind and its appropriate expression.]

23 But foolish and ignorant questionings refuse,—Things not taught by God are to be avoided because they breed strife and division.

knowing that they gender strifes.—[Paul correctly says that the effect of such disputes is to engender harsh contention and strife. Points of vital import can and should be discussed carefully and prayerfully by those who are diligently and prayerfully seeking the truth.]

tle towards all, apt to teach, forbearing, 25 in meekness ⁴correcting them
that oppose themselves; if peradventure God may give them repentance unto

⁴Or, *instructing*

24 **And the Lord's servant must not strive,**—The servant of
the Lord must not engage in bitter strife. [Everything which
is likely to be the cause of strife, heartburning, or hot words is
singularly out of place in the life of a servant of the Lord.
This, however is not out of harmony with the exhortation: "I
was constrained to write unto you exhorting you to contend
earnestly for the faith which was once for all delivered unto
the saints." (Jude 3.)]

but be gentle towards all,—Gentleness, with an appetite for
teaching, and patience toward those in error, and who oppose
the truth is compatible with firmness and fidelity in maintaining the truth. [Paul would press upon Timothy and his successors the great truth that was the Master's will that the nations of earth who sit in darkness and in the shadow of death
should learn by slow, though sure, degrees how lovely and desirable a thing it is to be a Christian—should come at length
to see clearly that Christ is the only lover and real friend of
man.]

apt to teach, forbearing,—[This is what the servant of the
Lord should really aim at being—the teacher rather than the
controversialist. Rather the patient endurer of wrong than
the fomenter of dissensions and wordy strifes.]

25 **in meekness correcting them that oppose themselves; if
peradventure God may give them repentance unto the knowledge of the truth,**—The feelings and impulses of the flesh, the
excitements and rivalries of controversy, the desire to expose
error, and to make it appear unworthy—all have a tendency to
lead us to forget that the Lord demands courteous consideration in our treatment of others. He demands that we give the
same consideration to the mistakes and faults of others that
we would like to receive and expect of them for our mistakes
and faults. It does not mean that we should overlook their
mistakes or let the faults go unreproved; but he demands that
we should treat them kindly and to respect their feelings in
correcting them. Wisdom demands this as well as the fundamental spirit of the Christian religion. Especially we should

the knowledge of the truth, 26 and they may ⁵recover themselves out of the
snare of the devil, having been ⁶taken captive ⁷by him unto his will.

⁵Gr. *return to soberness*
⁶Gr. *taken alive*
⁷Or, *by him, unto the will of God.* Comp. 2 Cor. 10. 5. Gr. *by him unto the
will of him.* In the Greek the two pronouns are different.

treat every man's religious feelings and practices with the respect and courtesy we would like to have shown us. This does
not involve any compromise of truth or righteousness or any
winking at errors. Every man wishes, if he holds error, to be
delivered from it. We desire it if we are true and honest. To
treat them as we would be treated demands that we should
show that we also desire to be freed from error. We should
do this as far as we are able. But we regard our religion as
sacred; we believe it true and holy. Others regard theirs in
the same way. Our duty is to treat them in trying to correct
their errors as we would have them treat us in trying to correct what they regard as error. None of us have room for
boasting of our knowledge. We should be modest, and while
striving to correct and teach others, we should do it in meekness and forbearance for those most confident in their knowledge and practice are most liable to err. So, instead of denouncing others with harsh words, let us seek to teach them
in meekness. [By "them that oppose themselves," it is not
likely that Paul alludes so much to those teachers of false doctrine as those led away by them. He says: "A factious man
after a first and second admonition refuse; knowing that such
a one is perverted, and sinneth, being self-condemned." (Tit.
3: 10, 11.) But the ones referred to in the passage before us
were to be dealt with in a different manner. Their treatment
was to be a gentle one. Nothing is said here of a first and
second admonition only; no hint is given that these are to be
shunned.]

26 **and they may recover themselves out of the snare of the
devil,**—[The sin which issues in unbelief is here represented
as a kind of drunkenness, and by repentance a man becomes
sober again, so Jesus calls it "when he came to himself."
(Luke 15: 17.) Again sin, so far from freedom to do as one
likes, is a state of being ensnared by the devil, from which he
is to be captured alive—to do the service of him whose service

is perfect freedom. Here we have the thought frequently enunciated by Paul that man being a creature cannot have real independence; his only freedom is to choose whom he will serve. He must cast down imaginations, and every high thing that is exalted against the knowledge of God, and bring "every thought into captivity to the obedience of Christ" (2 Cor. 10 : 5) or fall under the dominion of the devil. There is no other alternative. He cannot serve two masters, but he must serve one and his wisdom is to choose the service of the Father who created him and the Savior who died to redeem him.]

having been taken captive by him unto his will.—Men who turn from God and his ways to follow the ways of men are led by the devil. Under specious pretext of following their own wisdom, they are taken captive by him at his own will.

2. GRIEVOUS TIMES IMPENDING
3: 1-17

1 But know this, that in the last days grievous times shall come. 2 For men shall be lovers of self, lovers of money, boastful, haughty, railers, diso-

---

1 But know this,—Notwithstanding the hope just expressed in regard to the recovery of some who follow the ways of men, many evil men will arise in the church who will never be reclaimed.

that in the last days grievous times shall come.—This is the common designation in the Old Testament of the Messianic age—the time after the coming of the Christ into the world. It is thus used in the New Testament to designate the new dispensation, this being the last period of human history. The whole representation points to the immediate as well as to the remote future. Probably such "grievous times" would more than once occur, and the last occurring before the second coming of the Lord Jesus Christ may be the worst in the wide extent and terrible character of its error and sin.

2 For men shall be lovers of self,—Selfishness will be a general characteristic of the period. It denotes one who assigns to himself a larger share of wealth, honors, and bodily pleasures than 'to others. This trait is mentioned first because, as the root of the essence of all sin, it is the source of the other evil characteristics mentioned.

bedient to parents, unthankful, unholy, 3 without natural affection, implaca-

---

lovers of money,—Filled with selfish greed for the accumulation of wealth; improperly desirous of gain.

boastful,—These arrogate to themselves honors which do not fairly belong to them.

haughty,—These are they who contemptuously look down on others beneath them either in social position or wealth or in natural gifts.

railers,—Are scornful, insolent, and blame with bitterness. They carry the war of their tongues into the camp of the enemy and give vent to their vengeance against God or man. It is sinful in either case.

disobedient to parents,—No character has been more condemned by God that those disobedient to parents. Under the law of Moses the stubborn and rebellious son who would not obey his parents was to be stoned to death. (Deut. 21: 18-20.) The parents stood in the place of God to the child, and if it would not obey them they could not expect it to obey God. [Christ has set up a new standard of individual responsibility which sometimes makes it necessary for children, when they have come to years of responsibility, to act contrary to the wishes of their parents in order that they may obey God. The Lord said: "He that loveth father or mother more than me is not worthy of me; and he that loveth son or daughter more than me is not worthy of me." (Matt. 10: 37.) Yet parents have not forfeited all their natural rights, and in all matters where obedience to God is not at stake children are even more bound to yield them respect, obedience, and tender affection.]

unthankful,—[Children who begin life with disobedience to their parents with rare exceptions are ungrateful to all others who may show them kindness in their life journey. Ingratitude has always been regarded as one of the worst of crimes. It is said here that it would characterize that wicked age of which Paul speaks.]

unholy,—Not consecrated to God through their want of purity; defiled with sin, irreligious. [Those who scoff at holiness of life and character in its deepest sense.]

ble, slanderers, without self-control, fierce, no lovers of good, 4 traitors,

---

3 **without natural affection,**—Without affection for parents or children. The attachment of parents to children is one of the strongest in nature, and nothing can overcome it but the most confirmed and determined wickedness. [An affection which is common to every class of brutes, consequently men and women without it are worse than brutes.]

implacable,—Those who will not be bound by any oath or held by any engagement or obligated by any promise. They readily promise anything, but never intend to perform. Nothing could be more indicative of the lowest state of degradation than that in which all compacts and agreements are utterly disregarded.

slanderers,—Accusation maliciously uttered with the purpose or effect of damaging the reputation of another. As a rule, it is a false charge (Matt. 5:11), but it may be a truth treacherously circulated with the purpose of destroying the good reputation of another.

without self-control,—Persons of unbridled appetites and passions who do not control their evil propensities. [This seems to mean that in a man's soul there are two elements, a better and a worse, and when the better controls the worse, then he is said to be a master of himself. The lowest bodily pleasures are a sphere in which this virtue of self-control is specially displayed; that is those bodily pleasures which the other animals share with man and which are consequently shown to be slavish and brutal—pleasure of touch and taste. It is manifest that in order to be a virtuous man at all one must at least have control over one's own appetites. When this virtue is illuminated by the gospel its meaning is intensified. Its sphere is not confined to the lowest sensual enjoyments, self-mastery with regard to such things is still included; but other things are included also. There is a spiritual frenzy, and there are spiritual self-indulgencies analogous to spiritual madness and there are spiritual self-indulgencies analogous to bodily indulgence. For these things self-mastery is needed.]

headstrong, puffed up, lovers of pleasure rather than lovers of God; 5 holding a form of godliness, but having denied the power thereof: from these

fierce,—[In this resembling savages and wild beasts, the de-
nial of godliness ending in their having no power over their
angry passions.]

no lovers of good,—Hostile to every good thought and
work.

4 **traitors,**—Those ready to betray any person or trust committed to their keeping. Treason has been in all ages regarded as one of the worst crimes that man can commit.

headstrong,—[Stubbornly bent on pursuing one's own plans
or accomplishing one's own ends; obstinate; willful, ungov-
ernable.]

puffed up,—[Self-conceit, like smoke without substance,
puffed out into great volume, envelops and blinds them, dis-
torting and magnifying their views of themselves as compared
with others.]

lovers of pleasure rather than lovers of God;—More ready to
follow sensual pleasures than to follow the law of God. [They
are people who would make any sacrifice to procure a
fleeting pleasure and who would give nothing up in order to
do honor to the God and Father of the Lord Jesus Christ.
The sorrowful catalogue which has just passed before our
minds began with "lovers of self," that unhappy vice which
excludes all love for others, closes with the lovers of pleasure
which shuts out all love of God.]

5 **holding a form of godliness,**—All who so live while claiming to be Christians have the "form," the profession of godliness, while they fail to live according to its laws. [Keeping
up a show by formally keeping the Lord's appointment, but
renouncing its power and influence over the heart and life;
showing openly that they neither acknowledge its guidance or
even wish to do so. These claiming to be Christians, wearing
the name of Christ, but by their lives denouncing his name, do
the gravest injury to his cause. Another shameful catalogue of
vices Paul gives (Rom. 1: 28-32), but in that passage he
points to the sins of heathenism. Here he describes the characteristics of a class of people who went under the name of
Christ.]

also turn away. 6 For of these are they that creep into houses, and take
captive silly women laden with sins, led away by divers lusts, 7 ever learn-

---

but having denied the power thereof:—They deny its power
by failing to let its spirit well in their hearts, and its laws rule
in their lives. Anyone denies the power of godliness when he
professes to honor God, but refuses to obey his commandments.

from these also turn away.—These persons who, while pretending to serve the Lord, lived the degraded life of the heathen were to be shunned. No friendly intercourse was possible between the hypocrite and the devoted Christian. It was
a declaration that they had in vain exhausted all scriptural
means to save him before withdrawing; now this is the last
resort. Deliver him to Satan for the destruction of the flesh
that he may be saved. If they have followed the law of God
in the steps leading to it, their action has the full sanction of
the divine law, and their act is the act of God himself. A man
excluded by a church acting according to the divine law is excluded by God himself and without repentance as surely
damned as he will be when God says, "I never knew you: depart from me." The churches and individuals come to regard
this act too lightly. But the letter and spirit of God's law
should be followed in trying to save the sinner. When this is
done, it is an awful sentence of God himself as to his condition.

6 For of these are they that creep into houses,—The men
with these unworthy characters are described as insinuating
themselves into the homes of the Christians, and their influence must have been great, and the church suffered much.
The power they acquired over women of this type was great,
and their influence abounded everywhere in the apostolic age.

and take captive silly women—These hypocritical men bus-
ied themselves in securing popularity among the women of
the church. The way by which this was accomplished was
by easing their guilty consciences.

laden with sins, led away by divers lusts,—[As if sins were
heaped upon them. Their consciences were oppressed with
sins, and in this morbid state they lay open to the insidious
attacks of these corrupt men who promise them ease of con-

ing, and never able to come to the knowledge of the truth. 8 And even as
Jannes and Jambres withstood Moses, so do these also withstand the truth;
men corrupted in mind, reprobate concerning the faith. 9 But they shall

science if they will follow them.] Those who reject the truth
of God and are not subject to his authority are slaves of sin
and are led into the excesses and immoralities of lust.

7 **ever learning,**—Those who reject the authority of Jesus
Christ and the law of God as the standard of right have no
standard, and so led by their selfish desires and lusts are always reasoning, always speculating, and always learning.

and never able to come to the knowledge of the truth.—Because they reject the only standard by which to determine the
truth—the word of God. [As there lies in the womanly character the foundation for the highest development of the power
of faith, so also for the highest revelation of the power of sin.]

8 **And even as Jannes and Jambres withstood Moses,**—
These names are not mentioned elsewhere by name in the
Bible. They are supposed by early Jewish writers to have
been the magicians in Egypt that wrought wonders before
Pharaoh when Moses performed his miracles to cause him to
let the Israelites go. They used these magical arts to withstand Moses and prevent the delivery of Israel from Egypt.

so do these also withstand the truth;—So did these men
who now opposed Paul and sought to destroy his influence.
Probably they used some magical powers to deceive the people with the idea that they exerted miraculous powers as well
as Paul and others of the inspired men. God sometimes permitted evil men to manifest wonder-working power from the
devil which his servants wrought for him.

men corrupted in mind,—They were men who had once
been Christians, but had become corrupt in mind and were enemies of the truth.

reprobate concerning the faith.—Their faith had become so
perverted by sin that God condemned it as unworthy, leading
to ruin instead of salvation. It is possible for man to believe
that Jesus is the Christ and yet his faith is so mixed up with
error that it will not lead to salvation. This may mean that
they are so given over to sin that they lose he ability to distinguish between good and evil.

proceed no further; for their folly shall be evident unto all men, as theirs also came to be. 10 But thou didst follow my teaching, conduct, purpose,

9 **But they shall proceed no further:**—They shall proceed in their wicked course no longer. [After the apostle had pointed out the fearful ravages in the Ephesian church by the evil men, he proceeds to comfort Timothy with the assurance that, great as the mischief accomplished was, it should proceed no further. To human eyes such a state of things as here described would appear desperate. It was as though a deadly and incurable disease was eating away the life of the whole body of believers, but Timothy need nor fear—the evil would be allowed to reach a certain point. Since Paul thus wrote the same prophecy, not only at Ephesus, but in numerous other churches, has been fulfilled to the very letter. Still the same old foes under new leaders make havoc of the church. But, as a rule, they never advance beyond a certain point, and after all the centuries the church of the Lord Jesus Christ is still full of faith and life, bright, too, in spite of all the discouragements and the perpetual presence of these treacherous men with promise for future triumphs.]

for their folly shall be evident unto all men, as theirs also came to be.—Moses exposed the folly of Jannes and Jambres, and Paul will do the same to those perverters of the faith and bring heir evil ways to an end. Adam Clarke says: "As the Scriptures are the only rule of morals and doctrine, and shall ever be preserved, no sooner or later all false doctrines shall be tried by them; and the folly of men setting up their wisdom against the wisdom of God must become manifest to all. False doctrine cannot prevail long where the sacred Scriptures are read and studied. Error prevails only where the book of God is withheld from the people."

10 **But thou didst follow my teaching,**—Timothy followed the instruction given by Paul with full sympathy and approval. The reference is to Timothy's conversion of which the teaching, life, and sufferings of Paul were the means through which it was brought about. No other man knew the history of Paul's life like Timothy, who had been carefully trained to assist in carrying on the Lord's work after Paul should be removed. This earnest appeal to Timothy's recol-

faith, longsuffering, love, ⁸patience, 11 persecutions, sufferings; what things

⁸Or, *stedfastness*

---

lection of the past was for two distinct purposes: (1) it was to contrast the life of Paul, with which Timothy was so well acquainted, with the lives of the false teachers who were engaged in the destructive work in the Ephesian church; and (2) his memory of Paul and his devoted and self-sacrificing service of the Lord to stir Timothy to greater zeal in faithfulness in service to the Lord regardless of the cost of suffering and persecution in contending "earnestly for the faith which was once for all delivered unto the saints." (Jude 3.)

conduct,—Timothy had modeled his life after that of Paul's in teaching, fidelity to God, his long-suffering and bearing opposition, and his love and patience under all the suffering brought upon him.

purpose,—This refers to Paul's steadfast purpose to devote himself without reserve to the ministry of the gospel, to which the Lord had called him.

faith,—In the sense of fidelity to God; but probably to be taken in the usual sense of trust in God's word as an actuating principle of life taking God at his word.

longsuffering,—Long-suffering toward his many bitter adversaries, especially toward those of his own countrymen. In spite of all that unwearied, sleepless persecution which he endured at the hands of the Jews, he loved Israel to the end with a love as intense as it was changeless.

love,—It was with eager efforts that he ever sought to realize the wonderful grace of love by resisting temptations to any course of conduct that would hinder it and by using every opportunity to further it.

patience,—Paul bore patiently all things that came upon him. It is among the chief virtues and describes one who has been tested and who cannot be swerved from his course by any opposition or suffering. Jesus forewarned his disciples that they would have much to endure and had strengthened them by the promise that he who endured to the end would be saved. (Matt. 10:22.)

11 persecutions, sufferings;—[Not only were his plans

befell me at Antioch, at Iconium, at Lystra; what persecutions I endured:
and out of them all the Lord delivered me. 12 Yea, and all that would live
godly in Christ Jesus shall suffer persecution. 13 But evil men and impos-

foiled, his hopes baffled, his friends alienated through the per-
sistent enmity of his opponents, but bodily sufferings were inflicted on him—stoning, scourging, long imprisonments were
among the repeated sufferings he endured for his Master's
sake.]

what things befell me at Antioch, at Iconium, at Lystra;—
He recalls the persecutions and afflictions he had endured at
Antioch, Iconium, and Lystra. These were neighboring cities. Timothy was reared at Lystra and was no doubt acquainted with the facts, which are as follows: "The Jews
urged on the devout women of honorable estate, and the chief
men of the city, and stirred up a persecution against Paul and
Barnabas, and cast them out of their borders." (Acts 13: 50.)
"And when there was made an onset both of the Gentiles and
of the Jews with their rulers, to treat them shamefully and to
stone them, they became aware of it, and fled unto the cities
of Lycaonia, Lystra and Derbe, and the region round about:
and there they preached the gospel." (Acts 14: 5-7.) When
these persecutions occurred, Timothy may not have been a
member of the church, but lived at Lystra, and knew of them,
and at a subsequent visit of Paul and Silas became a companion of Paul and Silas. (Acts 16: 11.)

what persecutions I endured:—Timothy was acquainted
with the facts of Paul's persecutions, and he mentions them to
encourage him in his work and to strengthen him for the
trials which would certainly come upon him in his work.

and out of them all the Lord delivered me.—[He was cared
for by the Lord, who said: "All authority hath been given
unto me in heaven and on earth" (Matt. 28: 18), to whom he
belonged to order the earthly destiny of his servants. The
Lord, who had more work for him to do, delivered him out of
the hands of his enemies—gave him up to friends when he
was left for dead by his enemies.]

**12 Yea, and all that would live godly in Christ Jesus shall
suffer persecution.**—From this consideration of his own sufferings and afflictions for Christ's sake, he lays down this

tors shall wax worse and worse, deceiving and being deceived. 14 But abide
thou in the things which thou hast learned and hast been assured of, knowing

proposition. This truth is universal. A man that is faithful to
God in all things will be opposed and persecuted. The persecution takes different forms in different ages and countries.
Sometimes it is ridicule, oppositions of various kinds. Even
the light-minded and those in the church who lack devotion
and earnestness will ridicule, oppose, and persecute those who
seek to live and lead others to pure, holy, godly lives. There
is an antagonism between the flesh and the desires of the
spirit, so they oppose.

[It is the duty of the Christian so to teach and to live as to
commend himself to everyone in the sight of God, as Paul
says: "But we have renounced the hidden things of shame,
not walking in craftiness, nor handling the word of God deceitfully; but by the manifestation of the truth commending
ourselves to every man's conscience in the sight of God" (2
Cor. 4: 2), and thus compel the inward respect of even wicked
men for his sincerity and consistency; but a decided, earnest
Christian spirit and life will always evoke some form of opposition from the ungodly.]

13 **But evil men and impostors shall wax worse and worse,**
—Men who are given over to evil themselves and who beguile
and lead others into sin wax worse and worse. There is no
standing still morally or religiously. If a man is not improving, he is going backward. If he is going downward, he grows
worse and worse every day he follows this course.

deceiving and being deceived.—One who starts out in a
wrong course that seeks to deceive others deceives himself
worse than he does others. As a rule, men deceive themselves
as to their own course and character more than they deceive
their fellow men. When one imagines he gains anything by
deceiving others, he badly deceives himself. When a man
wrongs another, he commits a greater wrong against himself.
[He who perverts the truth in the very act destroys his own
power to see the truth and opens his soul to the influx of
error.]

14 **But abide thou in the things which thou hast learned and
hast been assured of,**—Paul had been Timothy's spiritual

of ⁹whom thou hast learned them; 15 and that from a babe thou hast known
the sacred writings which are able to make thee wise unto salvation through
faith which is in Christ Jesus. 16 ¹⁰Every scripture inspired of God *is* also

⁹Gr. *what persons*
¹⁰Or, *Every scripture is inspired of God, and profitable*

father and chief teacher in the gospel. He taught under the
direction of the Holy Spirit, and always maintained the divine
authority of that teaching, and reminded him to continue in
this teaching, which he had learned, and of which he had been
assured by the spiritual power manifested to confirm them.
This course would make Timothy grow better, wiser and
wiser, in contrast with the evil men who wax worse and
worse.

knowing of whom thou hast learned them;—This refers to
Paul, from whom Timothy had heard the gospel, as he had
learned the Scriptures of the Old Testament from his mother
and grandmother.

**15 and that from a babe thou hast known the sacred writ-
ings which are able to make thee wise unto salvation**—[These
words are corrective and explanatory of the foregoing assertion, indicating the only means whereby the salvation in question can be attained; provided we superadd faith in Christ
Jesus, who is "the end of the law unto righteousness to every
one that believeth." (Rom. 10: 4.) Thus we are drawn from
the letter of the law to its spirit in the gospel. (John 5: 39,
40, 46.) The apostle here grants that the Old Testament
Scriptures were able to make him wise unto salvation, but he
adds:

through faith which is in Christ Jesus.—[Wherefore, without the teaching of the New Testament that Christ hath
wrought the redemption of the world, which redemption the
Old Testament did foreshow he should work, it is not the Old
Testament alone which can perform so much as Paul claims
who presupposes this when he magnifies that so highly. Of
the intent of the Old Testament as compared with that of the
New Testament, the general end of both is one, the difference
between them consisting in this: the Old Testament did make
wise by teaching salvation through the Messiah that should
come; the New Testament, by teaching that Christ the Savior

profitable for teaching, for reproof, for correction, for [11]instruction which is in righteousness: 17 that the man of God may be complete, furnished completely unto every good work.

[11]Or, *discipline*

is come, and that Jesus, whom the Jews did crucify and whom God did raise again from the dead, is *he*.]

16 **Every scripture inspired of God is also profitable**—There have been doubts as to the proper translation of this sentence, but the translations—King James and the American Standard —make no material difference in the meaning. The two Versions give the point in the difference of translation. One says: "*All* scripture" (the Old Testament Scripture), referred to in verse 15, that had made Timothy wise unto salvation, "is given by inspiration of God, and is profitable." The other says: "*Every* scripture inspired of God is also profitable." They both declare the Scriptures of God that had gone before were profitable to the man of God—him who believed in Christ Jesus—for teaching. The same thing is in the following: "Now these things happened unto them by way of example; and they were written for our admonition, upon whom the ends of the ages are come." (1 Cor. 10: 11.)

for teaching,—The man of God can find teaching and example, warning and instruction in God's dealings with the Jewish people to help him in every temptation and trial through which he is called to pass.

for reproof,—For reproving mistakes and wrongs in ourselves and others.

for correction,—The Scripture is perceived as the rule of faith, convicting of error and guiding to truth.

for instruction which is in righteousness:—The Scripture trains by guiding and inspiring the soul in holiness and right living. These instructions are given as in accordance with the will of God as revealed through Christ Jesus and the Holy Spirit.

17 **that the man of God may be complete, furnished completely unto every good work.**—The teachings of Jesus and the apostles, in connection with examples, teachings, and the warnings of the Old Testament Scriptures, are sufficient to make the man of God perfect—perfect him in the knowledge

of God's will as revealed through Jesus Christ. Man should not treat the New Testament requirements in a way he does not find authority for treating them in the Old Testament. As God punished for disobeying, rejecting, turning aside, adding to or going beyond the requirements of the Old Testament, so he will punish for a similar course toward the requirements of the New Testament. As he blessed for faithful and trusting obedience to the Old Testament, so he will bless for faithful requirements of the New Testament.

3. CHARGE TO TIMOTHY TO FULFILL HIS MINISTRY
4: 1-8

1 [12]I charge *thee* in the sight of God, and of Christ Jesus, who shall judge the living and the dead, and by his appearing and his kingdom: 2 preach the word; be urgent in season, out of season; [13]reprove, rebuke, exhort, with all

[12]Or, *I testify, in the sight . . . dead, both of his appearing &c.*
[13]Or, *bring to the proof*

1 **I charge thee in the sight of God, and of Christ Jesus,**—Because of the all-sufficiency of the word of God to make the man of God perfect and to thoroughly furnish him for every good work, he gave him this solemn charge before God and the Lord Jesus Christ.

who shall judge the living and the dead,—Paul reminds Timothy of this judgment to be executed by Jesus Christ to warn him of the fearful responsibility resting on him to preach the word of God, for he would be held accountable for fidelity in this at the last day.

and by his appearing and his kingdom:—[This solemn charge was not because he suspected him of any unfaithfulness, but to show his own extreme solicitude for the preservation of the pure and unadulterated word of the Lord, and of the peace and prosperity of the church; and to leave in the divine record to proclaimers of the word in the succeeding ages a desire to be faithful and diligent in all their work.]

2 **preach the word;**—He was to preach the word that would make the man of God perfect, and that would thoroughly furnish him unto every good work. He was to preach this word as all-sufficient. It is a fearful thing to add to it or take from it or in any way to mutilate or change that word.

longsuffering and teaching. 3 For the time will come when they will not endure the [14]sound [15]doctrine; but, having itching ears, will heap to themselves teachers after their own lusts; 4 and will turn away their ears from

[14]Gr. *healthful*
[15]Or, *teaching*

be urgent in season,—Be ready on every favorable occasion to teach, exhort, and admonish; be urgent generally in the whole work of his ministry.

out of season;—Do not await favorable moments, but create them, to teach the word even under unfavorable circumstances. Eternal ruin is facing the world—await not for favorable circumstances to warn them of the terrible danger. [This, however, only touches a portion of the thought of Paul, who urges on God's faithful servants sleepless earnestness, which struggles on in the Lord's work regardless of bodily weakness and discouragement in face of dangers and bitterest opposition.]

reprove,—For wrong teaching with the idea of bringing the fault home to the offender.

rebuke,—For sins and wrongs persisted in. [A sharper and more severe word than reprove, generally with the idea of bringing the fault home to the offender.]

exhort,—Kindly encourage to greater fidelity those who are weak, disheartened, and ready to give up.

with all longsuffering and teaching.—Do this in a kind, forbearing, long-suffering spirit, striving to instruct and lead into the right paths while applying the word to the different conditions.

3 For the time will come when they will not endure the sound doctrine;—Paul urges that this be done the more earnestly while it may do good, for the time will come when these professed Christians will not endure the sound doctrine. Errors now just apparent, he must remember, would attain more formidable dimensions. The thirst for novelties in doctrine, the desire for a teaching which, while offering peace to a troubled conscience, yet allow the old self-indulgent life to go on, as before, would increase. In full view of this development of vicious error, in sure expectation of a future full of anxious care, Timothy and his fellow laborers must indeed be watchful and earnest in their teachings and ministrations.

the truth, and turn aside unto fables. 5 But be thou sober in all things, suf-

but, having itching ears, will heap to themselves teachers
after their own lusts;—They will serve teachers who will
gratify their own desires by teaching the things that please
their own fancy, that gratify the itching of their own ears.
The prophet describes them in the following terse words:
"My people are destroyed for lack of knowledge: because thou
hast rejected knowledge, I will also reject thee, that thou
shalt be no priest to me: seeing thou hast forgotten the law of
thy God, I also will forget thy children. As they were multi-
plied, so they sinned against me: I will change their glory
into shame. They feed on the sin of my people, and set their
heart on their iniquity. And it shall be, like people, like
priest; and I will punish them for their ways, and will requite
them their doings. And they shall eat, and not have enough;
they shall play the harlot, and shall not increase; because they
have left off taking heed to Jehovah." (Hos. 4: 6-10.) That
is, teachers can always be found who will teach what the people wish to be taught. As they are catered to, they grow
more and more depraved in appetite, and in hearing they will
wax worse and worse. When we leave the truth of God,
there is no stopping place.

4 and will turn away their ears from the truth,—They turn
away their ears wholly from the truth, and will give up
wholly to fables. A man begins to leave the plain and simple
truth of God and to turn from it and ends in wholly rejecting
it. Hence, the necessity of holding fast the form of sound
words.

and turn aside unto fables.—These fables were no doubt
purely rabbinical. It was said in the Jewish schools that an
oral law had been given on Mount Sinai, and that this law a
succession of teachers, from the time of Moses, had handed
down. This "law that is upon the lip," as it was termed, was
further illustrated and enlarged by the sayings and comments
of the more famous Jewish rabbis, and in the time of the Lord
Jesus Christ constituted a supplement to the written law of
Moses. For centuries this supplementary code was preserved
by memory or in sacred rolls and doubtless was constantly receiving additions. It contained, along with many wild and

fer hardship, do the work of an evangelist, fulfil thy ministry. 6 For I am already being [1]offered, and the time of my departure is come. 7 I have

[1]Gr. *poured out as a drink-offering*

improbable legendary histories, some wise teachings. This strange collection of tradition and comment was committed to writing in the second century by Rabbi Jehuda under the general name of the Mishna or "repetition of the law." Round this compilation a complement of discussions—the Gemara—was gradually formed and was completed at Babylon somewhere about the end of the fifth century A.D. These works —Mishna and the Gemara together with a second Gemara formed somewhat earlier in Palestine—are generally known to us as the Talmud. The influence of these traditions is alluded to by the Lord. (Matt. 15 : 3.)

5 **But be thou sober in all things,**—Those who are under the power and error of sin are mentally and spiritually living under the passions of drunkenness, while only such as are under the power of the truth and holiness are sober with clear vision and well-balanced mind. The word sums up all Paul's directions from 2: 14, in which he charged Timothy to abstain from striving about words to no profit, to the subverting of them that hear, and to confine himself to the simple word of truth, to avoid discussion which would lead to strife, and to be patient and gentle with all, and to keep steadily in the old paths in which the apostle had walked. He was to be ever watchful in all these things.

suffer hardship,—Bear persecutions that come for fidelity to the truth, which must be preached at any risk, and is thoroughly deserving of the greatest sacrifice.

do the work of an evangelist,—This includes all the teaching needed to make the gospel effective in the salvation of men. There was originally a distinction in the meanings of the words preach, evangelize, and teach. But the same person was called to all to such an extent that the words greatly lost their distinction and are used almost indiscriminately to refer to all the preaching and teaching to save men.

fulfil thy ministry.—This was to be done by devotion, zeal, and fidelity. He was to do the work faithfully, zealously, and courageously. Thus he would show his efficiency as a minis-

fought the good fight, I have finished the course, I have kept the faith: 8

ter of Christ by doing the full work to which he had been called.

6 **For I am already being offered,**—[In his first Roman imprisonment he thought a martyr's death was probable. At the time he now writes he says: "I am already being offered," which points to the drink offering of wine, which among the Jews accompanied the sacrifice. The allusion here is to Paul's bloody death. So certain was he that the time for his death was at hand that as he speaks he feels as though it was even then taking place. And he sees in his present suffering in the harsh treatment the beginning of that martyrdom in which his blood would be poured out. But he would not allow Timothy or the many Christians who loved him to be dismayed by his sufferings or tragic death. He would show them by his calm, triumphant courage that to him death was no terror, but only the appointed passage out of the body into the presence of the Lord as he said: "We are of good courage, I say, and are willing rather to be absent from the body, and to be at home with the Lord." (2 Cor. 5: 8.) So he speaks of his lifeblood being shed under the well-known peaceful image of the wine poured out over the sacrifice, the drink offering, the sweet savor unto the Lord. (Num. 15: 1-10.)]

and the time of my departure is come.—Paul's work was nearly over. He was soon to die for the cause of the Lord. His trial was near or past and he realized that he must soon die, hence the appeal to Timothy. As the old men fall out of the ranks, the young men must press forward to carry on the Lord's work and be watchful and faithful to the truth.

7 **I have fought the good fight,**—It was for the good of man to save him from sin and its fearful consequences. It was for the glory and the honor of God. [The struggle had been bravely sustained in the past, and was now being equally bravely sustained to the end. His claim to the crown was established.]

I have finished the course,—It was to do his duty as a conscientious and noble hero of faith. He had fought it to a good end. [How had he finished the course? The question is answered in Paul's own words, in which he explains his own

henceforth there is laid up for me the crown of righteousness, which the Lord, the righteous judge, shall give to me at that day; and not to me only, but also to all them that have loved his appearing.

course with joy as the ministry which he had received of the Lord Jesus. He says: "But I hold not my life of any account as dear unto myself, so that I may accomplish my course, and the ministry which I received from the Lord Jesus, to testify the gospel of the grace of God. . . . Wherefore I testify unto you this day, that I am pure from the blood of all men. For I shrank not from declaring unto you the whole counsel of God." (Acts 20: 24-27.)]

I have kept the faith:—He had been true to the faith through all the difficulties, conflicts, dangers, and temptations. He had not shrunk from confessing it when death stared him in the face; he had not corrupted it to meet the views of Jews or Gentiles. With courage and resolution and perseverance he had kept it to the end. To be faithful to God to the end is to succeed. That is the only true success.

8 henceforth there is laid up for me the crown of righteousness,—[Paul after speaking calmly of death, the bitterness of which he was already tasting, looks on beyond death and speaks of the crown which awaited him.]

which the Lord, the righteous judge, shall give to me at that day; and not to me only, but also to all them that have loved his appearing.—It is a crown that comes as a reward of the righteous life that he had lived. Such a crown was not only for Paul, but a similar one awaits all that have loved his appearing. The appearing of Jesus Christ will be the destruction of sin and the vindication of the righteous. It will be the establishment of the rule of right, justice, and mercy. All who are faithful and will look for his coming will desire it, will love it. For such the crown of righteousness is ready and waiting.

4. REQUESTS AND PERSONAL DETAILS
4: 9-18

9 Give diligence to come shortly unto me: 10 for Demas forsook me, hav-

9 Give diligence to come shortly unto me:—Paul, having given this exhortation to Timothy, asks him to use all dili-

ing loved this present ²world, and went to Thessalonica; Crescens to ³Galatia, Titus to Dalmatia. 11 Only Luke is with me. Take Mark, and

²Or, *age*
³Or, *Gaul*

gence to soon come to him. He wished to see his son in the gospel, with whom he had been so much in his labors and sufferings. once more before he left this world. It is natural to suppose that Timothy was equally desirous to see him once more in the flesh.

10 **for Demas forsook me, having loved this present world, and went to Thessalonica;**—Demas was once a faithful worker with Paul in Rome during Paul's first imprisonment there, and united with Paul in sending salutations from Rome to the Colossians and to Philemon. (Col. 4: 14; Phile. 24.) He is here described as having forsaken Paul when he was awaiting his trial before Nero. How sadly Paul now says that he "loved this present world, and went to Thessalonica." This is a sad statement.

Crescens to Galatia,—It is not likely that he had turned from following the Lord. He had possibly gone on a gospel mission.

Titus to Dalmatia.—Dalmatia was a province of Roman Illyricum, lying along the Adriatic Sea. Nothing is known respecting this journey of Titus. It was most likely with Paul's sanction, for we can hardly conceive of one who had been a trusted and honored companion of Paul and a Christian preacher as he had been had turned from following the Lord.

11 **Only Luke is with me.**—"Luke, the beloved physician" (Col. 4: 14), of all Paul's companions, seems to have been most closely associated with Paul. He was with him, we know, in his second missionary journey. Among Biblical scholars it is generally agreed that Luke was the author of the third gospel and Acts, both of which were certainly written by the same hand. (Acts 1: 1.) Accordingly we learn more of him in Acts in which he intimates his presence with Paul by the use of the pronouns "we" and "us." From these passages it is certain that Luke joined Paul at Troas and accompanied him to Macedonia (Acts 16: 10) and was with him in Philippi when Lydia and her household were baptized (16: 11-17);

bring him with thee; for he is useful to me for ministering. 12 But Tychicus I sent to Ephesus. 13 The cloak that I left at Troas with Carpus, bring
when thou comest, and the books, especially the parchments. 14 Alexander

---

joined him again at Troas (20: 5); and thence accompanied
him on his last journey to Jerusalem (20: 13, 14; 21: 1-17);
and accompanied him to Rome (27: 1 to 28: 16), and remained
with him till he was released as is shown by references made
to him by Paul written during that time (Col. 4: 14; Phile.
24). While these items seem relatively unimportant, they
show that Luke's fidelity to Paul kept him at his side through
the first imprisonment, and the verse before discloses him as
with the apostle at the end of the second imprisonment.

Take Mark, and bring him with thee;—Mark was the son of
the sister of Barnabas, over whom Barnabas and Paul disa-
greed and separated. (Acts 15: 36-41.) Paul then thought
him unwilling to endure hardness and danger. [Since that
time Mark had, by steady, earnest work, won back his place in
Paul's heart. After some twelve years we find him during the
first imprisonment with Paul at Rome. (Col. 4: 10; Phile.
24.)]

for he is useful to me for ministering.—Paul seems now to
appreciate him so highly that he is now summoned in his hour
of supreme danger, and in circumstances from which other
friends were ready to flee.

12 But Tychicus I sent to Ephesus.—Tychicus was with
Paul in his journey through Macedonia. (Acts 20: 4.) It is
not known how he came to Rome when Paul was a prisoner.
Paul sent him to report his condition to the churches and to
comfort them. (Eph. 6: 21.) He carried the letters to the
Ephesians (Eph. 6: 21) and to the Colossians (Col. 4: 7). [He
is mentioned also in Acts.(20: 4) and Titus (3: 12) so that he
too was one of the few found faithful to the end.]

**13 The cloak that I left at Troas with Carpus, bring when
thou comest,**—Paul in passing through Troas at some time,
left a cloak with Carpus. Winter was now coming on and
Paul in the cold damp prison, with few friends and scant re-
sources, remembered and wished for his cloak. (4: 21.)

and the books, especially the parchments.—We know not
what books he had. The parchments were probably some of

the coppersmith ⁴did me much evil: the Lord will render to him according to his works: 15 of whom do thou also beware; for he greatly withstood our words. 16 At my first defence no one took my part, but all forsook me:

⁴Gr. *showed*

his own writings. The writing was then done on parchments —dressed skins.

14 Alexander the coppersmith did me much evil:—He may have been a professed Christian who was a Judaizing teacher turned against Paul and made shipwreck of his faith. [Three men named Alexander are mentioned in connection with Paul's work, and we cannot positively decide which one is here denounced. They are: (1) Alexander of Ephesus, who was brought "out of the multitude, the Jews putting him forward" (Acts 10: 33) to defend them. The purpose of this was most likely to save the Jews from being mixed up with the Christians in the vengeance of the people. He may or may not have been the same as Alexander the coppersmith. (2) Alexander the coppersmith, of whom it is said he did Paul "much evil" (2 Tim. 4: 14). (3) Alexander, an early Christian who "made shipwreck concerning the faith" (1 Tim. 1: 19, 20), who did Paul "much evil" (2 Tim. 4: 14). Many attempts have been made to identify these men, but identification is simply a matter of conjecture.]

the Lord will render to him according to his works:—Paul leaves him with God to reward him according to his deeds, refraining from personal judgment, leaves him to the certain and holy judgment of God, assured that it will be according to his works.

15 of whom do thou also beware;—The opposition to the gospel which led him to withstand Paul would lead him also to oppose Timothy, and he gives this warning against him as a man not to be trusted. He was to be watched and avoided.

for he greatly withstood our words.—He violently opposed the teaching of Paul. Evidently he was an enemy of the gospel, and yet seemingly one who was disguised, for Timothy is put upon his guard against him.

16 At my first defence no one took my part,—At this first reply to the charges made against him in his trial, none stood firmly by him. [Accustomed to refer to his high spiritual priv-

may it not be laid to their account.   17 But the Lord stood by me, and
⁵strengthened me ; that through me the ⁶message might be fully proclaimed,

⁵Or, *gave me power*
⁶Or, *proclamation*

ileges, he speaks but little, and never in details of the outward incidents of his life. They did not belong to the world's
passing show, to the things which were seen and rapidly passing away. Two vivid touches alone reveal to us the nature of
the occasion. One is the shameful fact that not a single friend
had the courage to stand by his side. He had to defend himself singlehanded. No *advocate* would plead his case or speak
a word in his favor.]

but all forsook me:—[The position of Paul, a well-known
leader of the Christians in the year A.D. 66-67, was a critical
one, and the friend who dared to stand by him would be in
great danger. After the great fire in Rome (A.D. 64), the
Christians were looked upon as the enemies of the state, and
were charged as the authors of the terrible disaster. Nero, to
avert suspicion from himself, accused the Christians of the
awful deed. And as consequence a very great multitude of
Christians were subjected to terrible sufferings and death. It
is possible that Paul was eventually accused and arrested as
implicated in this crime and brought to Rome. But Paul, conscious of his own great peril, knew well that to stand by him
now, implicated as he was in this network of false accusations,
would be a service of the greatest danger to the Christians.]

may it not be laid to their account.—So he pleads for these
weak, unnerved Christians, who, through no ill will to the
cause of Christ, but solely from timidity, had deserted him, remembering, no doubt, the Lord Jesus, who, too, in his hour of
deadly peril, had been forsaken, said: "Behold, the hour cometh, yea, is come, that ye shall be scattered, every man to his
own, and shall leave me alone." (John 16: 32.) But like the
Master who proceeded to say, "I am not alone, because the
Father is with me," so Paul said to Timothy.

17 But the Lord stood by me, and strengthened me;—Notwithstanding the facts that his friends and brethren had forsaken him, the Lord stood by him and enabled him, now old
and feeble, to speak with clearness and force before the high-

and that all the Gentiles might hear: and I was delivered out of the mouth
of the lion. 18 The Lord will deliver me from every evil work, and will

---

est earthly tribunal in the capital city of the world filled with
a power that lifted him above fear and clothed him with a divine energy which his enemies could not resist. The following words of the Lord Jesus supported him on this trying occasion: "But when they deliver you up, be not anxious how or
what ye shall speak: for it shall be given you in that hour
what ye shall speak. For it is not ye that speak, but the
Spirit of your Father that speaketh in you." (Matt. 10: 19,
20.) And the great promise was fulfilled: "Lo, I am with you
always, even unto the end of the world." (Matt. 28: 20.)

that through me the message might be fully proclaimed,—
The strength and courage which the felt presence of the Lord
gave him enabled him on that momentous occasion, when
alone, friendless, accused of an awful crime before the highest
earthly court in the capital city of the world, to plead not only
for himself, but for the cause for which his Lord and Master
died on the cross. The great trial probably took place in the
Forum and in the presence of a great concourse of people
gathered from all parts of the empire.

and that all the Gentiles might hear:—This was apparently
the culminating point in Paul's lifework alluding primarily to
the vast audience which had listened to him on this solemn
occasion; but there is another and deeper reference to those
unnumbered peoples in the isles of the Gentiles (Isa. 11: 11;
24: 15; 51: 5), who, by Paul's work and teachings, would
come to the knowledge of the truth as it is in Jesus and be
saved.

and I was delivered out of the mouth of the lion.—It was
thought that the result of the trial would be that he would be
cast to the lions in the amphitheatre. In all his trials in Jerusalem and Caesarea his defense was that the gospel is true.
He preached that Jesus was raised from the dead as the vindication of his course. Many attended the trial of Paul, and by
his defense on that occasion his preaching became fully
known. All the Gentiles heard the truth and God delivered
him from the lion's mouth. The trial so resulted and his
preaching so affected the people and the judges that he was

save me unto his heavenly kingdom: to whom *be* the glory [7]for ever and
ever. Amen.

[7]Gr. *unto the ages of the ages*

not thrown to the lions. The customs of the country, the fate
of the Christians condemned, and the surroundings seem to
require this meaning.

18 **The Lord will deliver me from every evil work,**—The
evil design of casting Paul to the lions had been thwarted and
God would deliver him from all evil works. This does not
imply that God would save him from a violent death, but that
he would be with him and not allow any evil attempt against
him to succeed.

and will save me unto his heavenly kingdom:—[The issue,
so far as Paul was concerned, would be his entrance into
Christ's everlasting kingdom. This would be granted unto
him after and through death. The safe placing of Paul in
Christ's eternal kingdom is meant on the one side (2 Pet. 1:
11) removal from the sphere of evil, and on the other side
coming under the highest conditions of happiness in the enjoyment of Christ (Phil. 1: 21-23; 2 Cor. 5: 8, 9.)]

to whom be the glory for ever and ever. Amen.—[Dox-
ology is an accompaniment of the highest spiritual mood.
It is offered here to the Son of God as elsewhere to the
Father. For it was the Son's assistance that he had enjoyed
and still expected and into whose kingdom in heaven he was
by the same assistance to be safely brought. It will take the
ages of ages to declare all that Christ had been and was still
to be to him.]

5. SALUTATIONS AND BENEDICTIONS
4: 19-22

19 Salute Prisca and Aquila, and the house of Onesiphorus. 20 Erastus

19 **Salute Prisca and Aquila,**—These were two of Paul's
earliest friends after he had entered into his great work in the
service of the Lord Jesus. They were originally of Pontus
(Acts 18: 2); they had taken up their abode in Rome, where
Aquila exercised his trade as a tentmaker (Acts 18: 2, 3.).
They were driven from Rome by the decree of Claudius,

remained at Corinth: but Trophimus I left at Miletus sick. 21 Give diligence to come before winter. Eubulus saluteth thee, and Pudens, and Linus,
and Claudia, and all the brethren.

which banished the Jews from Rome; they came to Corinth,
where Paul became acquainted with them; they evidently
were Christians when Paul first met them; they were with
Paul at Corinth, at Ephesus (1 Cor. 16: 19), and Paul sends
greetings to them at Rome (Rom. 16: 3). They evidently
were among the many active and zealous teachers in the early
days of the church. That they were able and zealous is evident from the fact that it was they who taught the learned
Apollos the way of God more accurately. (Acts 18: 26.) In
this place and in others Prisca is named before her husband.
This seems to indicate that in this case the woman was the
principal worker in the cause of the Lord Jesus.

and the house of Onesiphorus.—Onesiphorus had been with
Paul in Rome (1: 17) and was now likely teaching or preaching, but whose family was at Ephesus. Paul evidently intends to compliment the family for its worth and holiness.

20 **Erastus remained at Corinth:**—Erastus had been a teaching companion of Paul and Timothy. He and Timothy were
sent by Paul into Macedonia, while Paul remained in Asia.
(Acts 19: 22.) Aftr teaching with Paul and Timothy for a
time, he settled down at Corinth. Paul tells this as interesting to Timothy.

but Trophimus I left at Miletus sick.—Trophimus went
with Paul to Jerusalem, was a Greek of Ephesus, and Paul was
accused of leading him into the temple and profaning it,
which brought on the tumult against him. He seems to have
been sent as a messenger between the churches and Paul.
[That he was left there in a state of sickness shows that
Paul's gift of healing was not permitted by God to be employed for private needs, even for the purpose of securing to
him the services of his closest friends, but was only to be
used when there was some clear intimation of the Spirit that
it was fitting.

21 **Give diligence to come before winter.**—Paul's life was
near to the end. Sailing and traveling were dangerous and

22 The Lord be with thy spirit. Grace be with you.

---

uncertain in winter. If he did not come before winter, he might be delayed another season.

Eubulus saluteth thee, and Pudens, and Linus, and Claudia, and all the brethren.—Nothing is known of Eubulus and of the others whose names are mentioned here. They all send greetings to Timothy. He had been with them and this was a kindly remembrance.

22 **The Lord be with thy spirit. Grace be with you.**—It is a peculiarity of the salutation that it is doubled—one to Timothy personally, the other to the church at Ephesus. [Thus closes our last authentic account of this great apostle. These are, perhaps, the last words of him who wrought a greater change in the condition of mankind by his writings and speech than any other man who ever lived. All honor to his blessed memory.]

COMMENTARY ON THE EPISTLE
TO TITUS

CONTENTS

INTRODUCTION TO PAUL'S EPISTLE TO TITUS

I. TITUS

Titus is not mentioned by name in Acts of Apostles, but is frequently referred to in Paul's Epistles. He was born of Gentile parents (Gal. 2: 3), and was one of the company from Antioch (Acts 15: 2) who accompanied Paul and Barnabas when they went to Jerusalem unto the apostles and elders about the question as to whether the Gentiles would be received into the church except they were circumcised after the custom of Moses (Acts 15: 1). He was possibly a native of Antioch, and since Paul calls him "my true child after a common faith" (Tit. 1: 4), he may have led him to obey the gospel by his preaching to him. He was a much younger man than Paul. When at Jerusalem his presence gave offense to the Judaizers, but the church refused to compel him to be circumcised, thus standing with Paul in his advocacy of receiving the Gentiles into the church without compelling them to be circumcised and obeying the law of Moses. (Gal. 2: 3-5.)

After this Titus remained Paul's companion, being perhaps with him when he wrote the Galatian Epistle (2: 3; 1: 2), and not mentioned again until the time of the incidents which caused the writing of the two Epistles to the Corinthians. At this time he paid three visits to Corinth and was one of the most active in spreading the gospel among the people that had hitherto sat in darkness and in the shadow of death. He was with Paul at Ephesus, thence sent on a special mission to Corinth, probably the bearer of the first Epistle to the Corinthians (2 Cor. 12: 18); with Paul in Macedonia (7: 6-15) and perhaps with him at Corinth. He had the superintendence of the work in Crete and was with Paul in Rome, thence sent by him to Dalmatia. (2 Tim. 4: 10.) His missions of investigation and love, his arrangement for the famous collection for the poor saints in Jerusalem were apparently undertaken spontaneously. (2 Cor. 8: 6, 16, 17.)

The appointment of Titus to the chief superintendence of the churches of Crete was one of singular fitness. There was a strong blending of races and religions in the island. There were many Jews, but the Gentile population outnumbered them. The congregations seem to have been numerous and full of life, but disorganized and troubled with disorders, misrule, and even dishonored with many excesses, utterly at variance with the doctrine of Christ. No one was so fitted to restore order and enforce a stern rule as Titus, who had already performed so great a work among the turbulent and licentious Christians at Corinth and had persuaded by his marvelous skill so many Gentile congregations to unite in helping with a generous liberality the pressing needs of their proud and haughty Jewish brethren who disdained them. (Tit. 1:4.)

II. DESIGN OF THE EPISTLE

The task which Paul committed to Titus when he left him in Crete was one of much difficulty. The character of the people was unsteady, insincere, and quarrelsome; they were given to greediness, licentiousness, falsehood, and drunkenness in no ordinary degree; and the Jews who had settled among them appear to have even gone beyond the native in immorality. Among such a people it was no easy work which Titus had to sustain when commissioned to carry forward that which Paul had begun, and to set in order the affairs of the churches which had arisen there, especially as heretical teachers had crept in among them. Hence, Paul addressed to him this Epistle, the main design of which was to direct how to discharge with success the duties to which he had been appointed. For this reason he speaks at some length on the qualification of elders and members and their functions with such local allusions as rendered these directions especially pertinent. Titus is enjoined to appoint suitable elders in every city, sound in doctrine and able to convict the gainsayers.

Paul then passes to a description of the coarse character of the Cretans as testified by their own writers and the mischief caused by the Judaizing among the Christians of the island. In opposition to this, Titus is to urge sound and practical Christianity on all classes—on the elderly men, on the older women, and especially in regard to their influence over the younger women, on slaves, taking heed meanwhile that he himself is a pattern of good works. The grounds of all this are given in the free grace which trains the Christian to self-denying and active piety, in the glorified hope of Christ's second coming, and in the atonement by which he has purchased us to be his people. All these lessons Titus is to urge with fearless decision.

III. PLACE AND TIME OF WRITING

The Epistle to Titus was evidently written very soon after Paul left Crete, and will most likely be dated from Asia Minor. Its own notices agree with this, for we find that he was on his way to winter at Nicopolis (Tit. 3: 12), by which it is most natural to understand the well-known city of that name in Epirus, and the notices of Second Timothy equally agree with such an hypothesis; for there we find that Paul had, since he last communicated with Timothy, been at Miletus and at Troas, probably also at Corinth (2 Tim. 4: 13, 20.) That he again visited Ephesus is on every account likely; indeed the natural inference from 2 Tim. 1: 18 that he spent some time in the companionship of Timothy, to whom he appeals to confirm what he there says of Onesiphorus.

The date of the Epistle cannot be determined with certainty, but it is usually believed, in the light of all the facts, that it was written in A.D. 67.

COMMENTARY ON THE EPISTLE TO TITUS

1. SALUTATIONS
1: 1-4

1 Paul, a ¹servant of God, and an apostle of Jesus Christ, according to the faith of God's elect, and the knowledge of the truth which is according to godliness, 2 in hope of eternal life, which God, who cannot lie, promised ²be-

---

¹Gr. *bondservant*
²Or, *long ages ago*

---

1 **Paul, a servant of God,**—[The full representation which Paul gives of his apostolic office is designed at once to mark the authority by which he gives the instructions that follow, and to serve as an index to the contents of the whole Epistle. He describes himself as "a servant of God." The title seems to mark the relation of (1) one who had once been a servant of sin, but having become free through Christ Jesus was still, so far as obligation, service, and life were concerned, a servant of God; (2) his devotion to God after the type of the Old Testament services, Moses and the prophets being preeminently called the servants of God; (3) his ministry in the service of a royal Master (Matt. 18: 23-35), who makes him a member of his household, a pillar in the temple, a sharer of his throne (Rev. 3: 21).]

and an apostle of Jesus Christ,—[This is a more exact definition of his office: (1) He had his commission from him. (2) He had all the signs and proofs of an apostle in him for he had received power to work miracles as well as to declare divine truth. (3) It is therefore, vain and deceptive for anyone to assume the name who cannot show the signs of an apostle.]

according to the faith of God's elect, and the knowledge of the truth which is according to godliness,—The faith of those chosen in Christ Jesus. It is a little difficult to see clearly how he was sent "according to the faith of God's elect." All critics think it means that he was sent in order to produce faith in those who would accept the gospel, and in order that others might acknowledge the truth that leads to godliness. This seems a little strained, but as nothing better is suggested all accept is as the true meaning.

2 **in hope of eternal life,**—The last dispensation of God was to be eternal. So before the introduction of the final dispensa-

fore times eternal : 3 but in ³his own seasons manifested his word in the
⁴message, wherewith I was intrusted according to the commandment of God
our Saviour : 4 to Titus, my true child after a common faith : Grace and
peace from God the Father and Christ Jesus our Saviour.

³Or, *its*
⁴Or, *proclamation*

tion—that through the Lord Jesus Christ—the promise of
eternal life was included in the eternal purpose of God, though
it was not revealed till after the creation of man in time and
in various dispensations granted to him. That which the
apostle had in view in prosecuting the work of his apostleship
is the hope for himself and for all believers of eternal life.
This is the glorious goal set before him and which in leading
men to the full knowledge of the truth he set before them
eternal life through Jesus Christ. Knowledge and faith as he
preached it, rested on a background of promise and hope,
which, in a manner, reached from eternity to eternity, having
God's primeval promise for its origin, and a participation in
this everlasting life for an end.

which God, who cannot lie,—The words are here used to
show the certainty of the fulfillment of the promise made before the ages. (Heb. 6: 18.)

promised before times eternal;—The promise of eternal life
was the result of a divine purpose fixed from eternity.

**3 but in his own seasons manifested his word in the mes-
sage, wherewith I was intrusted**—In the fitting seasons fixed
by God for the manifestation of the gospel in preaching the
message, Paul does not shrink from calling his preaching the
vehicle in which the word of the gospel was to be publicly
manifested because he was conscious of the fact that he was
divinely instructed in the secrets of the eternal counsels.

according to the commandment of God—[The commandment came direct from God: on the road to Damascus when
the Lord appeared to him (Acts 9: 5, 6) ; spoke encouragement to him at Corinth (Acts 18: 9, 10) ; and at Jerusalem
(Acts 23: 11).]

our Saviour;—[In this place and in 1 Tim. 1: 1, we must
understand that this refers to God the Father because through
the death of his Son he redeemed us from death and made us
heirs of eternal life. The Lord Jesus Christ is likewise a pos-

sessor of the title because he shed his blood as the price of our redemption and made us heirs of eternal life.]

4 to Titus, my true child after a common faith:—Paul had been instrumental in leading him to Christ and having thus been made a sharer of his faith. He was a faithful servant of God, and he calls him his true child after the faith common to all Christians. [Titus was a Gentile; and in "common faith" there is likely an allusion to the higher bond of unity by which this "common faith in Christ bound them, though one was a Jew and the other a Gentile." (Gal. 5: 6; Col. 3: 11.)]

Grace and peace from God the Father and Christ Jesus our Saviour.—Grace the favor and approbation of God, and peace, the consequence of this manifested favor of God, producing internal happiness, quietness, and assurance.

2. QUALIFICATION OF ELDERS
1: 5-9

5 For this cause left I thee in Crete, that thou shouldest set in order the things that were wanting, and appoint elders in every city, as I gave thee charge; 6 if any man is blameless, the husband of one wife, having children

5 For this cause left I thee in Crete,—Paul, clearly from this, had been at some time in the Island of Crete, south of Greece, and had preached the gospel there. Titus was with him, and he had left him to remain in the island for a time.

that thou shouldest set in order the things that were wanting, and appoint elders in every city, as I gave thee charge;—While there were persons from Crete in Jerusalem on the day of Pentecost (Acts 2: 11), it is likely that up to the time of Paul's visit but little effort had been made to spread the gospel. None among the Gentiles, who chiefly inhabited the island, had heard the gospel till Paul and Titus preached and planted churches there. Just when or how long Paul remained there we do not know, yet it is certain that he labored there for a time and planted churches. After preaching he hastened elsewhere before the Christians had time to develop themselves in the work of the Lord. So he left Titus, no doubt a gifted teacher, to supply the needed teaching, and as the members proved their capacity put them in the lead that were fitted to teach and lead in the work of the Lord.

that believe, who are not accused of riot or unruly. 7 For the ⁵bishop must be blameless, as God's steward; not self-willed, not soon angry, ⁶no brawler, no striker, not greedy of filthy lucre; 8 but given to hospitality, a lover of

⁵Or, *overseer*
⁶Or, *not quarrelsome over wine*

6 if any man is blameless,—Guilty of no wrong to his fellow men; he must be of such a character that no one can bring a reasonable accusation against him. Blameless must be his life, spotless his name.

the husband of one wife,—Having one wife only and faithful to her—a faithful husband.

having children that believe,—He must so bring up his children in the nurture and the admonition of the Lord that they are believing children.

who are not accused of riot or unruly.—The family is the nursery of the church and these two act and react upon each other so that a bad or weak father can never be an efficient elder. If he cannot "rule his own house, how shall he take care of the church of God?" (1 Tim. 3: 5.) His children ought to be believers that they "may adorn the doctrine of God our Saviour in all things." (Tit. 2: 10.) There must be evidence that they have been brought up in the nurture and admonition of the Lord.

7 For the bishop must be blameless, as God's steward;—Guilty of no wrong to his fellows. It is important that those entrusted as stewards with the truth of God should be honest and faithful in teaching all that God has revealed for the salvation of the world. He who refuses to teach the whole will of God is dishonest toward God and unfaithful to man.

not self-willed,—This does not mean that he is not to be firm and steadfast in his purpose, but that he must not be of such a stubborn spirit that he clings to his own will and refuses to listen to reason or facts. One in such position must have the sincere desire to fully investigate all sides, to know the full truth, and then be guided by it, and not by the self-will of his own.

not soon angry,—One who can restrain and govern himself [He should not be one ever ready with an angry, hasty word, remembering always his Master, "who, when he was reviled, reviled not again." (1 Pet. 2: 23.)]

good, sober-minded, just, holy, self-controlled; 9 holding to the faithful word

---

no brawler,—Not given to the use of wine. It was recognized as an evil, and one occupying the position of bishop must not be given to its use.

no striker,—No man of God should ever, even under sore provocation, so far forget himself as to raise his hand against his fellow man.

not greedy of filthy lucre;—Not anxious for gaining riches. He is to avoid gain by wrong means. A man who is anxious for riches is not fit for a bishop of a congregation of Christians.

8 but given to hospitality,—Ready to entertain strangers, and care for the homeless and needy. [The significance of the words have deeper meaning added to them in the following beautiful words: "Let love of the brethren continue. Forget not to show love unto strangers: for thereby some have entertained angels unawares." (Heb. 13 : 1, 2.)]

a lover of good,—A lover of good or benevolence generally. [The appellation points here to that large heart which finds room for sympathy with all that is good and noble and generous.]

sober-minded,—Not light and frivolous, but serious and sober in deportment. [In this expressive word mastery of self is especially implied—that self-command which wisely regulates pleasures and passions.]

just,—The one who is just is one who tries strictly to perform his duties toward men—the duties which integrity and justice seem imperatively to ask of him in his relation with his neighbor.

holy,—Devoted to God. The three words—sober, just, holy—present the three sides of human duty—duty to oneself, duty to men, and duty to God. In all these the man of God is to show himself a true man.

self-controlled;—Holding all his desires and appetites in restraint so moderate in their gratification. The bishop not only must be able to control his tongue, his eyes, and his hands, but must show a just and wise moderation.

which is according to the teaching, that he may be able both to exhort in the
¹sound ²doctrine, and to convict the gainsayers.

¹Gr. *healthful*
²Or, *teaching*

**9 holding to the faithful word which is according to the
teaching,**—God's truth is better expressed in the words which
the Holy Spirit chooses than in those of man's choosing.
While we, in our languages, have not the words used by the
Holy Spirit, still we have those in our languages into which
they have been translated to give the truth, and we should be
careful to hold fast to the faithful words God has given us,
that by these words of God we may be able to encourage to
the belief and practice of the same sound doctrine.

**that he may be able both to exhort in the sound doctrine,
and to convict the gainsayers.**—With the sound, healthful
teaching he was to exhort the adversaries; and with the same
true words he was to confute their arguments.

3. CHARACTER AND CONDITION OF THE CHURCH IN CRETE
1: 10-16

10 For there are many unruly men, vain talkers and deceivers, specially
they of the circumcision, 11 whose mouths must be stopped; men who over-

**10 For there are many unruly men, vain talkers and deceiv-
ers,**—There were many who did not reverence the word of
God. [They were nominally in the congregations of the
Christians, but in reality refusing all obedience, acting for
themselves, factious, and insubordinate, and unfortunately
their tribe is with us today. They have broken the peace of
many a home and disrupted the peace and prosperity of many
congregations.]

specially they of the circumcision,—The Judaizing Christians. These unhappy men evidently did not belong to the
stern and rigid Jewish party who bitterly hated all the followers of the Lord Jesus but were of the number of those vicious
opponents of Paul.

11 whose mouths must be stopped;—They must either be
convinced themselves so as to cease talking or they must be
so met and confuted that others will not listen to them. [Vain

throw whole houses, teaching things which they ought not, for filthy lucre's sake. 12 One of themselves, a prophet of their own said,
　　　　　Cretans are always liars, evil beasts, idle ªgluttons.

ªGr. *bellies*

talkers are the pests of churches and families, sowing the seeds of distrust and turning men's minds against the gospel.]

men who overthrow whole houses,—They not only destroy themselves, but they lead astray whole houses. [The mischief they were doing to the cause of Christ was incalculable. It was no longer individuals that their poisonous teaching affected, but they were undermining the faith of whole families.]

teaching things which they ought not, for filthy lucre's sake. —The subverted the truth for gain. [It is a significant fact that elders and teachers are to take heed to themselves and then to the church (Acts 20: 28), and to be ensamples to the flock (1 Pet. 5: 3), show that they are "doers of the word, and not hearers only," and that they have already reduced to practice the good lessons they are to teach others (1 Tim. 4: 12). It is a shame and a reproach upon the cause of Christ that some preachers and teachers at the present day seem to have but little sense of common honesty, honorable dealing, integrity, and uprightness; they do not attach sufficient importance to keeping their word and paying their debts.]

12 One of themselves, a prophet of their own, said,—The words quoted were written by the famous Epimenides of Grossus in Crete, about six hundred years B.C., who is called "a prophet of their own," for he is described by classic writers as a philosophic seer and priest, venerated for his predictions, around whose memory popular legends gathered, and to whom almost sacred honors came to be paid.

Cretans are always liars,—This terrible estimate of the Cretan character is amply borne out by the testimony of many profane writers. The word to "Cretanize," or to play the part of a Cretan, was invented as a word synonymous with "to deceive" or "to utter a lie."

evil beasts,—Not only liars, but gross and sensual, living in animalism and for it. All men may be called "beasts" who attend to their animal appetites as a means of gratification

13 This testimony is true. For which cause reprove them sharply, that they

rather than for relief. He who seeks happiness from his senses rather than from his spiritual nature is no better than a beast. [The happiness of a true man cannot stream from without; it must well up from his own spiritual nature enlightened by the word of God.]

idle gluttons.—Their gluttony made them dull, heavy, and indolent. These sins were true of the Cretans generally in their unregenerate state; but sins prevalent among a people before they become Christians will possibly be their besetting sins after they become such. The sins of lying and gluttony seem to indicate a ferocious and vindictive spirit, and that they were lazy and given to gluttony.

13 This testimony is true.—This was still true; they retained their evil characters; the Christians were still tempted into the sins which these qualities would lead; they were gross sins and demoralizing in their character.

For which cause reprove them sharply,—Because of this he admonishes Titus to rebuke them sharply—reprove all aberrations from the truth. [As the surgeon cuts out the diseased flesh in order, by the painful operation, to restore the patient to health, so must the words of Titus be severe when necessary. Titus had to deal with those who were rough and uncultivated, and therefore should be dealt with accordingly. There must be in reproving a distinguishing between sins; some are more gross and heinous in their nature or in the manner of their commission with openness and boldness to the greater dishonor of God and danger and hurt to men and between sinners; some are of a more tender and tractable temper, more apt to be wrought upon by gentleness and to be greatly discouraged by too much roughness and severity; others are more hardy and stubborn and need more sharp language to beget in them remorse and shame. Wisdom therefore is requisite to temper and manage reproofs aright as may be more likely to bring about the desired result. To that end the inspired directions are: "On some have mercy, who are in doubt; and some save, snatching them out of the fire; and on some have mercy with fear; hating even the garment spotted by the flesh." (Jude 22, 23.)]

may be *sound in the faith, 14 not giving heed to Jewish fables, and commandments of men who turn away from the truth. 15 To the pure all things
are pure: but to them that are defiled and unbelieving nothing is pure; but
both their mind and their conscience are defiled. 16 They profess that they

*Gr. *healthy*

that they may be sound in the faith,—That they may remain faithful and true to the faith in God as revealed through
Jesus Christ.

14 not giving heed to Jewish fables,—Jewish fables were the
traditions and practices that had through a long period of
time crept into their teachings and displaced the commandments God had given them. (Matt. 15: 1-10.) Christ gives a
sample of how they turned from and annulled the commandments of God by their traditions and myths. Jesus then
warns them: "But in vain do they worship me, teaching as
their doctrines the precepts of men." (Matt. 15: 9.)

and commandments of men who turn away from the truth.
—Every reasoning or influence that turns man from the word
of God is hurtful and ruinous. All the commandments of men
turn from the truth and are to be avoided. Any man who
puts the theories and devices of men upon an equality with
the commandments of God or who displaces the appointments
of God with the devices of man turns from the truth of God.

15 To the pure all things are pure:—The reference here is
to the use of meats as in Rom. 14: 13-23; 1 Cor. 10: 14-33. All
things indeed are pure; but "it is evil for that man who eateth
with offence." (Rom. 14: 20.) In the passage before us he
says: "To the pure all things are pure." It is the heart, not
the meats that must be clean to make the offering to the service acceptable to God.

but to them that are defiled and unbelieving nothing is
pure;—But unto those whose hearts are defiled and whose
lives are sinful, no offering they can bring to the Lord will he
accept as pure.

but both their mind and their conscience are defiled.—[The
mind is the willing as well as the thinking part of man. Defile-
ment of this mind means that the thoughts, wishes, purposes
and activities are all stained and debased. The conscience is
the moral conscience within, that which is ever bringing up

know God; but by their works they deny him, being adominable, and disobedient, and unto every good work reprobate.

the memory of the past with its omissions and commissions, its errors, its cruel, heartless unkindness, its selfish disregard of others. When this is defiled, then this last safeguard of the soul is broken down. The man and woman of the defiled conscience is self-satisfied, hard, and impenitent to the last.] Because when the mind and conscience are defiled and corrupt, nothing the man can do is acceptable to God.

16 **They profess that they know God; but by their works they deny him,**—This is all spoken of those claiming to be servants of God. One denies God in his works whenever he turns from God's laws, God's teachings, and God's ways to other ways. To own God in our actions is to obey him in all things, to prefer his ways above the ways of all other beings in the universe. To deny him in our works is to prefer other ways to his own ways.

being abominable,—This signifies that the actions of these persons, who professed to be his servants, had made them hateful in the sight of God.

and disobedient,—Rebellious and opposed to all law and order.

and unto every good work reprobate.—Given order to every evil work. Only the things God commands are good works. They are God's works, and he who prefers any other ways than God's cannot do God's works.

4. THE THINGS WHICH BEFIT SOUND DOCTRINE
2: 1-15

1 But speak thou the things which befit the 'sound °doctrine: 2 that aged

1 **But speak thou the things which befit the sound doctrine:** —[The false teachers were promulgating doctrines at variance with the teaching of the inspired Paul and his fellow apostles, and were also by their example and lives fatally lowering the standard of the Christian life. It was to the evil moral influence of these teachers that the attention of Titus was especially directed. These false doctrines were bringing forth already their sure fruit in the form of a life utterly unlike the

men be temperate, grave, sober-minded, ⁵sound in faith, in love, in patience:

⁵Or, *stedfastness*

pattern set by the Master. In contrast to this misleading doctrine, Titus is directed to exhort the various ages and different
sexes, the bond and the free to live such lives as will bring no
dishonor upon the name and cause of Christ. The strictly
practical nature of these charges is remarkable. He presses
home to the various ages and ranks the necessity of a quiet
and useful life. The sound doctrine by which Titus was directed to regulate his teaching stands in clear contrast to the
sickly, unhealthy teaching—fanciful and false—of the misleading teachers of Crete.]

   2 that aged men be temperate,—Not given to excess in anything. It is usually applied to drinking intoxicating spirits,
and it is right to apply it there as well as to other things, but
it means that we ought not to go to excess in anything. Why
was this applicable to old men more than to others? Sometimes people give way to excesses in youth when the flesh
is strong and its lusts almost uncontrollable, but after they
grow older and the will power is stronger they learn self-
control. Later they pass into a second childhood, the will
power fails, and they often fall into the same excesses they did
in youth. The people of whom Paul was writing had in youth
given way to excesses of all kinds. They were babes in Christ
and needed admonishing on many points.

   grave,—Reputable and serious demeanor, not given to lev-
ity or gay manners, but sober in speech, gesture, and dress.

   sober-minded,—Refraining from everything that is harmful
and injurious, and using that which will develop the faculties
and members to the highest degree of activity and efficiency.

   sound in faith,—Cheerful, contented trust in God should be
cultivated—a confidence that God overrules all, and that "all
things work together for good, even to them that are called
according to his purpose." (Rom. 8: 28.) A confidence that
God still overrules all things to the good of those who love
him should aid all God's children to look with a cheerful, contented spirit upon the affairs of this world, and thus drive out
all bitterness and anxiety about the misanthropic condition
that often beclouds and embitters life.

3 that aged women likewise be reverent in demeanor, not slanderers nor en-slaved to much wine, teachers of that which is good; 4 that they may train the young women to love their husbands, to love their children, 5 *to be* so-

in love,—Not bitter or vindictive. Christian love keeps the heart young and tender and sincere, and the aged illustrate its power through advancing in wisdom and kindness.

in patience:—They have to bear with many infirmities of the body with declining faculties; but cheerful patience must be more than a dull acquiescence with the inevitable; it must be cheerful acceptance of suffering that patience may have her perfect work in the closing days of life.

3 that aged women likewise be reverent in demeanor,—Elderly women by their very deportment, regulated by the will of God, were to teach the young women lessons of truth, faith, and love. [Paul, faithful to the instructions of the Holy Spirit, sets forth their position as fellow heirs in the church of Christ, and reminds them of their duties in the company of believers. They must remember that the position to which Christ had called them in his kingdom was not without grave responsibilities. There was a great and important work for them to do.]

not slanderers—There was danger that with the growing influence of years they would become bitter in their feelings and on light grounds bring accusations that were not true.

nor enslaved to much wine,—The women of Crete were given to wine drinking. Observe the fitness of the phrase "enslaved." The drunkard is thoroughly the slave of his appetite. (2 Pet. 2: 18, 19.) The religion of Jesus Christ has created a moral state lifting women out of their evil practices.

teachers of that which is good;—They are to be teachers by their example. The aged naturally are teachers to the young. They should be careful to teach only what is good by either precept or example. [This does not mean that they should be public instructors. (1 Tim. 2: 11, 12.)]

4 that they may train the young women to love their husbands,—Not only must they love their husbands, but they must do to them what love requires at their hands. She loves her husband who is his truest helper in attaining a true and

ber-minded, chaste, workers at home, kind, being in subjection to their own
husbands, that the word of God be not blasphemed : 6 the younger men like-

holy life. [This would be a matter requiring long time and
patience, and would follow as the result of the steady, faithful
performance of those quiet, everyday duties to which God had
in his providence called them.]

to love their children,—To love their children is to "nurture
them in the chastening and admonition of the Lord." (Eph.
6: 4.) Love is the fulfilling of the law. Love to the child is
to do what the law requires the mother to do for the child.
Often mothers from a selfish feeling spoil their children.
They deceive themselves, thinking it is from love. The Scriptures deal in practical questions, not mere sentiments. Solo-
mon said: "He that spareth his rod hateth his son; but he
that loveth him chasteneth him betimes." (Prov. 13: 24.)
That is, he that fails to restain his son and train him in the
right way hates him. Many parents will be made to realize at
the last day that they were the worst enemies of their children
and had led them to ruin; that their mistaken and selfish feeling for them was hatred and not love.

5 **to be sober minded, chaste,**—Well-balanced state of mind
resulting from habitual self-restraint, which gives no grounds
for evil reports.

workers at home,—That they be keepers or managers at
home; keep a neat, attractive house that will make her husband and children love home. Christian women should be the
best of housekeepers and should be models to all who know
them.

kind, being in subjection to their own husbands,—She must
be good and true in her character and recognize that God had
made her husband head, and she should take care that, as far
as in her lies, the law of subordination should be strictly
obeyed.

that the word of God be not blasphemed:—These words
refer to the clauses enforcing home duties. To fail to do them
would cause the word of the Lord which commands them to
be blasphemed—spoken against. Life is made up of small and
simple deeds. Character is composed of many simple quali-

wise exhort to be sober-minded: 7 in all things showing thyself an ensample
of good works; in thy doctrine *showing* uncorruptness, gravity, 8 sound

---

ties, and the honor of the name of the Lord is bound up with
the faithful discharge by Christians of the simple duties of
life. The family is the chief seat, and often the main test of
Christian character, and it is the distinctive feature of humility as ordained of God.

Christians are all built together as one body, sealed and ce-
mented together by the blood and Spirit of Christ, each to
help all others to grow into the body of the Lord Jesus Christ,
a dwelling place of God, through the Spirit on earth. Now,
brethren and sisters, between ourselves and God, how much of
this helping the weaker and tempted brethren and sisters have
we done? Whenever we have left others, especially the weak-
est and humblest ones, to strive alone, we have injured them,
but we have more seriously injured ourselves. When one
member sins all suffer. The spiritual ties are stronger than
the fleshly ones.

6 the younger men likewise exhort to be sober-minded :—
The tendency of youth is to lightheartedness and frolic that
lead to sin. While the Christian religion does not deny the
enjoyment of life to youth, it would hold in proper restraint
that they be sober-minded, and act as becomes Christians.
Because the true happiness here and hereafter is promoted by
restraining the tendencies to excess in lightness and frivolity.

7 in all things showing thyself an ensample of good works;
—While warning others he was to show himself a pattern in
all he taught by example as well as precept. A teacher ought
to practice what he teaches—to preserve his own character for
sincerity and honesty, and that his example may be added to
the precepts in his teaching.

in thy doctrine showing uncorruptness,—His preaching was
to be in maintaining the teaching of Christ as God gave it, unmixed with the teachings and philosophies of men. He must in
all those points of life which are connected with his teaching
show a purity and freedom from all interested motives; he
must be above seeking for popular applause, thus avoiding
the things the serious hearer could condemn.

speech, that cannot be condemned; that he that is of the contrary part may
be ashamed, having no evil thing to say of us. 9 *Exhort* ⁰servants to be in
subjection to their own masters, *and* to be well-pleasing *to them* in all
things; not gainsaying; 10 not purloining, but showing all good fidelity; that

⁰Gr. *bondservants*

---

gravity,—In his public teaching and private intercourse
with the people he must never forget he was the teacher of
the message of eternal life, and that he must have a dignified
manner that vindicates his profound seriousness of purpose
and devotion.

8 sound speech, that cannot be condemned;—In his teaching he was to use sound speech such as produced a good influence, conformable to the word of God.

that he that is of the contrary part may be ashamed,—That
it may be so good in its influence that those who oppose may
be ashamed of the opposition [when he finds neither in the life
nor in the teaching that he can fairly criticize as hurtful to
anyone].

having no evil thing to say of us.—[The "of us" associates
Paul and others with Titus. The evil thing which might have
been said against Titus in reality would be spoken against
Paul and the other apostles, for they all taught the same
thing. The teaching and life of Jesus are so pure and holy, so
unselfish, and so full of goodness that no one can oppose or
deny it. The pure life of the child of God will put to shame
opposition to Christ.]

9 Exhort servants to be in subjection to their own masters,
—Slavery of a bitter form existed at the time of Jesus and the
apostles. While the fundamental principles of the teaching of
Jesus Christ are contrary to the principles and practice of
slavery, Jesus and the Holy Spirit did not propose to violently
break existing relations or disrupt the institutions of earth. It
sanctified and softened all relations of life and gradually cor-
rected the evil through the Spirit of Christ. Slaves were held
by virtue of the political governments. The Christian religion
recognized both parties to the relation as Christians and
brethren. It did not break the relationship, but put into action a spirit of love, gentleness, and fidelity that melted and
brought about the destruction of the relation.

they may adorn the doctrine of God our Saviour in all things. 11 For the grace of God ⁷hath appeared, bringing salvation to all men, 12 instructing us,

⁷Or, *hath appeared to all men, bringing salvation*

---

and to be well-pleasing to them in all things;—The servants were to be faithful and obedient, to seek fidelity of service to please them well [especially they should study to make their service acceptable to the master, avoiding a contrary spirit, or the disposition to set up their own will against the will of the master. It is obvious that "all things" is here limited to things not contrary to God's law. According to the principle, "We must obey God rather than men." (Acts 5 : 29.)]

not gainsaying;—They should obey cheerfully, willingly, without sullenness; not thwarting or setting themselves against their master's plans, or desires, or orders.

10 not purloining,—Taking little things which they think are so small as to be unnoticed. Stealing is a sin to which slaves are especially liable. They reason that they have labored for it without pay and there is no harm in their taking a portion of their own labor. While this seems plausible, the Holy Spirit forbids it.

but showing all good fidelity;—[Many slaves in the days of Paul were entrusted with the property of their masters as merchants, physicians, and artists. Thus they had many ways of showing their honesty. It was in their power to defraud them by embezzlement, or to waste the property, or to allow it to be wasted without check or rebuke. Servants were to have family interests at heart, and they were thus to commend themselves to the love and confidence of their masters.]

that they may adorn the doctrine of God our Saviour in all things.—They are to show all fidelity in their position that they may adorn the teaching that God has given to the world and commend it by their conduct to their masters. [A slave cheerfully accepting his hard lot, and striving to please and advance the interest of his earthly master only for the love of Christ, must have been in those days a silent, yet a most powerful influence which could so mold a character so degraded that scarcely were they considered to rank among men at all. "They were ranked as possessions just like sheep and cattle."]

to the intent that, denying ungodliness and worldly lusts, we should live soberly and righteously and godly in this present ⁸world; 13 looking for the
blessed hope and appearing of the glory ⁹of the great God and our Saviour

⁸Or, *age*
⁹Or, *of our great God and Saviour*

11 **For the grace of God hath appeared,**—God's favor of love
to man appeared in the person of Jesus Christ. The power of
God was manifested and so was the law, but not fully and
clearly his love till Jesus came.

bringing salvation to all men,—Salvation is open to all men,
but man accepts or rejects as he sees fit. The choice is with
him. Jesus opened the door, pointed out the way, and invited
man to return to the Father's home and to the blessings he
enjoyed in heaven. This is what Jesus did for us.

12 **instructing us,**—[Educating us by a life of sad experiences. God's grace is in truth a stern discipline of self-denial
and training for higher and better things.]

to the intent that, denying ungodliness—There is a feeling
in the flesh of rebellion against God. To restrain this feeling
and bring it under subjection to God is to deny ungodliness.

and worldy lusts,—The lusts for the fleshly, worldly things
—lust of the flesh, lust of the pride of life, lust for power, for
riches and honor. To deny ourselves these—to turn from
them—is what the Lord teaches us.

we should live soberly—To live soberly is to discharge the
duty one owes to himself. He is not to give way to appetites,
passions, and lusts, but to so live that by a moderate use of
his faculties he will develop them to the highest point of
strength and activity. He must do his duty to himself before
he can do his duty to others. He who does not live soberly
cannot live righteously. He cannot do his duty to his fellow
man until he discharges those he owes to himself. A drunken
man cannot do his duty to his wife, to his children, to his
neighbors, to his God; but the man who properly controls
himself can discharge his duty to all others.

and righteously—To live righteously is faithfully to discharge our duty to our fellow men in all the relations of life.

and godly—To live godly is to discharge our duties to God.
The obligation and duties we owe in these several relations

Jesus Christ; 14 who gave himself for us, that he might redeem us from all

---

interweave into and overlap each other. They depend upon each other, yet they are distinct and cover man's whole duty.

in this present world;—In the physical world God has ordained that men shall live by food and exercise. The soul takes food in approaching God in worship, which consists in the earnest and devout study of God's word, in prayer, songs of praise to God, and in continuing "stedfastly in the apostles' teaching and fellowship, in the breaking of bread and the prayers." (Acts 2:42.) This food gives no strength without it is assimilated to the wants of the spiritual works which consists in restraining our appetites and passions within proper bounds, in acting kindly toward all men, in showing kindness to those in need, and in actively carrying the word of life to all in darkness. The doing of this spiritual labor in turn gives appetite for earnest and true worship and enables the soul to appreciate its benefits. The best preparation the child ever receives for profitable attendance on the Lord's-day service is attained through fidelity in discharging the duties they owe to their fellow men and to God through the week. It enables them to live soberly, righteously, and godly. As in this world, so in the spiritual world, food gives strength to labor, labor gives appetite for food, and assimilates the food received to the nourishment and growth of the spiritual body.

13 looking for the blessed hope and appearing of the glory of the great God and our Saviour Jesus Christ;—As an incentive to and reward for this faithful discharge of his duties, the faithful Christian is to look forward to that blessed hope and glorious appearing of the great God and our Saviour Jesus Christ. He told them he would come again in the clouds of heaven, and that his appearing would be a glorious one. (Mark 13:26, 27.) He will come to redeem from the grave and crown with everlasting glory and righteousness those that were faithful to him.

14 who gave himself for us,—The fundamental idea of the bloody sacrifice is that he for whom the sacrifice is made deserved death for his sins and the death of the victim is accepted in lieu of that of the sinner. The animals were ac-

iniquity, and purify unto himself a people for his own possession, zealous of
good works.

cepted as temporary and typical sacrifices for sin. They were
temporary, as they took away finally no sin, but only freed
them from it for a season. The sin was rolled forward and
the sinner was held guiltless until the day of atonement, when
there was a remembrance of the sins again, and a sin offering
was made for it anew. It was typical in as much as it pointed
forward to the sacrifice of the Son of God, the shedding of his
blood for the sins of the world. The blood of Jesus alone can
take away sins. So all sins previous to the shedding of his
blood were rolled forward until he came and took away sins
once for all. Then there was no more remembrance of sins
that had been forgiven. To shed his blood for sin was to give
his life for the life of the sinner. Jesus did this for man. Man
had sinned, sold himself to the devil, brought himself under
bondage to him as his servant became subject to death, received the wages of sin so that he died.

that he might redeem us from all iniquity,—To redeem from
iniquity is to lead from all wrongdoing to our fellow men, and
just to the extent that he delivers us from wrongdoing he delivers us from sin and suffering.

and purify unto himself a people for his own possession,—
[As Israel was represented as God's chosen people, his peculiar treasure (Ex. 19: 5, 6; Deut. 7: 6; 14: 2), so Christians are
Christ's own possession, given him by the Father (John 6: 37;
17: 6-8), forming the body of which he is the head (Eph. 1: 22,
23; Col. 1: 18), and made to him "an elect race, a royal priesthood, a holy nation, a people for God's own possession, that
ye may show forth the excellencies of him who called you out
of darkness into his marvellous light: who in time past were
no people, but now are the people of God: who had not obtained mercy, but now have obtained mercy" (1 Pet. 2: 9,
10).]

zealous of good works.—Doing the works of God. They
are good because they conform to the likeness of God and
make us good to man. Nothing brings good to man except
the things commanded by God. To do them honors God and
benefits man. God's honor and man's good are joined to-

15 These things speak and exhort and reprove with all [10]authority. Let
no man despise thee.

[10]Gr. *commandment*

gether in the work he does. The humble can do good works
as well as the mighty. Indeed, exalted positions carry with
them strong temptations, of which we in the humbler spheres
of life know nothing. God requires us to strive day by day to
do something that will help others. If we do so from the
right motives, do it in the name of the Lord, whether it benefits others or not, we shall save our own souls because in so
doing we fit ourselves for a home with God.

15 These things speak and exhort and reprove—The truths
were to be made to bear upon the conscience and to result in
right conduct. He enjoins to dwell on the doctrine of edifica-
tion and never to grow weary because it cannot be too much
inculcated. He likewise bids him to add the spurs of exhortation and reproof for men are not sufficiently admonished as to
their duty if they be not solemnly urged to the performance of
their responsibility.

with all authority. Let no man despise thee.—[The exhortations and reproofs must be characterized by authority so
that none might regard lightly the apostolic instruction. He
must speak with the authority which comes from a knowledge
of the divine will and of the saving purpose of God.]

5. SUNDRY INJUNCTIONS
3 : 1-11

1 Put them in mind to be in subjection to rulers, to authorities, to be
obedient, to be ready unto every good work, 2 to speak evil of no man, not to

**1 Put them in mind to be in subjection to rulers, to authori-
ties, to be obedient,**—At the time this letter was written Nero
was emperor, who was a persecutor of Christians. Paul had
just been released from prison yet showed feeling toward the
rulers or authorities. Jesus and the apostles early in their
ministry taught by precept and example that they should submit to the civil rulers save when they required something of
them contrary to the will of God. Then they "answered and
said unto them, Whether it is right in the sight of God to
hearken unto you rather than unto God, judge ye: for we can-

be contentious, to be gentle, showing all meekness toward all men. 3 For we

not but speak the things which we saw and heard." (Acts 4: 19, 20.) Here he teaches them to be subject to them. They are to conduct themselves thus toward the governments that are seeking to destroy the religion of Christ from the earth. It does not then involve the support or approval of the governments or of their courses, but God directs them to quietly submit to these powers in whatever they require of them, save when they demand something contrary to the law of God.

In view of the fact that the civil government is an ordinance of God, even to the infamous Nero, a minister of God, we must be subject, not only for wrath (for fear of punishment), but also for conscience's sake. That is, as a duty we owe to God, we must submit to them in the place God has put them. Jesus set the example, paying tax. (Matt. 17: 24-27.) Although in doing so he classed himself as a stranger and not a child of human government, the same government concerning which Paul now writes to Titus to instruct the Christians in Crete to be obedient. The same relationship and duties are required by Peter. (1 Pet. 2: 13-16.) Christians are to submit quietly to the ordinances and laws of human governments, seeking to live a quiet and peaceful life. This involves no support or participation in the strifes and conflicts of the governments of the world.

to be ready unto every good work,—This is connected with and defines the works which the Christians may perform in obedience to the civil powers. They could not do an evil work.

2 to speak evil of no man,—They were not to speak evil or contemptuously of these rulers.

not to be contentious,—Not to be guilty of noisy strife in opposing the civil rulers when they are compelled to refuse obedience.

to be gentle,—Their obedience must be in a gentle, kind spirit.

showing all meekness toward all men.—The meekness signifies kindly forbearance, a gentle unresentful spirit under evil treatment unto all men. God's law is that Christians should

also once were foolish, disobedient, deceived, serving divers lusts and plea-sures, living in malice and envy, hateful, hating one another. 4 But when the kindness of God our Saviour, and his love toward man, appeared, 5 not by works *done* in righteousness, which we did ourselves, but according to his

submit to the human governments so far as obedience to God will permit, then when loyalty to God demands disobedience to human governments, the refusal to obey is to be accompa-nied with passive unresisting submission to their penalties.

3 **For we also once were foolish,**—He reminds them that be-fore they became servants of Christ they were without under-standing. "We" refers, as many think, to the Jews. It may mean as showing the feelings cherished in all Christians, Jews and Gentiles alike. They had all been without what God or-dained for good.

disobedient,—Disobedient to the authorities, even when they required nothing wrong at their hands.

deceived,—Deceived as to what was pleasing to God in such matters.

serving divers lusts and pleasures,—Serving their own prej-udices and passions rather than God.

living in malice and envy, hateful, hating one another.— Cultivating malice and envy toward those who had the rule over them, making themselves hated and hating one another. This refers chiefly to the spirit of envy and insubordination that the Jews cultivated toward the Roman rulers. Paul cor-rects all that temper among Christians and tells them that the kind, gentle spirit is that which conquers even the civil rulers.

4 **But when the kindness of God our Saviour, and his love toward man, appeared,**—But after God had shown his kind-ness and love to man in the coming of Jesus Christ to suffer and die for men, Paul came to see that the spirit of envy and hatred was contrary to God and his spirit of dealing with men. God's love to man while yet in enmity toward him, his over-coming men's hatred with love, with a new revelation to man as to how he should conquer hatred and overcome evil.

5 **not by works done in righteousness, which we did our-selves,**—God saved men from this sinful course that cultivated the spirit of hatred and bitterness to the civil rulers and to-ward all that evil entreated and opposed them.

mercy he saved us, through the [11]washing of regeneration [12]and renewing of the Holy Spirit, 6 which he poured out upon us richly, through Jesus Christ

[11]Or, *laver*
[12]Or, *and* through *renewing*

but according to his mercy he saved us,—Christ saved them from the course of wickedness, not through works of righteousness which they had done before the coming of Jesus that merited salvation.

through the washing of regeneration and renewing of the Holy Spirit,—Moved by his own mercy, he saved us through the washing of regeneration and the renewing of the Holy Spirit. There are two applications of the word righteousness in the Scriptures. Here the washing or bath of regeneration refers to baptism. It means the washing or bath connected with regeneration. Here the righteousness which we did that did not bring salvation is placed in contrast with baptism. When Jesus came to John to be baptized of him, "John would have hindered him, . . . but Jesus answering said unto him, Suffer it now: for thus it becometh us to fulfill all righteousness" (Matt. 3: 14, 15), making baptism a part of righteousness. There is a righteousness of God, and there is a righteousness that comes through the ways and works of man. Baptism is a part of God's way of making man righteous. So is a renewing of the Holy Spirit. The Jews were not saved on account of any righteousness they had done before Christ came to merit it but moved by his own mercy to men he saved them through the washing of regeneration and renewing of the Holy Spirit. He first sent his Spirit to renew man. The Spirit came to the apostles, through them preached Christ to the world, produced faith, changed the heart, directed the life anew, and the heart renewed, the person was baptized into Christ, put off the old man of sin now dead, was buried with him in Christ, washed away his sins, and arose to a new life in Jesus Christ. The relation of these facts to each other and the connection of each of them to the remission of sins, entrance into the name of Christ, God, and salvation by the same word, settle beyond dispute that they are for the same end or thing. Man must believe into Christ, but his believing carries him through repentance and baptism before he is in

our Saviour; 7 that, being justified by his grace, we might be made [13]heirs according to the hope of eternal life. 8 Faithful is the saying, and concern-

[13]Or, *heirs, according to hope, of eternal life*

Christ. Repentance comes from faith, but it leads through baptism to the remission of sins. Faith that stops short of repentance and baptism does not carry the believer into Christ. These facts settle the office of faith, repentance, and baptism.

6 **which he poured out upon us richly,**—God shed forth his Holy Spirit through Jesus Christ abundantly on the apostles at Pentecost. The power was shed forth in such abundance that they were overwhelmed, baptized in the Spirit.

through Jesus Christ our Saviour;—Jesus Christ said: "I will pray the Father, and he shall give you another Comforter, that he may be with you for ever." (John 14: 16.) "But when the Comforter is come, whom I will send unto you from the Father, even the Spirit of truth, which proceedeth from the Father, he shall bear witness of me." (John 15: 26.)

7 **that, being justified by his grace, we might be made heirs according to the hope of eternal life.**—The Holy Spirit was bestowed to guide those justified by the mercy of God to fit them to be heirs of God of the eternal life that had been promised those who love God. [This life eternal is still for us in the future, though ever present in respect of hope; children we indeed are and sharers in many good gifts of our Father, but eternal life, that glorious inheritance, is still in the future; but it is a sure hope, eternal life, the hope of which is the mainspring of all Christian work and activity, though it includes it, of course, is something far more than merely endless existence. A veil, impenetrable to mortal eyes in the Father's house of "many mansions." (John 14: 2.) "It is not yet made manifest what we shall be. We know that, if he shall be manifested, . . . we shall see him even as he is" (1 John 3: 2), "and so shall we ever be with the Lord" (1 Thess. 4: 17). And with these thoughts and words we are to comfort one another.]

8 **Faithful is the saying,**—That which he had just said is a faithful saying, and he desired these truths to be taught confidently that they who have believed in God might be careful to

ing these things I desire that thou affirm confidently, to the end that they who have believed God may be careful to ¹maintain good works. These things are good and profitable unto men: 9 but shun foolish questionings, and genealogies, and strifes, and fightings about the law; for they are unprofita-

¹Or, *profess honest occupations*

maintain good works. "For we are his workmanship, created in Christ Jesus for good works, which God afore prepared that we should walk in them." (Eph. 2: 10.)

and concerning thse things I desire that thou affirm confidently,—[He willed that over and over again these words be repeated by the faithful believers in the Lord to remind them, not only of the glorious hope of eternal life, but also to bring him to their remembrance to whom they owed this glorious heritage. And as they repeat or hear these words, telling of the wondrous mercy showed to them for no merit of their own, they will the more willingly think thankfully of and act loyally with other people still living in that deep and loathsome darkness where they once dwelt until God in his mercy sent unto them the message of life and delivered them.]

to the end that they who have believed God may be careful to maintain good works.—All incentives to a life of loyal obedience comes from a sense of God's grace in bringing to us the message of salvation. "We love [God], because he first loved us." (1 John 4: 19.) "For the love of Christ constraineth us; because we thus judge, that one died for all, therefore all died; and he died for all, that they that live should no longer live unto themselves, but unto him who for their sakes died and rose again." (2 Cor. 5: 14, 15.) The doctrines which unfold to us that marvelous self-moved grace, therefore, are to be strongly and constantly insisted upon to incite to a life of holiness. Good works, not merely benevolence, but an honorable and holy life.

These things are good and profitable unto men:—They were ordained for man's good. It profits man to walk in them.

9 but shun foolish questionings, and genealogies,—The Jews especially were given to questions of genealogy, still relying on descent from Abraham.

ble and vain. 10 A factious man after a first and second admonition ²re-
fuse; 11 knowing that such a one is perverted, and sinneth, being self-condemned.

²Or, *avoid*

---

and strifes, and fightings about the law;—Connected with
these were many foolish, frivolous, unprofitable questions not
taught in the Scriptures and bringing no good to men.

for they are unprofitable and vain.—These, as all questions
of human reasoning, are unprofitable and vain. [These dis-
turb and embitter the feelings; they lead to the indulgence of
a bad spirit; they are often difficult to be settled; and they are
of no practical importance even if they could be determined.]

10 A factious man—A factious man is one that creates strife
and division. These questions and practices not taught by
God all gender strife. He who persists in introducing these
subjects not taught in the Scriptures is a heretic and excites
division.

after a first and second admonition refuse;—He is to be admonished as to the evil of his course a first and second time,
and if he does not desist, he is to be rejected. Introducing
questions and practices not required by the word of God is a
cause of strife and division, and the man who cannot be convinced that he is wrong in doing it must be excluded from the
membership of the church. The failure to do this brings division and strife into the churches.

11 knowing that such a one is perverted, and sinneth, being
self-condemned.—He that brings such things in the church is
turned away from the way of salvation. The way of salvation
is to walk only in the way God has marked out—do only the
things he has required. A man who persists in introducing
things not commanded by God walks directly against the way
of salvation, sins, and brings condemnation upon himself.

6. DIRECTIONS RESPECTING INDIVIDUALS
AND BENEDICTION
3: 12-15

12 When I shall send Artemas unto thee, or Tychicus, give diligence to

---

12 When I shall send Artemas unto thee, or Tychicus,—Artemas is not mentioned elsewhere. Tychicus is mentioned

come unto me to Nicopolis: for there I have determined to winter. 13 Set forward Zenas the lawyer and Apollos on their journey diligently, that nothing be wanting unto them. 14 And let our *people* also learn to ¹maintain good works for necessary ²uses, that they be not unfruitful.

²Or, *wants*

several times as a messenger of the churches in carrying the contribution to Jerusalem and in communicating with Paul. (Acts 20: 4; Eph. 6: 21; Col. 4: 7; 2 Tim. 4: 12.) Artemas doubtless served the same offices.

give diligence to come unto me to Nicopolis:—The Nicopolis to which Paul urged Titus to come is probably the city of that name situated on the southeast promontory of Epirus in Greece. If this view is correct, Paul's labors most likely extended to Italy. Nicopolis was situated only a few miles from Preveza, the chief city of Epirus today.

for there I have determined to winter.—Nicopolis is in a warm climate, and Paul was now old and feeble and enjoyed the warm weather.

13 Set forward Zenas the lawyer—It is quite likely that before Zenas became a Christian he had been a Jewish lawyer. The lawyers were a class of Jewish teachers who were especially learned in the Mosaic law, and who interpreted that law and taught it to the people. Nothing more is known of Zenas than is contained in this passage.

and Apollos on their journey diligently, that nothing be wanting unto them.—Apollos is mentioned as a colaborer of Paul on several occasions. They were traveling together somewhere and Paul directs Titus to bring them on their journey diligently, and see that they were in want of nothing. They were doubtless on a journey preaching, and, possibly like Titus, going to see Paul for the last time.

14 And let our people also learn to maintain good works for necessary uses, that they be not unfruitful.—Let Christians turn to work at things that are good to supply needful purposes. In this help rendered to others, they are not unfruitful. [These injunctions laid the foundation of those great works of love—all undreamed of before the death and resurrection of Jesus Christ but have been for nineteen centuries the glory of the religion of the Lord Jesus Christ, one grand result of the

15 All that are with me salute thee. Salute them that love us in faith. Grace be with you all.

Master's coming to this earth, which even his bitterest enemies admire with a grudging admiration. In these "pastoral Epistles" we have eight special reminders to be earnest and zealous in good works. There was evidently in the mind of Paul as guided by the Holy Spirit an anticipation that some who professed to be followers of the Lord would content themselves with a dreamy acquiescence in the great truths, while the life remained unaltered. It is noteworthy that in these Epistles containing so many urgent exhortations to work for Christ are among his last inspired utterances. The passages are 1 Tim. 2: 10; 5: 10; 6: 18; 2 Tim. 2: 21; Tit. 1: 16; 2: 7, 14; 3: 14.]

15 **All that are with me salute thee.**—All the brethren where Paul was sent salutations to Titus. They are not named because the individuals composing the company of Paul were most likely known to Titus.

Salute them that love us in faith.—An inclusive greeting, embracing each member of the church in Crete, whose love to Paul was based upon the common faith in the Lord Jesus.

Grace be with you all.—He prays that God's favors and power might rest upon all of them.

COMMENTARY ON THE EPISTLE
TO PHILEMON

CONTENTS

INTRODUCTION TO PHILEMON

Paul may have written many private letters during his long life, but only one has come down to us, and that one is very brief and weighty. It was addressed to Philemon at Colosse, one who had become obedient to the faith through the labors of Paul. He was a zealous Christian, in whose house the church met. The Epistle was written and sent at the same time as that to the Colossians.

It was a letter of commendation of a slave of Philemon, who had run away from his master on account of some offense which he had committed. By some means he fell under the influence of Paul in Rome, who taught him the gospel, to which he became obedient, and then desired to return to his master.

The Epistle is purely personal, yet very significant. Paul omits his usual introductory words—"an apostle of Jesus Christ"—and substitutes the touching designation, "a prisoner of Jesus Christ," thereby going directly to the heart of his beloved friend and brother in Christ.

The Epistle introduces us into a Christian household consisting of father (Philemon), mother (Apphia), and son (Archippus) who was at the same time a fellow soldier, a Christian minister, and a slave (Onesimus). This shows the effect of Christianity upon society at a crucial point where heathenism was utterly helpless. It touches on the institution of slavery, which lay like an incubus upon the whole heathen world, and was interwoven into the whole structure of domestic and public life.

The effect of the gospel upon this gigantic social evil is that of a peaceful and gradual cure from within, by teaching the common origin and equality of human beings, their common redemption and Christian brotherhood, by emancipation of them from slavery unto spiritual freedom, equality and brotherhood in Christ where "there can be neither Jew nor Greek, there can be neither bond nor free, there can be no male and female; for ye all are one man in Christ Jesus." (Gal. 3: 28.) This principle and the corresponding practice wrought first an amelioration and ultimately the abolition of slavery. The process was very slow and retarded by the counteracting influence of love of gain and power and all the sinful passions of men; but it was sure and is now almost, if not complete, throughout the Christian world, while paganism and Mohammedanism regards slavery as a normal state of society, and hence do not make even an attempt to remove it. It was the only wise way to follow in dealing with the subject. A proclamation of emancipation from them would have resulted in a bloody revolution in which Christianity itself would have been buried.

Paul accordingly sent back Onesimus to his rightful master, yet under a new character, no more a contemptible thief and runaway, but a new man in Christ Jesus and a beloved brother, with a touching request that Philemon might receive him as kindly as he would Paul himself, yea as his own heart. (16, 17.) Such advice took the sting out of slavery; the form remained; the thing was gone. What a contrast! In the eyes of the heathen philosophers, Onesimus, like every other slave, was but a chattel; in the eyes of Paul, a redeemed child of God and an heir of eternal life which is far better than freedom.

This Epistle was written from Rome some time in the year 62 at about the same time that Ephesians and Colossians were written.

COMMENTARY ON THE EPISTLE TO PHILEMON

1. SALUTATION
1-3

1 Paul, a prisoner of Christ Jesus, and Timothy [1]our brother, to Philemon our beloved and fellow-worker, 2 and to Apphia [2]our sister, and to Archippus our fellow-soldier, and to the church in thy house: 3 Grace to you and peace from God our Father and the Lord Jesus Christ.

[1]Gr. *the brother*
[2]Gr. *the sister*

1 **Paul, a prisoner of Christ Jesus,**—Paul was now a prisoner at Rome. It is interesting to note the name "prisoner" is here used instead of "apostle" as in the Colossian Epistle written at the same time. There Paul's captivity is dwelt upon mainly as a ground of thankfulness. Here on the contrary in this personal Epistle and in accordance with his courtesy not to command, but for love's sake to entreat.

and Timothy our brother,—Timothy may have written this Epistle as he did those written to the Ephesians and Colossians.

to Philemon our beloved and fellow-worker,—Philemon was evidently a man of some wealth and standing in the city and church, and was an earnest worker for the Lord Jesus Christ. On account of his devotion to Christ, he calls him "our beloved," and on account of his labors for the advancement of the cause of Christ "and fellow-workers." In that age all Christians were expected to be active in the service of the church, and the distinction between "the clergy and the laity" was unknown. The probabilities are that Philemon was a public teacher in the church at Colosse and probably a laborer in the surrounding country and towns.

2 **and to Apphia our sister,**—It is safe to conclude from the connection of the names that Apphia was the wife of Philemon.

and to Archippus our fellow-soldier,—It is not known who he was, but it is supposed that as a member of his household he was a son.

and to the church in thy house;—A church met in Philemon's house, as they frequently met in the houses of prominent and active members in the church. [We have here a glimpse of a quiet Christian home in the early days of the church. The gospel makes the most solid progress when the family is converted and consecrated to Christ. The gospel impresses upon the sacred duty of showing piety at home. As the joining of Timothy's name is giving the salutation did not prevent the Epistle from being Paul's only, so the church in the house in receiving the salutation does prevent its being addressed only to Philemon and his family, who were, like himself, interested in Onesimus.]

3 **Grace to you and peace from God our Father and the Lord Jesus Christ.**—[Grace is the unmerited but all-comprehensive favor of God and peace an enjoyment resulting from grace and a blessing to be diligently sought and increasingly cultivated. Grace and peace comprise heaven's choicest benedictions.]

2. THANKSGIVING FOR PHILEMON'S LOVE AND FELLOWSHIP
4-7

4 I thank my God always, making mention of thee in my prayers, 5 hearing of ³thy love, and of the faith which thou hast toward the Lord Jesus, and toward all the saints; 6 that the fellowship of thy faith may become effectual, in the knowledge of every good thing which is in ⁴you, unto Christ. 7

³Or, *thy love and faith*
⁴Many ancient authorities read *us*

4 **I thank my God always, making mention of thee in my prayers,**—[The frequent expression of Paul's thanks and prayers indicates his habitual devoutness of spirit. A prayerful heart is keenly appreciative to the least evidence of Christian excellence, and joyfully thanks God as the source and giver of all good. Prayer and gratitude are usually blended together.]

5 **hearing of thy love, and of the faith which thou hast toward the Lord Jesus, and toward all the saints;**—His thanksgiving for them and prayers in their behalf were aroused to greater activity by hearing of the love and faith they manifested by their labors and sacrifices for the sake of the Lord Jesus and toward all the saints.

6 **that the fellowship of thy faith may become effectual, in the knowledge of every good thing which is in you, unto**

For I had much joy and comfort in thy love, because the hearts of the saints
have been refreshed through thee, brother.

Christ.—The followship of the saints, to which his faith in
Christ led him in helping them. Paul had heard, and because
of this, he prayed that it might become effectual in leading
others to practice every good thing in them in Christ Jesus
that his example might lead others to practice all good that
was in him for the Lord.

**7 For I had much joy and comfort in thy love, because the
hearts of the saints have been refreshed through thee,**—Paul
uses the word "refreshed" to express the relief and rest given
by Philemon because he had encouraged and refreshed the
souls of the saints by his labors and gifts in their behalf.

brother.—The term "brother" is applied to Philemon here
and in verse 20 with a marked emphasis of affection evidently
implying some special intimacy of friendship and love. In
this place the title "brother" has a peculiar appropriateness,
for Paul had been speaking of the love of Philemon, which
made him a brother indeed to all the spiritual family of God.

3. INTERCESSION FOR ONESIMUS
8-22

8 Wherefore, though I have all boldness in Christ to enjoin thee that
which is befitting, 9 yet for love's sake I rather beseech, being such a one as
Paul [5]the eged, and now a prisoner also of Christ Jesus: 10 I beseech thee
for my child, whom I have begotten in my bonds, 6 Onesimus, 11 who once

[5]Or, *an ambassador, and now &c.*
[6]The Greek word means *Helpful.* Comp. ver. 20 marg.

**8 Wherefore, though I have all boldness in Christ to enjoin
thee that which is befitting,**—While, owing to the fact that he
had been instrumental in converting Philemon, he might be
bold to urge him to do the thing that is proper toward
Onesimus.

**9 yet for love's sake I rather beseech, being such a one as
Paul the aged, and now a prisoner also of Christ Jesus:**—Paul
preferred asking Philemon through love, rather than commanding him because of any authority he might have over
those whom he had taught the truth, to do what was proper in
that concerning what he writes to him.

was unprofitable to thee, but now is profitable to thee and to me: 12 whom I
have sent back to thee in his own person, that is, my very heart; 13 whom
I would fain have kept with me, that in thy behalf he might minister unto
me in the bonds of the ⁷gospel: 14 but without thy mind I would do nothing;

⁷Gr. *good tidings.* See marginal note on Mt. 4. 23

10 **I beseech thee for my child, whom I have begotten in my
bonds, Onesimus,**—His entreaty was in behalf of Onesimus,
whom Paul during his imprisonment had converted to Christ.
He calls it a begetting. [The wish of love is all-powerful with
loving hearts, and its faintest whisper louder and more con-
straining than all the trumpets of Sinai.]

11 **who once was unprofitable to thee, but now is profitable
to thee and to me:**—Onesimus was a slave belonging to Philemon. He had run away from him, and while in that rebellious
spirit was unprofitable to him. But he had gone to Rome,
met Paul, who taught him the gospel, and since his conversion to Christ would render service that would be profitable
both to Paul and Philemon. He had already been helpful to
Paul after his conversion. How he returns to Colosse to serve
his master with the fidelity of a Christian. This will render
his service profitable.

12 **whom I have sent back to thee in his own person, that is,
my very heart:**—Paul sent him back to his own master to
serve him. The Christian religion does not destroy the relations regulated by the civil laws. It sanctifies, makes the
Christian use them for the good of others, and with the fidelity with which he would serve God. The Spirit through Paul
says: "Servants, obey in all things them that are you masters
according to the flesh; not with eye service, as menpleasers,
but in singleness of heart, fearing the Lord: whatsoever ye do,
work heartily, as unto the Lord, and not unto men; knowing
that from the Lord ye shall receive the recompense of the inheritance: ye serve the Lord Christ." (Col. 3: 22-24.) This
shows that God takes the service as rendered to himself and
requires it to be with the fidelity with which he requires service to himself. Paul sent him to Philemon and asked him to
receive him in the kindness of love—my own best beloved—
begotten of myself.

13 **whom I would fain have kept with me, that in thy
behalf he might minister unto me in the bonds of the gospel:**

that thy goodness should not be as of necessity, but of free will. 15 For
perhaps he was therefore parted *from thee* for a season, that thou shouldest
have him for ever; 16 no longer as a ⁸servant, but more than a ⁸servant, a
brother beloved, specially to me, but how much rather to thee, both in the
flesh and in the Lord. 17 If then thou countest me a partner, receive him as

⁸Gr. *bondservant*

——Onesimus was a helper to Paul in his bonds. Paul was now
becoming old and needed help. He intimates that Philemon
would and should help him if he were near, and he felt that
Philemon would not object to his retaining Onesimus to minister to him in his stead, but, lest help so rendered might appear to be forced and not voluntary, he refused to retain him
and sent him to his master—the bonds of the gospel—the
bonds to which fidelity to the gospel brought him.

14 but without thy mind I would do nothing; that thy goodness should not be as of necessity, but of free will.—This
shows that he required Onesimus to return to the relation
which the civil law imposed upon him. He did not permit
Onesimus to surrender his right. He required both to act in
the relation according to the spirit of Christ. True fidelity and
love in both parties to it.

15 For perhaps he was therefore parted from thee for a season, that thou shouldest have him for ever;—His running
away, Paul suggests, was a departing for a season that he
might receive him again in a condition that he will never seek
to evade the duties pertaining to his responsibilities again.
[The phrase "for ever" is the word always used for "eternal."
The contrast with "for a season" might be satisfied here by
the merely relative sense of "perpetual" or "lifelong service";
but considering that the phrase is used in direct reference to
the brotherhood in Christ, it is better to take it in its absolute
sense of fellowship in the life eternal.]

16 no longer as a servant, but more than a servant,—Not
now simply as a slave, but as a brother in Christ to be trusted
and loved in the station he occupies. In these words we have
the principle which is absolutely destructive of the condition
of slavery—a condition which is the exaggeration of natural
inferiority to the effacement of the deeper natural equality.

a brother b e l o v e d,—T h e s e natural ties are not only
strengthened by duty, but made living ties by the love which

myself. 18 But if he hath wronged thee at all, or oweth *thee* aught, put that to mine account; 19 I Paul write it with mine own hand, I will repay it: that I say not unto thee that thou owest to me even thine own self besides. 20 Yea, brother, let me have ¹joy of thee in the Lord: refresh my heart in Christ.

¹Or, *help.* Comp. ver. 10 marg.

delights indeed to respect the rights of others, but is not content without willingness to sacrifice even our own rights to them.

specially to me, but how much rather to thee,—Paul first emphasizes his own love for Onesimus, which, indeed, breathes in every line of the Epistle; but then goes on to infer in Philemon a yet greater affection toward Onesimus, a spiritual love toward the "brother beloved."

both in the flesh and in the Lord.—But if beloved and trusted by me for my sake, how much rather on your own account, as he is connected with you both in the flesh according to the civil government that regulates his fleshly relation and according to the law of God regulating your spiritual relations.

17 If then thou countest me a partner, receive him as myself.—If therefore you have a fellowship for me, treat him as you would me. This does not break the civil relation, but receive him as you would receive me were I related to you as he is.

18 But if he hath wronged thee at all, or oweth thee aught, put that to mine account;—If he has wronged you by fleeing from you, or is indebted to you in any way, put that on my account. He had received service from Onesimus and was willing to assume obligations that he had evaded by running away. So he says charge it to my account. Paul placed Onesimus in a position where he could return without being called upon to suffer for failures while he was in Rome, where he was converted to Christ.

19 I Paul write it with mine own hand, I will repay it:—Paul says he wrote this proposition with his own hand and would repay the injury done by his running away. He intimates to him that he (Paul) was instrumental in saving Philemon so he was under obligations to him for the salvation of his own soul. Philemon could afford to accede to his request.

21 Having confidence in thine obedience I write unto thee, knowing that
thou wilt do even beyond what I say. 22 But withal prepare me also a lodging: for I hope that through your prayers I shall be granted unto you.

**that I say not unto thee that thou owest to me even thine
own self besides.**—He admonished him to do what he had requested and so let him have joy of him in the Lord—gratify
the desires of my heart in that I will be refreshed and cheered
in Christ by your course in this matter.

20 **Yea, brother, let me have joy of thee in the Lord: refresh
my heart in Christ.**—In these words he admonishes Philemon
to do as he requested—gratify the desires of my heart that I
will be refreshed and cheered in Christ by your course in this
matter.

21 **Having confidence in thine obedience I write unto thee,
knowing that thou wilt do even beyond what I say.**—[In
verse 8 he had waived his right to enjoin, for he had rather
appeal through love and request. But here he sounds the note
of authority and then passes to affection and trust. He here
uses the word obedience, and in such a way as to connect it
with love and the privilege of his friends. He trusts Philemon's obedience because he knows his love and is sure it is
love of such devotion that it will not stand on the exact measure, but will delight to do even more than is asked. Men will
do much to fulfill generous expectations. When love enjoins,
there will be trust in its tones, and it will act like a magnet to
draw into duty and obedience. A heart truly touched by the
love of Christ never seeks to know the lowest limit of duty,
but the highest possibility of service.]

22 **But withal prepare me also a lodging:**—Paul expected
soon to visit Colosse and to be with Philemon at his home so
admonishes him to have a room ready for him when he should
come. [It is most likely that this clause was added that Philemon might be moved with joy at the prospect of his coming
at an early date, and also that he might be the more zealous to
do everything that Paul desired him to do that nothing
should be lacking when he comes.]

**for I hope that through your prayers I shall be granted unto
you.**—The efficacy, which is ascribed to prayer, is a great encouragement to God's people to have recourse to prayer in

their trials, agreeable to the exhortation and example of Christ and his apostles. But effectual prayer must be offered "in faith" (James 1: 6)—in full persuasion of the goodness and power of God. Jesus said: "If ye abide in me, and my words abide in you, ask whatsoever ye will, and it shall be done unto you." (John 15: 7.) And it must be according to his will, for the inspired man of God says: "And this is the boldness which we have toward him, that, if we ask anything according to his will, he heareth us." (1 John 5: 14.) Our petitions, whether for ourselves or others, are to be offered with submission to the will and wisdom of God; and the highest confidence which can be entertained concerning them is that which Paul here expresses: "I hope that through your prayers I shall be granted unto you." Certainly Paul was satisfied with the outcome, for he said, as the Holy Spirit moved him: "And we know that to them that love God all things work together for good, even to them that are called according to his purpose." (Rom. 8: 28.)

4. SALUTATIONS AND BENEDICTIONS
23-25

23 Epaphras, my fellow-prisoner in Christ Jesus, saluteth thee; 24 *and so do* Mark, Aristarchus, Demas, Luke, my fellow-workers.

23 Ephaphras, my fellow prisoner in Christ Jesus, saluteth thee;—He calls Epaphras "my fellow-servant" in Col. 1: 7; 4: 12. Here he calls him "my fellow-prisoner in Christ Jesus." He lived at Colosse. He seems to have been a messenger going between Paul and the churches, and may have been imprisoned at this time, or he may have suffered imprisonment at some former period, and Paul called him his fellow prisoner on that account.

24 and so do Mark,—Mark had aforetime been unfaithful to Paul (Acts 13: 13; 15: 36-41) which caused a serious breach between Paul and Barnabas. [But at a later time he is marked out as useful as ministering. (2 Tim. 4: 11.) Paul's firmness in refusing at whatever cost to take with him an unworthy man we may presume had aroused Mark to a better spirit.]

Aristarchus,—He was a Macedonian, had accompanied Paul in his return from Macedonia. (Acts 19: 29.) He had accom-

25 The grace of [2]our Lord Jesus Christ be with your spirit. [3]Amen.

[2]Some ancient authorities read *the*
[3]Many ancient authorities omit *Amen*

panied him on his journey to Jerusalem as one chosen to go with him to carry the bounty of the Macedonian churches to the poor saints in Jerusalem. (Acts 20: 4.) He was with Paul when he was taken prisoner, and was either himself sent as a prisoner or voluntarily accompanied him to Rome and remained with him during his imprisonment. (Acts 27: 2.)

Demas,—Demas was one of Paul's companions in Rome (Col. 4: 14), but seems after Paul's second imprisonment to have forsaken him, "having loved this present world." (2 Tim. 4: 10.)

Luke, my fellow-workers.—Luke was doubtless the beloved physician (Col. 4: 14) and the traveling companion of Paul, who wrote Acts of Apostles and the Gospel of Luke, and during his second imprisonment (2 Tim. 4: 11) was the only one of Paul's companions who remained with him. He here calls all these his fellow laborers.

25 **The grace of our Lord Jesus Christ be with your spirit. Amen.**—This includes with Philemon, Apphia, Archippus, and the church in the house of Philemon. It invokes on their spirit the free, rich favor of Christ, with all the fullness of the blessing it brings.

APPENDIX

APPOINTMENT OF ELDERS AND THEIR DUTIES

There lies before me the following inquiry: "Our congregation recently having had what seems to me an unusual experience, I write to request that you give your views on a question which has disturbed our minds very much. On account of some differences, our elders thought best to resign and offered their resignations, which were accepted. No others as yet having been found who were willing to undertake the work of the eldership, our deacons, thinking that too much responsibility would be thrown upon them, asked that an *advisory committee* be chosen by the church in order that some older brethren might be present at the official meetings to give their advice and vote upon questions affecting the welfare of the church. This course was adopted, the committee chosen, myself being of the number. I declined to serve, thinking it an unscriptural position—that if adopted by the church and found to work satisfactorily, they might conclude they would need no elders in the future.

"There seemed to me to the danger of God's plan of church government being set aside, superseded by men's plans, some of whom unfortunately appear willing to try to correct the mistakes that God has made in matters pertaining to the church. I held that until we appointed elders our deacons could consult with the whole church or any older members without naming a 'committee' as a substitute for the eldership.

"I do not wish to occupy a wrong position in the matter; if you differ with me, I would be thankful for any light you may be able to give on the subject."

We cannot be too cautious in adding functions to the church not ordained by God. The failure or perversion of those created by God does not justify our setting them aside or superseding them with an order not ordained by God. The judges of Israel were appointed by God. But when the sons of Samuel walked "not in his ways but turned aside after lucre, and took bribes, and perverted justice," the people desired to change the order and make a king rather than live under the rule of the judges. "And Jehovah said unto Samuel, Hearken unto the voice of the people in all that they say

unto thee: for they have not rejected thee, but they have rejected me, that I should not be king over them. According to
all the works which they have done since the day that I
brought them up out of Egypt even unto this day, in that they
have forsaken me, and served other gods, so do they also unto
thee. Now therefore hearken unto their voice: howbeit thou
shalt protest solemnly unto them, and shalt show them the
manner of the king that shall reign over them." (1 Sam. 8:
3-9.)

God's spiritual order now is sealed by the blood of Jesus
Christ. It is more sacred than the old order sealed by the
blood of bulls and goats. Because it may fall into improper
hands, be ineffective or be perverted at times, is no reason it
should be set aside. It is better to bear with evils and trust
with patience and time to correct the wrongs that afflict than
to change God's order. To change God's order puts the matter in such shape that all work, all effort or success works
harm, leads from God.

When the order is changed, and a wrong plan is put in operation, the more successfully it works, the farther and farther
it gets away from God. It is like finding a bad place in the
right road. If we, to avoid the place, take another road, the
smoother it is, and the greater speed we make on it, the farther we go wrong. The only way of safety before God is to
take his appointed way and resolutely stick to it, even though
the places seem to be rough and many obstacles lie in the
way.

The question of changing an eldership is one of the most
difficult problems connected with church work. We find
nothing concerning the matter in the New Testament, either
by precept or example, save the admonition that an accusation
against an elder is not to be received save on the testimony of
two or three witnesses. I make this the occasion to speak of
the duty of the elders. I am not sure that it is right for an
eldership to resign. If one or two inefficient members are
among the elders, they ought to be kindly and frankly conferred with on the subject, and induced to withdraw, or with
the consent and agreement of the elders and of the older members of the church, one might be dismissed from the eldership.

But it would be a rare case that a whole eldership would be of such character that all should be dismissed.

Some may be fitted for the eldership and others not. Those fitted should not be treated as those unfitted are. That would be unjust and disastrous to the order of God.

These resignations are usually based on the idea of popular rule in the church. The idea is the elders have received their authority by the popular election of the church from the multitude of disciples and when dissatisfaction arises they return it to those from whom they received it. The elders do not receive their authority by the popular vote of the church. They receive their authority from the Lord. "Take heed unto yourselves, and to all the flock, in which the Holy Spirit hath made you bishops." (Acts 20 : 28.)

The Holy Spirit makes men overseers of the flock of God just as much now as he did in the days of the apostles.

When the apostles of teachers needed help at Jerusalem to look after the Grecian widows that were neglectd he gave the qualifications and told the disciples to look out among them men possessing these. They did so and they appointed them to the work. This was done by the Holy Spirit. (Acts 6: 1-4.) Whenever a church under the same directions of the Holy Spirit selects men having the qualifications given by the Spirit, the Spirit appoints them just as much as it did at Jerusalem. Inspired men did not select. The disciples selected under direction of the Spirit.

This selection was made under the restrictions that the younger were to submit to the older, and that God did not permit women to teach or exercise authority in the church. This would limit the selection to the older men of the congregation. When they selected they were to look out among them men of certain qualifications. "Look ye out" carries the idea of consulting among themselves, and reaching an agreement. This consulting and conferring must be had with the younger and the women that there may be no accusation against those selected. But the older men must make the decision, not by a vote, but by agreement reached through this consulting and seeking out.

There is no provision or example of how a mistake in the selection could be rectified, but it is reason the same class ought to decide whether they made a mistake in selecting, or whether some worthy had turned from their steadfastness.

Unanimity should be sought for in the selection or in the setting aside one selected. Elders are placed in position by the Spirit of God to rule under the divine law. This means to hold in restraint the unruly and to check the currents of excitement that would carry the multitude in wrong courses. For elders to resign, simply because they sometimes were compelled to stand against the current of the multitude, would be to shrink from the work to which they were especially appointed.

If rulers in human governments resign every time the current of popular opinion is against them, they defeat the very ends for which constitutions and laws and rules are made. They are made to restrain the passions and excitements of the multitudes within the limits and restrictions of right as defined in the laws. For the elders to resign because the people go wrong is to fail of the chief end and the special occasions for which God appointed them. It is to break down all rule and respect for God's law and to work the ruin of the church. While everybody is going in the right way, and of their own accord doing right, laws and rulers are not needed. The elders are appointed by God to teach and lead them in the way of truth, and to stay the current when the people go wrong. If they resign when trouble comes and the people go wrong, they fail in the vital point of duty.

The tendency now is to let the women, and the preacher run the church. They supersede the eldership, displace them in their work. The women and the preachers try to displace all elders who refuse to submit to their dictation. It is the duty of the elders firmly to rsist this tendency and to refuse to surrender the trust committed to them. They should maintain the divine order, and if any become so dissatisfied with that order as to create division and strife, let them go out; but to the elders, the trust of preserving the church in its integrity and fidelity to the word of God is committed, and to resign the trust, when the divine order is threatened with subversion

and destruction, is to be recreant to duty. A church not true
to the word of God, that deliberately turns from God's order,
is not a church of God, and unless it repents, the sooner it dies
the better. If it does not die, it must be rejected as apostate.

The elders are the scriptural representatives of the church.
The presumption is with them. The courts of the country so
regard them. And if they surrender the church to the rule of
the women and children and the preacher, the blame is theirs.
Elders sometimes go wrong. They oftener do it under the
idea that they ought to compromise the law of God for the
sake of peace than on any other ground. They do it to please
the preacher and the young folks. They are ordained to God,
to maintain, teach, and enforce the laws of God, never to compromise or yield them.

The elders are the undershepherds to watch over and feed
the flock of God. In accepting the work of the elders they
bring themselves under the most sacred and solemn obligations possible to men to guard and maintain the honor of God,
to keep his teaching and his service pure from all innovations
of men. As shepherds and teachers of the flock, they assume
the most sacred and solemn obligations to the flock to feed the
flock with the pure milk of the word of God, that by this they
may grow; to guard against all teaching and practices that
rest on human authority as vitiating the service of God and
defiling the spiritual nature of the taught, and cutting them
off from the blessings of God, which come to men only
through the appointments of God unmixed with human inven-
tions and traditions. A sadder perversion of a sacred trust is
never seen than when elders and teachers forget the sanctity
of their obligations both to God and his church, and, as his
trusted servants and chosen teachers, encourage the introduction into his service of practices not authorized by God, so destroying his authority as lawgiver, and, as a consequence,
hurtful and poisonous to the spiritual nature of men.

INDEX TO COMMENTARY ON FIRST THESSALONIANS

INDEX TO COMMENTARY ON SECOND THESSALONIANS

INDEX TO COMMENTARY ON FIRST TIMOTHY

INDEX TO COMMENTARY ON SECOND TIMOTHY

INDEX TO COMMENTARY ON TITUS

INDEX TO COMMENTARY ON PHILEMON